# SLAVERY AND WAR
# IN THE AMERICAS

**A NATION DIVIDED:**
**STUDIES IN THE CIVIL WAR ERA**

Orville Vernon Burton and Elizabeth R. Varon, Editors

# SLAVERY AND WAR

## - IN THE - AMERICAS

RACE, CITIZENSHIP,
AND STATE BUILDING
IN THE UNITED STATES
AND BRAZIL, 1861–1870

## VITOR IZECKSOHN

UNIVERSITY OF VIRGINIA PRESS
Charlottesville and London

University of Virginia Press
© 2014 by the Rector and Visitors of the University of Virginia
All rights reserved
Printed in the United States of America on acid-free paper

First published 2014

1 3 5 7 9 8 6 4 2

Library of Congress Cataloging-in-Publication Data

Izecksohn, Vitor.
Slavery and war in the Americas : race, citizenship, and state building in the
United States and Brazil, 1861–1870 / Vitor Izecksohn.
pages    cm. — (A nation divided : studies in the Civil War era)
Includes bibliographical references and index.
ISBN 978-0-8139-3585-0 (cloth : acid-free paper) — ISBN 978-0-8139-3586-7 (e-book)
1. United States—History—Civil War, 1861–1865—African Americans. 2. Paraguayan
War, 1865–1870—Blacks. 3. Brazil—History, Military—19th century. 4. United States—
Race relations—Political aspects—History—19th century. 5. Brazil—Race relations—
Political aspects—History—19th century. 6. Nation-building—History—19th century.
7. Slavery—Political aspects—History—19th century. 8. Soldiers, Black—History—
19th century. 9. Recruiting and enlistment—History—19th century.
10. Citizenship—History—19th century. I. Title.
E540.N3I93 2014
973.7'415—dc23
2013049975

*For Júlia, with unconditional love*

# Contents

# Acknowledgments

This work has been a long time in the making. It resulted from years of research and certain of my obsessions. In the beginning, grave illness was an unexpected complication. Thanks to many people and many academic, research, and medical institutions, I was able to overcome initial obstacles, stay patient, maintain focus, and conduct research in two countries, while simultaneously writing in English. Many years have passed since that first New England winter. Some friends took different paths; others have passed away. Trajectories have changed, and people have moved on with their lives. To honor them all would require writing another book, a memoir. Perhaps that is in the future. Here, credit is given to those more consistently involved, although debts incurred are also well known.

My interest in comparative history and military issues dates back to early contacts with maps and the way countries were drawn across continents. Later, when I started serious research on the Rio de La Plata Wars and the nation-building push across South America, I was lucky to have Hendrik Kraay and Peter Beattie as friends and academic interlocutors, eventually publishing with both of them. Peter, who identified himself as an outside reviewer, deserves my sincere gratitude for comments and suggestions that materially improved the quality of this book. Later on, Todd Diacom, Dain Borges, Seth Garfield, Bryan McCann, Marshall Eakin, and Matthew Barton discussed my ideas in several graduate seminars. Their invitations permitted me to visit a number of U.S. universities and broaden my research.

## Acknowledgments

This investigation began in the Graduate Program at the University of New Hampshire. There I developed an interest in U.S. history and the ways in which American exceptionalism could be contested. As a foreign researcher in a domestic field I was welcomed, and my early inquiries were well received and benefitted from generous observations and discussions. With his prodigious knowledge of the Brazilian military and keen memory, Frank D. McCann was a valuable resource and a good friend. J. William Harris was fundamental in keeping this work going on. An attentive reader, he gave me many helpful hints about American history, U.S. Southern history, and the history of slavery. W. Jeffrey Bolster, Lucy Salyer, Douglas Wheeler, and Stephen Reyna all made helpful comments during the early phase of this research. Later on, conversations with Thomas Bender, Anthony Pereira, Don Doyle, and the late Charles Tilly refined my arguments, reinforced my determination, and kept me acquainted with new lines of inquiry.

During the project's early stages, my parents and sisters believed in it and encouraged me to continue despite illness and adversity. I deeply regret that my sister Denise did not live to see the book completed. Her early departure from this life gave me an inordinate sense of urgency that kept me pushing ahead.

At the University of Maryland's Freedmen's and Southern Society Project, Steven Miller and Leslie Rowland guided me through the records of the National Archives. While in Maryland, I also benefitted from the generosity of Phyllis Held, who made me feel at home while snowstorms closed the Archives and most of the Washington, D.C., area.

Support from the Conselho Nacional de Desenvolvimento Científico e Tecnológico (CNPq) of the Brazilian Ministry of Science and Technology, and the Coordenação de Aperfeiçoamento de Pessoal de Nível Superior (CAPES) of the Brazilian Ministry of Education made it possible to live and work in the United States. I am proud of the confidence in me shown by these two pivotal Brazilian development agencies. I am also grateful to the staff of the following Brazilian libraries and archives for help researching this material: Arquivo Nacional, Arquivo Histórico do Museu Imperial, Arquivo Público do Estado do Rio de Janeiro, Arquivo Público do Estado do Pará, Arquivo Público Mineiro, Biblioteca Nacional, Museu Histórico Nacional, Museu Casa de Benjamin Constant, Arquivo Histórico do Rio Grande do Sul, and Arquivo Público do Rio Grande do Sul.

The Programa de Pós Graduação em História Social of Universidade Federal do Rio de Janeiro has been my working place for a decade now. Its support during the final stages of writing was particularly welcomed. I am especially grateful to Manolo Florentino, Maria Beatriz de Mello e Souza, and Monica Grin, among many other colleagues, as well as to students and staff. I am also grateful to the Instituto de História at UFRJ.

In the United States, fellowships from the Gildher Lehrman Institute of American History and the Fulbright Commission provided opportunities for teaching and research. The Gilder Lehrman staff made possible access to its excellent collection stored at the New-York Historical Society. As a researcher and visiting professor, I am grateful to the Department of History, Brown University, for its stimulating academic environment. In Providence, Jeremy Mumford, Michael Vorenberg, Corey McEleney, Eliza Childs, and James Green took valuable time to comment on first drafts of the manuscript. My special appreciation goes to Jimmy for his help, friendship, and access to his office facilities and to Jose Itzighsohn for comradeship and permanent exchange of ideas.

At UVA Press I counted on the confidence of Dick Holway, who believed in the book from the beginning. Vernon Burton, Raennah Mitchell, Morgan Myers, Mark Mastromarino, and the two anonymous readers materially improved the quality of this book as well.

Through their companionship, my friends Bill Leavenworth, Darryl Thompson, and Vladmir Pistalo made my life in America much easier than I had expected it to be, sharing their suggestions, observations, and wisdom with me. We share a past, the same memories, and a kind of language, something close to a common heritage.

My student assistants Aline Goldoni, Felipe Brito Vieira, and Guilherme Sedlacek collaborated in collecting documents and discussing related questions in seminar meetings. Miquéias H. Mügge drafted the maps with his habitual care and competence. This book benefited enormously from his knowledge of Geographic Information Systems (GIS) and other graphic programs, as well as his capacity for meeting last-minute deadlines.

Writing in a second language demanded cooperation, serenity, and love. This work would not have been possible without the help, care, and attention of my dear friend Karen Alexander. She was a comrade, an editor, and a joy during all these years. She was also a good reader, an excellent copy editor, and a counselor. No words can express my gratitude to my friend, whose skills made my prose sharper and my ideas clearer.

This book is dedicated to my daughter, Júlia, because she is the greatest gift I've ever received.

# SLAVERY AND WAR
# IN THE AMERICAS

# Introduction

The 1860s were difficult times for the Western Hemisphere's two largest countries, the United States of America and the Brazilian Empire. During that decade, both nations were involved in long, costly struggles that challenged their national unity and their internal political cohesion. In the United States, the sectional crisis that had festered since the founding of the nation reached its peak after the 1860 presidential election. The victory of the Republican candidate, Abraham Lincoln, ignited old fears among Southern leaders committed to states' rights and the survival of slavery, about federal interference in local affairs. These concerns were not new, but the election of the first Republican president, and his association with free-soil messages, limiting slavery's expansion to the western territories, soon led to the secession of several states, the formation of a new country, and finally to a devastating civil war that would cost more than 600,000 lives.

A few years later, in the hemisphere's southern cone, Brazilian interference in the intermittent Uruguayan Civil War transformed what had been a permanent institutional crisis into a fierce interstate conflict that came to involve four countries and affect power arrangements in ways previous South American conflicts had not. The subsequent Paraguayan invasion of Brazil's western and southern provinces and further attacks on northern Argentina started a war most Brazilians and Argentineans thought would be short and easy to win. Later developments would show how naïve these early projections had been. In the midst of the fighting, old collections of semi-independent provinces turned into state-led nations; entire populations were removed arbitrarily from their hometowns; and hunger and disease decimated the Paraguayan people, affecting demography as well as changing existing patterns of regional organization and power distribution in the Southern Cone.

This book tells the story of these wars, emphasizing the permanent negotiation that took place between each respective nation-state and the people involved in the recruitment efforts for the Union and the Imperial armies. It compares the impact of the U.S. Civil War (1861–65) and the Triple Alliance War (1864–70) on civilian populations in the American Union and Brazil. These two remarkably different countries had similar war experiences in terms of recruitment, centralization, and military hierarchy. Both the Union forces and the Imperial armies faced recruitment crises related to the scarcity of volunteers, which prompted both governments to shift from early appeals to patriotism to painful impressments and, eventually, to the enrollment of freedmen of African descent as soldiers. If the Brazilian army, which had long recruited from the lower sectors of society, was less reluctant to conscript civilians and to free slaves for military service, the Union army had to overcome constitutional obstacles and racial prejudice before recruiting a much larger number of African Americans, most of whom came from the Southern states. The ramifications of these policies were felt far beyond the war years and contributed powerfully to emancipation and reform in the defeated South and to the erosion of monarchical legitimacy and representative parliamentary government in Brazil.[1]

Wartime necessities led to centralized recruitment in both countries, which strengthened each national government and profoundly affected the lives and customs of populations subjected to the draft. Because both countries depended on small central or national bureaucracies, each central government needed the support of local authorities to reach the population. Thus in many ways the U.S. Civil War resembles the War of the Triple Alliance more than any other armed confrontation of the nineteenth century.

Also known as the Paraguayan War, the Guerra Grande, or the Damned War, the Triple Alliance War was the longest large-scale international conflict in the history of the Americas. Four countries—Brazil, Paraguay, Argentina, and Uruguay—were drawn into fighting that lasted five years and four months. As with the Union, Brazil had superiority in manpower and resources, but these were not sufficient conditions for a quick victory.

To secure victory, the Brazilian government had to mobilize men and re-sources at unprecedented levels. Mobilization was based on mass recruit-ment, and a military infrastructure was created to oversee the war effort from the rear. This resulted in the construction of long lines of supply su-pervised by the central state. Financial resources and production necessary to fund and fuel the Brazilian war machine were redirected until Paraguay was defeated. As with the Union, decisions that would lead to uncondi-tional victory prevailed over alternative proposals envisioning a negotiated peace. In this sense, Brazil's war effort displayed many elements of a total war, although it never quite reached that point. The Union came close to achieving it, but in the long run, relative bureaucratic weakness and lack of infrastructure kept the Brazilian and the Union militaries from maintain-ing full strength for the duration of each conflict. But unconditional sur-render became a goal, a situation that would change social and economic parameters in the defeated countries. War demands touched on delicate issues for these victorious contenders: nationalism and patriotism were normally counterbalanced by personal attachments to regions, states, or towns. Bureaucratic efforts depended on negotiations between delegates of the central state and local authorities. Party allegiance played strong roles in the citizens' willingness to help the war efforts.

Increasing government intervention during wartime normally leads to a temporary suspension of local prerogatives through the recruitment of soldiers and the confiscation of material resources. Political centraliza-tion, a consequence of war, frequently results in the loss of local autonomy. These actions encountered different social organizations in each of the countries analyzed. Politics in the United States was based on beliefs that emphasized localism through states' rights and regional institutions, only a few of which, such as the parties and the courts, had national expression. Brazilian politics was nominally more centralized with provincial presi-dents appointed by the Cabinet in power. But the Imperial government engaged with its provinces only through negotiations and compromises. The aftermath of war generated similar dilemmas for Rio de Janeiro and Washington. Structural limitations to the recruitment and supplying of troops affected the distribution of power and the construction of racial identity. Each national state tried to circumvent these limitations by using complex strategies, the failure of which comprises an important element of this book's narrative.

Each of these wars has been extensively analyzed, but the two have

never before been systematically compared. Despite clear parallels between them, no historian has undertaken a significant comparison of the
Union and the Brazilian Empire during the wars of the 1860s, and no published work has displayed short-term comparisons, such as those that were
made between the U.S. Civil War and the wars of German Unification.[2]
In 1986, Herman Hattaway and Archer Jones argued that the Confederacy
could have resisted much longer if the Confederates had been willing to accept the almost 70 percent mortality rate that the Paraguayan population
suffered. Twelve years later, while underlining the demise of the Confederate will, James McPherson called attention to the fact that the Confederate
war effort, in which 5 percent of the population perished, seems feeble
when compared to the 56 percent of Paraguayan adults who died in that
conflict. Although McPherson's data can be contested, the Paraguayan
numbers still provide a good contrast to the demise of the Confederate will
to fight, raising the issue of the degree to which territorial defense can fuel
national sacrifice. McPherson called for a comparison of the Paraguayan
War and the U.S. Civil War, but the response was limited.[3]

This book is based on research conducted in archives in the United
States and Brazil. It also relies on the pioneering works of other scholars,
essential for grasping the main debates evolving from each war. A comparative analysis of military enlistment overcomes some of the problems that
afflict single-nation studies of collective action and bureaucratic organization. Comparing both countries offers different perspectives on national
trajectories, their differences and similarities, and the specificity of each
case. Comparative analysis is a powerful tool to understand the history of
societies as intertwined channels of influence operating on the vast experience of human diversity. Comparisons reveal configurations that otherwise go unnoticed.

This particular comparison of two wars in the Americas is relevant because it responds to a new research agenda established by historians interested in connecting American challenges to similar processes and conflicts
taking place in other regions.[4] Connecting warfare and emancipation in
the two largest countries of the Western Hemisphere places the American
Civil War in the larger context of the long and troublesome processes of
national unification and slave emancipation. Moreover, this comparison
with a centralized monarchy helps refine our understanding of American
republicanism in wartimes and the meaning of its political appeal, the

4

ways in which civic culture operated, and the delicate balance between democratic ideals and the realities of state-led warfare. The enrollment of former slaves in the military and the conditions governing their emancipation became government policy in both the United States and Brazil, but a host of contingencies ensured different social and political responses.

This book compares several distinct perspectives, including those of the full range of people in both societies involved with military recruitment: soldiers, officers, journalists, writers, religious and political activists, bureaucrats, slaves, and freed people. All of them faced changing realities and had to adapt to or fight in new social environments. It also emphasizes state-building limitations faced by centralizing elites, highlighting the strategies they used to overcome or circumvent eventual obstacles. The negotiations undertaken by government officers and local leaders in their recruitment efforts stressed selective recruitment, exemptions, targeting the constituencies of the opposition, and distributing financial benefits. As the wars stretched on, the use of such tools shrank, forcing governments to rely more on coercive practices, which in turn generated growing resistance.

Compared to the rich historiography of the American Civil War, the historiography of the Triple Alliance War is still relatively small. Furthermore, few authors have studied the Paraguayan conflict in relation to other contemporary processes of military and social mobilization.[5] A comparative analysis of Brazil and the United States is essential for grasping the full significance of military mobilization, state centralization, and political reform for the men and women whose lives were affected by these events. The Union exhibited institutional change amid the industrial revolution, but the Brazilian stage was very different. If the industrial revolution in the Northern states increased war capacity by producing modern equipment and technological expertise, what was the strategy for an agricultural country like Brazil, which bought European weapons but rarely produced them at home?[6]

For the United States and Brazil, countries with decentralized military traditions, these wars raised challenges that forced each government to review old practices and customs. Decentralization was based on local organization through militias, locally raised troops under the command of regional bosses. As the wars demanded growing numbers of men and resources, they exposed the inadequacy of government structures in both countries, each of which lacked the means to recruit the forces needed to fight enemies that organized cohesive armies and were motivated to keep the fight going without any real possibility of victory. But anti-professionalism was strong and derived from historical experience, political ideology, lack of resources, and pragmatism. It posed the strongest challenge to each country's efforts to fulfill their war aims.

ONE

# Military Traditions Confront
# Mass Mobilization in the United States
# and Brazil

In Brazil and the United States, popular distrust of a professional military took root and grew from the late colonial period to the 1860s. Both societies developed suspicion, resentment, or opposition to national armies and favored local military units commanded by local officers. British North Americans and Luso-Brazilians both organized locally controlled military institutions during the late colonial period and after independence. Comparing connections between the development of different levels of administration in each empire and the distinct social responses to those innovations provides a brief introduction to the social and constitutional problems that limited the expansion of national armies in the mid-nineteenth century, and that so effectively obstructed the two countries' war efforts in the 1860s. Several questions emerge: What was the status of civilian-military relations in each colonial dominion? Were antimilitary attitudes among British and Portuguese Americans similar? How did such attitudes adapt to the transition from Imperial rule to independence?

The diversity of regions that formed these large empires is an important consideration. British and Portuguese America consisted of mosaics of collectivities weakly connected to each other. Regional variations in demographic patterns and social structures make it difficult to generalize, yet, despite, or perhaps because of, this enormous diversity, in both North America and Brazil the center did not hold, at least not when it came to war or the provision for war. In these colonial arenas, military activities involved less centralization and less accumulation of coercive powers by central authorities than occurred in Europe's absolutist monarchies, where, in Charles Tilly's formulation, "War wove the European network of national states, and preparation for war created the internal structures of the states within it."[1]

In contrast to European efforts to establish direct government through the creation of strong central bureaucracies, cooperation between royal agents and locals was the norm for colonial and national defense in both Portuguese and British North American settings. Such cooperation resulted in small professional armies and heavy imperial dependence for colonial security on unspecialized auxiliary forces such as militias, armed bands, and National Guards. But parallels can be deceptive. Despite similarities in indirect government and the decentralized character of military mobilization, the steps taken toward this balance of authority were not identical. Each colony achieved cooperation at the local level from different entities in different ways. Luso-Brazilian and British–North American colonists established patterns of military organization that differed from each other, just as they diverged from the European paths of militarization.

Deficiencies in the professional military capacity made each imperial power heavily dependent on the assistance of private locally raised and led militia companies to reinforce public authority as well as maintain external defense and internal order. These groups transmitted commands and regulated both colonial and national policies through complex bargaining that connected the interests of local communities to the prerogatives of royal agents.

When faced with inevitable wartime demand for men and resources, each society responded in ways that were intertwined with customary patterns of justice and primary collective identities. The most delicate aspect of colonial militarization was the transfer of men from the auxiliaries to permanent army units. To be moved into the professional army brought the risk of fighting in distant places under the command of strangers. The transfer of local troops to frontline combat units constituted one of the main problems faced by all colonial officials involved in the administration of war and defense. Examining the rules and circumstances of such transfers allows a broader understanding of the impact of war on colonial ways of life, as well as on changing perceptions of military obligations, political rights, and patriotism. The negotiations among different levels of authority undertaken to transfer local soldiers to permanent army units and the claims generated among local bosses and their constituents, preserved in government records, reveal how ordinary people understood their rights and obligations vis-à-vis the central authority of the state and their local communities. Such collaboration was particularly intense in the thirteen British colonies during the last decades of imperial rule. This contrasts with normal conditions prevailing in Portuguese America, where only those who wanted to escape hunger and poverty, or expected to obtain freedom from servitude, were willing to serve far from home for extended periods of time.[2]

Brazil and the United States followed patterns of military organization that differed from the great Military Revolution that had been taking place in Continental Europe since the sixteenth century. In Europe, the strong centralized monarchies of the emerging states of France, Sweden, Prussia, and Russia created powerful military organizations built to wage war, which they accomplished by extracting funds and power from subjects and vassals. In contrast, British-American and Luso-Brazilian colonies maintained decentralized structures of defense. While the European Military Revolution reinforced the direct power of the state, the United States and Brazil relied consistently on intermediaries, who helped to enroll, house, drill, and provision soldiers and, when necessary, commanded them in the field.[3]

Changes in the organization of the military forces after independence did not substantially transform patterns established during the colonial period. These patterns reflected the limited capacities of the new central governments to accomplish tasks associated with military defense and extraction, the coercive recruitment of men from society.

In order to control large territories with limited financial resources, authorities had to rely on the help of the local community leaders. Effective territorial control was achieved through alliances with entrepreneurs, party bosses, and other sectors of the local elites. By the 1860s, political parties provided the main channels through which social forces were mobilized. As such they could be an asset or a burden, depending on the state of political affairs and the willingness of the local leadership to cooperate with the central government.

Particularly where recruitment for the army was concerned, concessions had to be made in the ways recruits were obtained. Local discretionary practices defined who should and who should not be sent, sparing certain individuals whose loyalty was too important to ignore. Such exemptions made enlistment less universal and less democratic, and favored categories of recruits based on marital status and occupation. When it came to federalizing the militia, limitations faced by nationalist elements throughout the United States, as well as widespread Brazilian resistance to war mobilization during Pedro I's reign, reveal a stubborn and universal intolerance of professional armies during the Era of Independence. Facing mounting resistance in their struggle to create professional military institutions, progressive or nationalist elements ended up acquiescing to consensual power sharing.

By the middle of the nineteenth century, considerable segments of Brazilian and American elites opposed the organization of strong military institutions in their countries. The strategic advantages of maintaining large professional armies were outweighed by serious arguments emphasizing the potential threats they posed to both internal stability and social hierarchy. Those concerned with stability feared the constriction of public order and perversion of civic virtue by ambitious officers in command of a powerful centralized military. Those concerned with social hierarchy associated standing armies with the turmoil, riots, and anarchy that could result from arming the poor and slaves. Common wisdom concluded that strong military forces were expensive, unreliable, and inherently risky to liberty and the maintenance of order. Enduring mistrust of an essential tool of modern nations made the state-building processes in Brazil and the United States unlike the trajectories taken by France and Prussia. While these European monarchies built their states from war, centralization, and citizen disarmament, American and Brazilian elites built states that kept small regular armies in the barracks.

Anti-professionalism, a legacy of the colonial experience, prevailed in both nations after independence, with brief periods of militarization followed by demobilization and a permanent reduction of the rank and file. But it should be emphasized that a political consensus on demobilization was not reached in either case. Federalists in the United States and conservative forces in Brazil never completely accepted disbanding of the army. But problems with mobilizing troops in countries like these, with large territories, scattered populations, and weak central governments, made it difficult to supplant decentralized alternative systems for internal defense and national security, which were already in place and strengthened by tradition.

Antimilitarism was not rigid or doctrinaire but derived organically from the colonial experience. Scarcity of resources was a chief reason for opt-ing for weaker professional military institutions, and civic conceptions of nationhood also made it impossible for governments in the Americas to emulate the countries that had successfully undertaken the Military Revolution in early modern Europe.

In spite of the similarities between Brazil and the United States, the long-term implications of demilitarization for each country were very different. In America, service in the militias was considered an honorable obligation, well suited to citizens, but the Brazilian vision of military service was derogatory.[4] Even auxiliary militias, such as the Brazilian National Guard, made clear that this option chiefly provided a way to avoid service in the national army. Except for a short interval between 1831 and 1850, service in the Brazilian National Guard did not materially integrate civic or political life within the nested levels of provincial and imperial authority. Rather, exemptions from professional military service reinforced seigniorial power, and increased client dependency on the wealth and prestige of local bosses.

The pivotal differences between the United States and Brazil were located in common attitudes toward military service. While American elites shared with the white population an apprehension about the potential growth of a despotic power supported by a standing army, Brazilian antiprofessionalism was more elitist and less ideological. Those who opposed the growth of military institutions were primarily concerned with the lack of financial resources and the risks to the political order and national unity. Consequently, whereas American antimilitarism could be more consistently attributed to ideas and religious traditions, Brazilian demilitarization resulted from an elitist decision based on the experiences of the first decade after independence. These differences opened the window for widespread enrollment of free people of color in the Imperial army, while its American counterpart remained a segregated institution.

The sources of Brazilian anti-professional attitudes were substantially different from those present in the American political tradition. Localism was not especially valued as a nation-building ideology. By the middle of the nineteenth century, large sectors of Brazilian elites saw a strong central government as the best guarantee of both national integrity and social order.[5] American hostility toward standing armies resembled the position of mid–nineteenth century Brazilian liberals in many respects, but differed fundamentally in one: Americans reserved much more power to local government than Brazilians did. Americans elected state governors, and these governors controlled state militias, whereas in Brazil provincial presidents were chosen by a regent or by the emperor himself. American prejudices against standing armies resulted from their suspicion of centralized power, a concern shared by both the elites and the people; in Brazil, demobilization stemmed from the need to preserve its centralized monarchy menaced by a turbulent military. Local elites in most Brazilian provinces viewed the military service of their dependents as a lesser evil. They compromised with provincial leaders in the name of hierarchical institutions such as slavery and patronage, while leaders in the American states directly controlled their militias and either offered or withheld their services.

As we shall see, both countries entered the 1860s with small regular armies unfit for the large military campaigns to come. These campaigns would challenge the accepted standards of service, pushing transformations in the nature of military obligations. But the power of inertia would prove to be a formidable obstacle to institutional and social change, creating tension between the center and its peripheries. Local bosses, who feared a permanent extension of central powers, viewed even small changes with suspicion. Such patrons had defended their closest clients against recruitment and possible relocation to the front lines since colonial times; how could they surrender these powers to a distant government? For their part, individuals and communities noticed the changes and reacted according to their capacity and interest in order to prevent the removal of recruits to the front.

## The Triple Alliance War

The longest international war in South American history, the Triple Alliance War, set the Paraguayan Republic against the Triple Alliance, formed by the Brazilian Empire, the Argentinean Republic, and the Republic of Uruguay. Although it was fought by preindustrial societies it nevertheless showed many mechanisms characteristic of modern warfare, such as mass enrollment, intense use of new technologies like the telegraph and steamboats, and deliberate manipulation of public debates through propaganda in the press.[6]

In all belligerent countries, different sectors of society participated intensely both as soldiers and civilians, including disenfranchised people such as women and slaves. Consequently the "home front" became an integral support of warfare. In Paraguay, women took over the agricultural production that supplied the army, even as the population was decimated by hunger, fatigue, disease and battle causalities. The war destroyed the first Paraguayan Republic (1811–1870) as well as the majority of its male population.[7]

The Triple Alliance War grew out of changes in the regional power structure. During the 1860s Paraguayans felt threatened by political reconfigurations taking place in the Rio de La Plata. More-conservative agrarian elements, the Blancos in Uruguay and Federalistas in Argentina, were losing influence to more-liberal urban elements in these countries, a centralizing influence propelled by elites situated in Atlantic port cities. These divisions were exacerbated by shifts in Paraguayan foreign policy that ended with the catastrophic decision of President Francisco Solano López to engage in a war that his armies could not win.

Since independence, Paraguay had adopted a heavily centralized style of government. Paraguay's first dictator, José Gaspar Rodriguez de Francia (1766–1840), framed state control and centralization through territorial surveillance and repression of any form of opposition. No other institution, not even the Church, could challenge the supreme government. Militarization of Paraguayan society played a pivotal role in centralizing its politics. According to Luc Capdevila, under Francia's rule the army's main mission "was the control of the interior space."[8] As Fernando López-Alves pointed out, these exceptional circumstances differentiated Paraguayan national organization from that of other countries in the Rio de La Plata basin.[9] Its precocious centralization and territorialization were unmatched by any of its neighbors.

Paraguayan independence helped crystallize a national identity rooted in the ethnic composition of its population, most of whom descended from Spanish creoles and Guarani natives, and the widespread use of the Guarany language in everyday life. In his efforts to avoid being absorbed by Buenos Aires, Francia gave special attention to the peasantry. The dictator developed a policy of access to land to the lower classes and supported a flourishing subsistence economy to expand the social basis of his support among his countrymen. These measures, allied with strict surveillance, strengthened the links between government and population. Thus reinforced, patriotism became a pivotal element in sustaining national resistance against invasion decades later.

Francia was succeeded by Carlos Antonio López (1792–1862), who ruled Paraguay for twenty-one years. Having inherited a small, unified nation, López was free to pursue economic development. Monopolies on yerba mate and tobacco production gave the government the income necessary to import guns and machinery.[10] Yet C. A. López's brand of authoritarianism was not particularly cruel, and his foreign policy approaches were moderate in comparison to further developments.

During the 1850s, foreign engineers, most of them British, supervised a program of national modernization. Major government projects included Asunción's arsenal and shipyard, the Ybicuy ironworks, and the construction of the Asunción–Vila Rica railroad. All had military applications, a logical policy in view of the unstable political situation in the surrounding Argentinean provinces and territorial disputes with Brazil.

In spite of the high degree of state control, Paraguayan resources were limited, especially when compared to Argentina and Brazil. The country was poor, and, despite widespread militarization, weapons were old and inadequate. Furthermore, ammunitions were scarce due to civil wars in Argentina that periodically stopped traffic on the Rio de la Plata, Paraguay's primary commercial link with the outside world.

When Paraguay's second dictator, Carlos Antonio López, died in 1862, his legacy was progressive in terms of economic development and greater social stability. Paraguay's independence had been recognized by its neighbors, and foreign relations were established with the United States and European nations. When Francisco Solano López succeeded his father as president, essentially as dictator, Solano López inherited a country with few internal problems and a high degree of social cohesion. Ironically, this basic unity probably encouraged the new dictator to enter a war that would destroy his country.

In contrast to his father's diplomacy, Solano López's aimed to increase Paraguay's regional influence. Under his leadership, foreign affairs assumed a central role in the formulation of Paraguayan internal politics. Expanding the army required increasing the enrollment of soldiers, a serious issue in a country with a small population who were needed for agricultural work. According to James Schofield Saeger, even before the outbreak of the war, "Francisco López drafted so many men into the armed forces that Paraguay became 'overmobilized.'"[11]

Solano López favored a militaristic approach to diplomatic issues and began extensive mobilizations of the Paraguayan population in the countryside, especially at the military training camp established near a railway depot at Cerro León.[12] Nevertheless, Paraguayan diplomacy even under Solano López seems to have been governed by a sincere wish to keep a fictitious balance of power in the region at any price.[13] The dictator's labors to end the Argentinean Civil War in 1862 underscored his efforts to set up, in the Argentinean Federation, a rival power to counter Brazilian influence.[14] Events proved this to be López's fatal mistake.[15]

*

## The Uruguayan Crisis

Life along Brazil's southern borders could be described as in "a violent state of peace." Tensions dated from colonial times when Portugal and Spain competed to control access to the Rio de la Plata watershed. After the loss in 1828 of the Cisplatine Province (current-day Uruguay), Brazilian foreign policy was redirected toward opening internal navigation on the river and settling border disputes with neighboring republics. Conflicting land claims caused intermittent skirmishes over badly delineated international boundaries. More important, as the rivers provided the quickest route between Rio de Janeiro and the large frontier province of Mato Grosso, far in the Brazilian west, access to navigation routes was essential to integrate Brazilian hinterlands with coastal regions. However, some of these routes lay outside Brazilian boundaries.

To open navigational channels, Imperial authorities combined diplomatic missions with the intermittent use of force. Because the Imperial army was small, cooperation between local and national authorities was vital to safeguarding Brazilian interests in the Rio de la Plata basin. To maintain the integrity of the southern border, the monarchy relied on National Guard units raised and controlled by cattle ranchers and merchants from the province of Rio Grande do Sul, whose loyalty was rewarded with titles of nobility, land grants, and sinecures. Military honors granted for leading successful skirmishes reinforced the authority of the local bosses over the men they led, providing them with enough prestige to maintain provincial authority and strengthening their links to the monarchy.[16]

Uruguay and Argentina were still unstable republics in the making in the 1850s. Struggles among territorial strongmen, commonly known as caudillos, frequently disturbed commerce and navigation. Some of these caudillos fought for federalism and decentralization, and others sided with forces pushing for centralized national governments in these fractured republics. Many Brazilian gauchos from Rio Grande do Sul owned ranch land in Uruguay and needed open international borders in order to transport cattle and slaves to distant markets. Disruptions of commerce and navigation hurt the frontier economy and constantly drew Brazilian landowners into Uruguayan and Argentinean border conflicts.[17]

Even after Uruguayan independence in 1828, Brazilian forces had intervened many times in that country's affairs, with the basic aim of defending gaucho interests. When Uruguay freed its slaves in 1842, Rio Grande do Sul acquired a second border problem. Freedom to the south attracted escaped slaves, despite the risk of impressment into Uruguayan militias. Some slaves crossed the frontier to freedom, and occasionally Brazilian gauchos mounted cross-border raids to catch the runaways. At first, institutional weakness in Uruguay's fragile republic prevented occasional border invasions from constituting an international dispute. But political strife in Uruguay soon attracted the attention of neighboring governments, and local clashes over territorial sovereignty became the epicenter of complex international confrontations.

In 1863, a civil war started in Uruguay involving the Blancos, then in power, and urban-based Colorados, merchants and landowners whose leader, Venancio Flores, had once fought with Argentinean liberals. Flores, a close friend and ally of the Argentinean president Bartolomé Mitre, mounted a new rebellion against the Uruguayan republic. Such factional schisms in the republic's troubled politics were not new. What was new, however, was the attention Flores's rebellion received from other nearby nations. The Paraguayan dictator Solano López offered to mediate the dispute, but Brazil did not seriously consider his proposal. The monarchy was interested in a fast and permanent solution to the Uruguayan crisis.

Brazilians were the most important foreign element living in Uruguay, accounting for 10 to 20 percent of its population and controlling 30 percent of Uruguayan land. Furthermore, gauchos had never acknowledged the territorial boundary dividing Brazil and Uruguay. The Blanco party, in power in Montevideo, attempted to institute a policy of "border nationalization," which taxed Brazilian citizens and threatened to control movements of their cattle and slaves in Uruguayan border regions.[18] In retaliation, gaucho leaders pressed the Imperial government to support the Colorado party, which favored their interests, but was out of power. Accordingly, José Antonio Saraiva, the Brazilian plenipotentiary in Uruguayan matters, "appealed" to the Blanco government on May 12, 1864, to "take into consideration our complaints over the serious offenses made against Brazilian subjects residing in Uruguay, whose property, honor, and life did not find protection, protection warranted by the Constitution of the same republic, in reason of which Brazil and the Argentinean Confederation consented to her political existence."[19]

Three months later, the Imperial military intervened in Uruguay to overthrow the Blanco government in favor of the Colorados, with the energetic support of gauchos from Rio Grande do Sul. Brazil's intervention in Uruguay and the military support given to Venancio Flores deeply offended the Paraguayan government, which had a treaty of mutual defense with Uruguay and viewed the invasion as a threat to its national sovereignty.[20]

However, Paraguay's evaluation of the 1864 crisis failed to account for important institutional transformations taking place in the region. Consolidation and centralization within national states decreased the power of provincial leaders. The emergence of Bartolomé Mitre as president of a semi-united Argentina advanced these structural changes in government through a program of "modernization" and "civilization" that transformed Argentina by integrating it into the capitalist world system. Tempted by progress, modernization, and material gain, many provincial Argentinean leaders opted for submission to the new centralized order. In addition, rebellious Rio Grande do Sul had been reintegrated into Brazil by 1845, fully restoring the Empire's capacity for intervening in border conflicts. Cavalrymen from Rio Grande do Sul were potentially an important asset for Brazil. Although national integration was still far from complete, Brazil and Argentina were much more stable by the middle of the 1860s than they had ever been.[21]

The Paraguayan government counted on the support of Argentinean "Federalist caudillos," dissenting oligarchs who opposed centralization in Buenos Aires's long struggle for nationhood. In his war plans, Solano López counted on support from his political ally Justo José de Urquiza, governor of Argentina's Entre-Rios province, to counter Brazilian intervention in Uruguay. But Urquiza's support never materialized. Over time, he had gradually accommodated to the new political realties in Argentina, which brought greater prosperity on the pampas (and adjacent regions) even as they diminished the ability of local bosses to stand up against national interests. López also expected that slaves would undermine the operational capacity of the Brazilian army, but his calculations were based on outdated international relationships and did not take into account changes in the region.

Paraguay reacted quickly to Brazil's intervention in Uruguay. In November 1864, Paraguayan authorities in Asunción took possession of the Brazilian merchant vessel *Marquês de Olinda*. In December, a naval expedition landed in Coimbra, in the Brazilian province of Mato Grosso, and proceeded to invade large portions of the province. Most southern and western areas of Mato Grosso quickly fell into Paraguayan hands. (See map 1.)

In early 1865, Lopez requested Argentina's permission to send an army across its province of Missiones in order to aid the Blancos, who were losing badly to the Colorados and their international allies. But Mitre refused. Argentina's unification party, the Unitarians, supported the Colorado rebellion in Uruguay because they saw the Blancos, historical allies of Argentinean Federalistas, as a threat to modernization.

As a result, Paraguayan troops invaded the Argentinean province of Corrientes in April 1865. This created an alliance between the two most powerful nations in Rio de La Plata that cut most international contacts with the Paraguay—perhaps the worst possible outcome. Isolation was aggravated by the destruction of the Paraguayan fleet in the battle of Riachuelo in June 1865.

In less than six months, reckless military decisions led Paraguay into a two-front, international war against larger and better-equipped nations, a strategy that wasted valuable resources. Consequently, the Blancos were defeated, and a Colorado government installed in Montevideo. The Colorado allegiance with Argentina and Brazil created the Triple Alliance. Allied forces would put down their arms only after inflicting total defeat on the Paraguayan government.

Paraguayan troops staked their chances for victory on swift, early offensives on both fronts, but the troops and ordinance squandered in Matto Grosso and Corrientes proved disastrous. The lack of basic war matériel forced Paraguayans to improvise to keep the army in the field. But it was difficult to compensate for the shortages of essential items such as boots, surgical supplies, ammunition, and uniforms. Epidemics, hunger, and the lack of warm winter clothes and equipment victimized many troops.[22] Having crossed vast frontier territories without adequate transport and supplies, the outnumbered army lost its best men and ammunition without destroying vital enemy resources or lines of supply.[23]

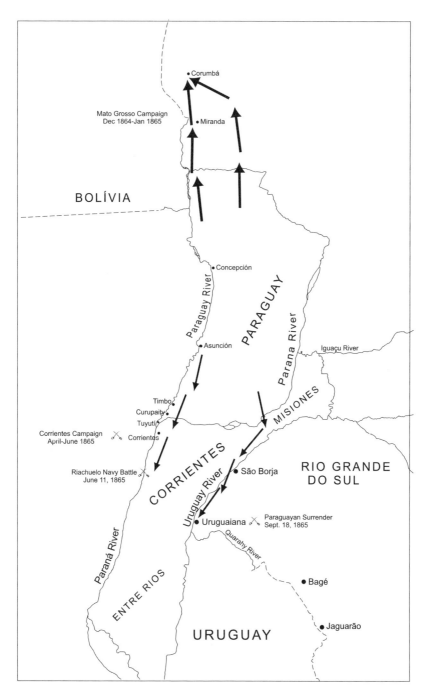

MAP 1. Paraguayan offensives (1864–1865). (Courtesy of Miquéias Henrique Mügge)

The Paraguayan army never reached Uruguay. By November, most of the remaining soldiers had been pulled back to defend the southern frontier against invasion. The remaining expeditionary forces were isolated in distant Mato Grosso garrisons.[24]

Incredibly, subsequent phases of the war were even bloodier and more difficult. The Allies turned to the invasion and conquest of Paraguay, commencing a long and bloody campaign that lasted four more years. During that period, the Paraguayans offered a fierce resistance to the invading troops. Solano López aimed at a negotiated peace, an alternative rejected by the alliance leaders, especially Pedro II. The war finally ended on March 1, 1870, when Solano López was killed at Cerro Cora while crossing the country with the remains of his army.

Paraguayan demographic losses remain the subject of intense debates. Vera Blinn Reber estimated that the war took between 8.7 and 18.5 percent of the prewar Paraguayan population. This data is contested by the research of Thomas Whigham and Barbara Pottash, who estimated that the war losses amounted to as much as 60 to 69 percent of the Paraguayan population. These findings reinforce estimates made by Wanderley Guilherme dos Santos and Luc Capdevila, that Paraguay lost at least half of its prewar population. What is clear from the testimony of travelers is that a demographic catastrophe had taken place, which created an enormous imbalance between males and females in the following decades.[25]

The Triple Alliance Treaty consolidated military, political, and diplomatic agreements that would long be in effect. It forbade Paraguay from keeping a regular army and navy, and solved boundary disputes by dismembering nearly 50 percent of Paraguayan territory and distributing it amongst the victors.[26]

The harsh treaty provisions denounced in the Paraguayan press became the departure point for an entire revisionist historiography of the war. During the 1970s, historians influenced by dependency theory saw the struggle as resulting from British influence in South America. From this perspective, Paraguay was a progressive nation fighting against imperialism. However, contemporary sources do not corroborate British intervention or even the will to intervene.

The Paraguayan War, the last crisis in the Rio de la Plata region, can be better described as the final step in the long process of state formation. The longest conflict in South America brought changes to all participant countries. Even the winners had to face the burden of economic crisis, veterans' demands, and military interference in domestic politics.

## Brazilian War Conduct

Even without its allies, Brazil far surpassed Paraguay in population, trade, wealth, and productive capacity. This superiority led Brazilian elites to believe that the war would be quickly concluded, but the Paraguayans fought a tenacious defensive war that took the Triple Alliance years to overwhelm. After a series of victories, the Triple Alliance forces were defeated at the battle of Curupayty. This marks the long, sixteen-month siege of Humayta fortress, surrounded by swampy terrain. Even after conquering Humayta, the Alliance forces had to face the dismembered Paraguayan army in a series of battles that extended the war until the last of Solano López's troops were destroyed at Cerro Cora. Instability in Uruguay and Argentina meant that Brazilians ultimately bore the brunt of the war.[27] (See map 2.)

Providing the resources required by the campaign would ultimately pose challenges to traditional social hierarchies on the Brazilian home front, especially for the free poor who depended heavily on personal networks to protect their social and economic status. The Brazilian Imperial State had problems mobilizing its population for war. Consequently, it could fight only what the sociologist Miguel Centeno defined as a "limited form of warfare," that is, a partial mobilization of population and material resources that never seemed to be enough. This permanent demand made the war unpopular on the home front.

The Brazilian government mobilized around 140,000 men to fight on the Paraguayan front. This was less than 2 percent of Brazil's estimated 9.1 million inhabitants in 1865. However, according to 1872 census records, only about 4.2 percent of the population—including slaves—were males of military age (fifteen to thirty-nine years old). At that rate, the mobilization still called up only about 3.3 percent of Brazilian males of military age.[28] Nonetheless, this relatively small mobilization would create serious strains on Brazil's social, institutional, and political structures.

For Brazilian society, the war contrasted a rising patriotism with racial and social segregation, creating challenges that were exacerbated by deficiencies in infrastructure. The defense of national borders was framed in terms of national honor, which appealed to and united different parts of

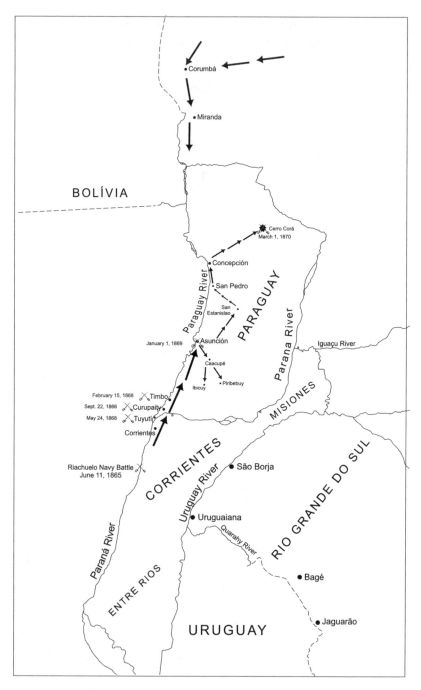

MAP 2. Triple Alliance's offensives (1866–1870). (Courtesy of Miquéias Henrique Mügge)

society. However, geographical realities made it difficult to frame the idea of a serious external threat coming from such a small nation. Thus, patriotic appeals to national honor and defense of border integrity appeared in proclamations that emphasized Brazil's role as defender of civilization against barbaric Paraguayan invaders. It is difficult to measure the force of such appeals, especially in small towns and on farms located far from major cities and provincial capitals.

## Issues in the American Civil War

This discussion of the American Civil War will be brief, as the subject is already well known and its literature voluminous. The conflict resulted in part from the escalation of tensions around the expansion of slavery into unincorporated western territories. These tensions led to the erosion of the Second Party System and the creation of a new, more-radical political force in the North, the Republican Party, whose main aim was to contain slavery within regions where it already existed. Republicans were also interested in the old Whig agenda that included support for industrialization, market expansion, a new banking system, and public works.

Would the economy and society of the United States be based on free and wage labor, or would slavery remain central to Southern political and social organization and continue to play a controversial role in territorial expansion? The Civil War decided the country's future direction. It started as a limited war to restore the Union, but it ended by fundamentally changing the fabric of American society. What started as a limited war to re-establish sovereignty over the Confederate states became a war to reshape Southern society, and resulted in a war that shaped the United States as a modern capitalist nation.

Early military units were recruited by local religious, ethnic, and fraternal organizations, as well as by political parties and leaders, who appealed to state militia units for volunteers. However, volunteer units proved unable to cope with modern industrial warfare. Drafts and other forms of compulsory recruitment became necessary to replace soldiers on the front, and for a time coercive enlistment measures enhanced the federal government's control over the lives of its citizens. Those conflicts were especially dramatic in the years 1862–63, before a system of bounties, the recruitment of African Americans, and other selective incentives placated tensions. The industrial, standardized economy developing in the North also demanded new ways of control and discipline that proved incompatible with traditional military organization based on localism and volunteerism. On the Northern home front, limits to the nation's power to conscript became a contentious issue in areas less willing to accede to federal demands.

The origins of the American Civil War differ remarkably from the origins of the Triple Alliance War. The Civil War was preceded by long disputes involving different visions of the national organization of the United States, while the Triple Alliance War resulted from territorial disputes, struggles concerning the control of the rivers, and extraterritorial influences. The countries in the Rio de la Plata basin presented different degrees of institutionalization, as central governments were still dependent of local sovereignties.

The main differences with the Triple Alliance War lie in the centrality of slavery to American sectional disputes. Slavery was seen as a hindrance to Northern economic development. Although it was still important to the Brazilian economy in the 1860s it was little more than a secondary factor in the crisis that brought war to the Rio de La Plata region. Also, Americans fought over diverging conceptions of the future of the nation, while the Triple Alliance contenders fought over the consolidation of territorial boundaries and state control. Of course, patriotism and nationalism were present in the South American conflict, but the meanings of these terms, and the involvement of public opinion during the period preceding the outbreak of the Paraguayan War, were limited. In the long run, the South American struggle brought changes to national organization in all the countries involved, but no nation's identity was built on derogatory and racist assumptions about its enemies.

To understand how recruitment transformed society and government during the Civil War in the United States and the War of the Triple Alliance in Brazil, it is necessary to follow the course of the wars. How effective and permanent were these changes in each country? Which hierarchies were challenged? How did people respond to the changes affecting their daily lives? The following chapters will try to answer these questions by examining military activity on the home fronts, particularly how recruitment and intervention by central governments affected civilians' lives.

24

# TWO

# The Crisis of the American Recruitment System

## Union Army Recruitment, April 1861–July 1863

On November 10, 1862, a hostile crowd surrounded William A. Pors, a longtime resident of the town of Port Washington in Ozaukee County, Wisconsin, as he entered the courthouse. Weeks before, Pors, a local attorney, had been appointed the district draft commissioner by the Wisconsin governor Edward Salomon. Early that morning, a large group of men armed with stones and clubs made their way through the town in an ad hoc procession. The crowd congregated in front of the courthouse, where it confronted the commissioner. A group of women unfurled a banner inscribed "No Draft." Pors was warned at the courthouse door that "should he go to the court-house he would be a dead man." He tried to persuade the crowd to disperse, but to no avail, and "as soon as they saw the draft-box they made a rush for it and knocked it in pieces." The women assaulted Pors, pushing, kicking, tearing out his hair, rending his clothes, and knocking him on the head. The draft commissioner made his way through the crowd as best as he could but was thrown down the courthouse steps.

Outside, the crowd turned uglier. Twice Pors was hit on the head with stones. Despite his injuries, the beleaguered man raced to the post office for refuge as the mob tore down the draft lists. After destroying the lists, it turned against the building that housed the post office. The crowds intended to hang the commissioner but were prevented by the postal clerk, a German immigrant, who denied them entrance. Later that day, Pors escaped to Milwaukee in a covered carriage prepared by "the good citizens."

After the commissioner left town, a crowd of "several hundred" turned on his residence, doing "a good deal of damage" to a mill it attacked on the way there. The mob broke into the commissioner's house and destroyed everything inside. Two pet canaries were torn into pieces; the chimneys, the windows, and all the furniture were demolished. Finally the mob turned on the property of several other citizens who were identified with the Republican Party. The party of Abraham Lincoln was then associated with government policies that demanded more recruits for the Northern armies. The riots lasted two more days before order was restored by six hundred soldiers who imposed martial law.[1]

As harrowing as these events were, Pors met a kinder fate than other commissioners who were killed for enforcing the draft. But his case is emblematic of conflicts that arose as the Republican administration increased the scale of the federal government's military mobilization in its struggle with the Confederacy. Many northern and western communities reacted against what they saw as unacceptable changes in the socially constructed rules connecting military service, volunteerism, and citizenship. Struggles arising from the centralization of military recruitment and against the imposition of rigid discipline were common in other countries.

Such struggles also existed in Brazil, but there, recruiting agents normally targeted individuals who were not protected by a local leader or affiliated with a National Guard unit, a fluid but significant part of the population that can be called the "unprotected poor." Their status depended on personal connections with patrons. In the United States, recent immigrants were in a similar condition as Brazil's unprotected poor, but, except in urban areas, they were a minority of the population. Unlike in Brazil, most white adult males in the United States had actively participated in elections since the 1830s. Thus, the Civil War is unusual because authorities had to negotiate with a majority of enfranchised citizens from the beginning. In both countries, innovations in recruitment procedures conflicted with rooted concepts of individual freedom, local power, and the idea of nationhood.

As with the Brazilian situation during the Paraguayan campaign, the consequences of the Civil War were not confined to the defeated regions of the South. The conflict would bring unintended effects to most areas of the Union as it challenged the authority of states over state militias and introduced a different balance of power between federal and state governments. In the same way, Brazilian war efforts would bring some of the Northern provinces to the edge of rebellion as recruitment challenged some traditional political privileges, even if temporarily.

The scale of social and governmental transformation was completely underestimated because everybody thought both wars would end quickly. Initial strategies and troop movements showed a level of misunderstanding difficult to comprehend today as most in the Union, the Confederacy, the Brazilian Empire and even Paraguay counted on a short war with a few great battles that would define the outcome and enhance national honor. Time would prove them all tragically wrong, as the spectators out for the afternoon to witness the Battle of Manassas were the first to realize.

## The Background

The Civil War was the most intense conflict faced by the American nation during the nineteenth century. As a large, multifront war, it required unprecedented levels of mobilization, recruitment, and training. Civilian populations—as victims and as supporters—became entangled in the war, which resulted in more American casualties than almost all twentieth-century contests combined. Union losses alone were nearly as great as all U.S. losses in World War Two. The conflict demanded a state structure capable of coping with a vast and integrated war effort, leading to spectacular changes in bureaucratic organization and the workings of government. These changes redefined national sovereignty in such areas as the nationalization of the relationship between government and citizen and the transformation of slaves into soldiers.

Some of these changes affected traditional assumptions on such vital matters as local governance, states' rights, conscription, personal liberty laws, the centralization of national power, and the voluntary character and composition of the army. They also reinforced the role of the federal government as the main recruiting organization of the armed forces. The emphasis on states' rights was progressively replaced by centralization, with the federal government taking charge of military affairs, fiscal policy, the procurement system, and economic development.[2]

These changes affected the lives of people living in loyal states in many ways. They interfered with usual policy-making practices, thus affecting relations between individuals and their communities. These transformations were profound enough to affect the social basis of community support for efforts to feed and expand the army. As a consequence, simultaneous with the struggle against the Confederacy there was, within Northern states, a conflict over the identity of the Union itself, a conflict Lincoln called "the fire in the rear."[3]

Although much has been written about the economic transformation of the North spurred by the war, in the last three decades more attention has been paid to the changes that occurred in military recruitment and its impact on American social organization. How was the control of recruitment transferred from the states to the federal government? What kind of conflicts resulted from that transfer of authority? Under what conditions did cooperation between local leaders and federal officers become possible? What kind of transformations operated under traditional assumptions and on accepted institutions? How did the local population react to the growing intrusion of the central government in their lives?[4]

This new situation was caused by the failure of volunteerism and the introduction of the Union's first draft system, through the Enrollment Act, in March 1863.[5] Congress's approval of this important war measure was part of a more general shift in the nature of the war: its transformation into a general effort to destroy the basis of Southern society. From this perspective, military events and the politics of war assume a greater historical significance because they reveal how military mobilization promoted political centralization and established more direct links between citizens and the federal government. They also produced social conflict on a scale not previously experienced by common citizens in antebellum America. Finally, they helped to delineate the multiplicity of issues that emerged as a result of the constantly changing and complex interaction between the growing military needs of the Republican administration and the strong commitment of citizens to their communities.

Because recruitment was such a critical issue in the sectional conflict, it demands a broad and multilayered consideration. As in the Brazilian case during the Paraguayan Campaign, the Civil War period has to be looked at not as a single, unbroken development cycle but as a fluid situation, changing according to diverse circumstances. When circumstances were adverse to the Union efforts, the federal government needed to create the conditions required to keep the war effort at full strength. Creating and enforcing a national conscription system in a government traditionally based on the preeminence of states' sovereignty raised constant problems for the administration and created a paradox for political leaders. In his December

28

1861 report as secretary of war, Simon Cameron foreshadowed this paradox, stating: "While it is admitted that soldiers in the Regular army, under the control of officers of military education and experience, are generally better cared for than those in the Volunteer service, it is certain that the popular preference is largely given to the latter. Young men evidently prefer to enter a corps officered by their friends and acquaintances."[6]

## Setting the Stage

According to Herman Hattaway and Archer Jones, the summer of 1862 marked "the greatest Confederate and poorest Union efficiency" of the conflict.[7] Successful Confederate resistance on the battlefield caused a shift by the Lincoln administration in the direction of emancipation and "total war," the most important social and political consequences of the war. Both objectives required a strong commitment from Northern society to the "new" war goals, as well as a federal government strong enough to support them. During that period, the Republican administration resorted to a series of unprecedented measures to enforce its authority in the face of the escalating costs of war.

The Republican action after 1863 was described as a fusion of party and state; by imposing its national vision, a sectional party connected the ideals of Union and Liberty to a new conception of American nationhood.[8] This vision was national in scope, demanding the centralization of some political and administrative procedures. But riots and popular revolts in five states demonstrated that many would resist the increasing sacrifices demanded by the quest for reunion.

The new form of nationalistic activism was not always compatible with the well-established notions of individual rights and local power. The dilemma faced by Lincoln and his supporters lay in the fact that the greater war effort tested the limits of state power in such areas as "personal liberty laws" and the control of state militias. There was considerable resistance at the local level to the idea that the nation's defense was a primary responsibility of every citizen, not one reserved to a distant central state, and where the notions of freedom and localism were intertwined. An anonymous pamphlet published in Rhode Island during the heat of the conscription debate provides an example of that kind of local discontent: "The present [law] is the first attempt in this country to create a regular army by arbitrary conscription, and it is such an audacious onslaught upon state rights and personal liberty as was never before witnessed in any free government."[9]

Although most authors agree about the importance of these transformations in the nature of the war, their effects on the civilian populations of the North are still subject to extensive debate. All social groups experienced personal sacrifices, but some authors question whether the burden was evenly distributed among classes, regions, and ethnic minorities. Was it a rich man's war but a poor man's fight, as some say? Were other alternatives for recruitment feasible or compatible with the government's bureaucratic structure?[10]

## The North and the Politics of Secession

For about six weeks, from December 20, 1860, to February 1, 1861, the secession of South Carolina and the rest of the lower South shook Northern public opinion while it divided Southerners over the risks associated with territorial disintegration.[11] In spite of the gravity of the situation, it was not clear then whether secession in the lower South would prevail or whether decades of political disagreement would finally lead to war. Most Northern political factions favored some sort of negotiation, envisioning an "acceptable compromise" capable of restoring the old Union. The Democratic Party, still a relevant political machine, was strong in both sections of the country. During previous crises, compromises had been reached, and it was expected that the conciliatory forces would again prevail. Simultaneously, many groups in the upper South opposed secession.[12] These "reluctant Confederates," as the historian Daniel Crofts has designated Southern Unionists, feared the risks of a civil war and the resultant destruction and bloodshed. According to Crofts, "the survival of competitive Opposition parties in the upper South . . . during the 1850s provided institutional barriers against secession."[13]

Even within the states of the lower South that followed South Carolina into secession, there were some areas with strong pro-Union minorities. The vote for secession had been surprisingly close in Georgia and in certain parts of the cotton kingdom, not to mention the Border States, where slavery was not so significant but links with the South were strong.[14] More important, both sections shared a language, a memory of the common inheritance, national symbols, and devotion to the same forefathers. Both also shared a reverence for what they believed to be American republican culture.[15] But these initiatives and points of convergence could not ignore a basic question: Would the Southern elite concede control of the government to a hostile antislavery majority? One of the strongest fears among Southerners was that a Republican administration in Washington would lead to a wave of slave insurrections supported by the federal government.[16]

Notwithstanding its small size and decentralized structure, the antebellum federal government was strong enough to provoke slave owners' fears of a disruption of their social order, their ascendancy over socially subaltern groups. Potential federal interference might come through the operation of government institutions, such as the mail and the courts systems, or through manipulation of traditional patronage practices involving the states and the federal government. According to David M. Potter, by 1860, the Southern elites feared above all "the power to appoint Republican judges, custom collectors, and postmasters in the South."[17] Such power, they believed, could disrupt their control of their plantations. Their state of mind was well captured in an editorial published by the *Charleston Mercury* in October 1860: "If, in our present position of power and untidiness, we have the raid of John Brown . . . what will be the measures of insurrection and incendiarism, which must follow our notorious and abject prostration to Abolition rule at Washington, with all the patronage of the Federal Government, and a Union organization in the South to support it?"[18]

The Georgian Thomas R. R. Cobb summarized the precariousness of the pro-slavery position under a Republican executive: "The Executive branch of the Government alone can protect us. The President only can call out the Army and the Navy. The President only can appoint Commissioners, and Marshals, and Judges, to execute the Fugitive Slave Law. The President only can protect us from armed invasions and secret incendiaries. I admit that it is so feeble that we can hope but little from it, even with a friend as President—with a foe, what we can hope?"[19]

The Republican Party had come to power in northeastern and middle western areas of the country on a platform of limiting slavery to the states where it existed, restraining its expansion into the western territories, and sweeping the "slave power" from the federal government. The party was deeply committed to strong federal intervention in infrastructure and in the judicial system. Certain sectors tried to picture the party as "the defender of the white man," in a clear rejection of slave labor. Others openly criticized the Southern social order as an inferior and backward social experiment. Lincoln himself recognized in February 1860 that a Republican victory would put clear limits to slavery, affirming, "The Federal Government . . . has the power of restraining the extension of the institution."[20]

In spite of the great tension that existed in the country, there was a predisposition to compromise, especially given the indeterminate position of the upper Southern states, in particular the most important of them, Virginia. Many people believed that if the upper South stayed in the Union, secession could not last long. Such a perspective prevailed long after the opening of the Civil War showed the extent of Confederate commitment to independence. This belief in compromise had enormous consequences for the Union; because as a result, its leaders were slow to shift toward total war and abolition during the first year of the conflict.

## First Phase: Enthusiasm

By 1861, the North was a heterogeneous, multi-ethnic society involved in a relentless process of economic development and territorial expansion. Most Yankees subscribed to a doctrine of localism that was basic to their civic culture. Robert H. Wiebe has described the antebellum social organization as made up of "island communities," as the establishment of a national market had not yet destroyed the parochial structures prevalent in most states.[21]

The U.S. Census of 1860 recorded a population of 22,339,989 for the entire region, excluding the areas of western Virginia, eastern Tennessee, and other Confederate pockets loyal to the Union. The Northern railroad network encompassed 21,973 miles, and the North's 1,300,000 industrial workers were employed in 110,000 manufacturing establishments. Northern states manufactured 97 percent of the country's firearms in 1860, 94 percent of its cloth, 93 percent of its pig iron, and more than 90 percent of its boots and shoes. In spite of such impressive numbers, the evolution of the war would show how little superiority in resources meant when confronted with a cohesive enemy determined to achieve and maintain its independence.[22]

When supporters of the Confederate cause opened fire on Fort Sumter on April 12, 1861, the act propelled loyal Northern sentiment by giving the Union a cohesive cause, something that had become lost during the winter of 1861 as compromise was debated. By attacking, Confederates became the aggressors, traitors to both the American flag and the nation's cause. Patriotic feelings united the North and penetrated deeply into most towns and counties. During the first two years of the conflict, most soldiers who enlisted in the North did so because they "chose to do so."[23] Alfred Bellard, an apprentice carpenter from New Jersey, wrote in his diary: "When Fort Sumter was fired into by the Rebels . . . my military spirit along with the rest of the Northern states rose to boiling pitch."[24]

President Lincoln, emulating previous presidential rhetoric, particularly a 1790 message by George Washington, announced on April 15 that "combinations too powerful to be suppressed" existed in the South, and called for 75,000 troops for a three-month term of service.[25] This call is normally recognized as the official inauguration of Northern mobilization. But informal actions taken by some state governors were already positioning state militias for war. Governor John Andrew of Massachusetts, a Republican deeply committed to abolitionism, was also an enthusiast of state militias. In January 1861, Andrew informed the state legislature, "In respect to good conduct, discipline, spirit and capacity proportioned to its numerical force, I am advised that our active citizen soldiery was never in a condition of greater efficiency."[26]

These state governors, many of whom had taken office before Lincoln's inauguration, were not limited by the clauses that restricted preemptive action coming from the president or his secretary of war. Consequently, they took steps to transform their local militias into combat units, anticipating the presidential call. During the war's first months, state leaders also controlled the procurement system to supply troops. After the presidential call and for most of the first year, governors proceeded with the utmost energy in their recruiting activities, always keeping the responsibility for the raising of troops in their own hands.

As in Brazil's war against Paraguay, initial calls produced enormous mass meetings and farewell ceremonies at which regimental flags were presented, soldiers were praised, and speeches were delivered. Even for a society used to volunteerism, the first exhibitions of enthusiasm surprised many observers. A Wisconsin newspaper reported: "The North is rousing to the task. From Maine to Minnesota, in every village and hamlet the signal of arms is sounded; and hundreds of thousands are enrolling themselves for the struggle. Every State and every section is to be taught the great lesson that it is no light thing to trample upon the Constitution and the laws; and that every attempt to break up the Union will be visited with fearful retribution."[27]

During these first weeks, the call for soldiers encountered few problems. Feeling outraged by the machinations of the "southern conspiracy," thousands of volunteers enlisted spontaneously in militias organized under state auspices. These volunteers had scarcely any military experience because, for the most part, militia activities in peacetime were very limited, rarely reaching the point of real military training. At the time of the first call-up, the general feeling was that the war would be short and the rebels would soon be brought back into the Union. James McPherson portrayed that way of thinking as the "rage militaire"—an expression commonly associated with the French experience in combat. Knowing nothing of the risks and consequences of total warfare that they would experience, many volunteers thought about the war experience as an adventure, an opportunity to see a world very different from that of their daily lives.[28]

Meetings in support of the Union spread around the country. War fever extended to all ages and classes, crossing party lines. An Indiana newspaper reflected the nonpartisan spirit in April 1861: "Now, looking at the North, we find men almost unanimous for the Government. Party lines are obliterated." In the same month, a paper in Springfield, Massachusetts, proclaimed divisions in the North were no longer partisan, noting: "We know no names but patriots and traitors . . . Once we suffered ourselves to be made mean by party spirit, and to become corrupt through it. Now, moved by a common impulse, we rally for the defense of our country; and the shackles of party fall off. Thank God for this."[29]

Lincoln's call for troops was also eagerly answered in areas where Democratic Party forces prevailed. Such was the case in the coal-mining districts of Pennsylvania. Grace Palladino's study of draft resistance showed how the initial call for troops was enthusiastically answered in this region. These districts had a significant foreign population, with Irish Catholics predominating. By June 1861, a Republican newspaper not known for its sympathy to Catholic immigrants noted, with approval, that English, French, German, Scotch, Irish, and Welsh "have banished all differences and [are vying] with each other in their expressions of loyalty to the country of their choice."[30]

At this point, raising troops was fully in the hands of state governors. According to David Osher, this state of affairs reflected the "privatization of civic responsibility," that is, a compromise between a fragile federal organization and empowered local communities.[31] But political cooperation between the federal government and the states was made easier by the fact that by 1861 all Northern governors were Republican, and as such represented both the state organizations and the national coalition responsible for bringing Lincoln to Washington.[32] According to Dora L. Costa and Matthew E. Kahn, an enlistee was more likely to be from a Lincoln town, that is, a town with Republican sympathies that had supported Lincoln during the 1860 election.[33] Social homogeneity and Protestantism favored this kind of civic commitment, although the first months of mobilization were rich in examples of Catholic and immigrant pronouncements in favor of the Union cause. Personal commitment and local party structures were the best sources of successful recruitment. As a county-wide Republican convention proclaimed in 1862, "the Republican organization, in all its principles, in all its practices, and by all its members, is committed to the preservation of the Union and the overthrow of the Rebellion. It is the power of the State and the Power of the Nation."[34]

Although the governors controlled the process of recruiting, they depended on the goodwill of local political bosses or prominent men who aspired to become officers in the newly formed military companies. At the local level, recruitment was connected to the popularity of local notables, whose prestige was fundamental to the success of those regiments that were raised and equipped. Paul Ledman has shown the force of personal prestige in Cape Elizabeth, Maine. In this relatively wealthy coastal community, prominent citizens advertised in local newspapers, appealed to acquaintances, and spent their own money in "raising expenses." In reward for their services, such notables often achieved the rank of colonel in the new regiments. Ledman has demonstrated that without the commitment of such persons, the initial recruitment would have been a much more difficult task.[35]

The force of localism was so strong that in most companies officers were recruited in the same communities as their soldiers, a military tradition dating from colonial times. This circumstance strengthened the parochialism normally associated with the act of mustering in, common to prewar militia service. Consequently, both a chain of command and a complex network of kinship governed relations among members of these locally raised units. These links were strengthened by the practice, common at the beginning of the war, of electing junior officers. As James McPherson has explained: "In the American tradition, . . . citizen soldiers remained citizens even when they became soldiers. They voted for congressmen and governors, why should they not vote for captains and colonels?"[36]

Local and ethnic pride reinforced the links among soldiers. Local ties impelled many men to enlist and at times kept them in their units far beyond the dictates of their personal interests. Fear of acquiring a reputation for cowardice in the eyes of associates forced many men to come to terms with their fears of battle and to fight alongside neighbors, relatives, and acquaintances.[37] This particular discipline was reinforced by the fact that many units were organized around communal activities, such as temperance associations, Sunday Schools, and churches. In other cases, regiments were recruited from ethnic communities, reinforcing the links between immigrant commitment and local pride. The relation between the first volunteers and their communities remained strong until the end of the war. It helped to keep many veterans committed to the Union cause, allying the national pursuit of the war with a strong sense of group identity.[38] A volunteer from Iowa explained his motives in a letter to his mother, assuring her that, "never . . . [had] men [a] nobler or more sacred cause for which to fight, and die. And we should bless fortune that the opportunity is ours, of devoting our lives to the maintenance of that Government which our fathers purchased with theirs."[39]

## Northern Public Opinion and War Limits

As Republican governors lobbied for more recruits, thousands flocked to enlist. The capitals of loyal states turned into big camps. In such a spirit, Governor William Dennison of Ohio answered the Lincoln administration's first call for a quota of thirteen regiments by declaring, "Owing to an unavoidable confusion in the first hurry and enthusiasm of . . . our people, a much larger force had already mobilized." The governor added, "Without seriously repressing the ardor of the people, I can hardly stop short of twenty regiments."[40] So strong was the general enthusiasm, and so precarious was the military organization during these first months, that William Pitt Fessenden a conservative Republican U.S. Senator from Maine, exhorted Secretary of War Cameron to increase recruitment quotas: "The People are now at your back, full of enthusiasm and wrath. Take advantage of it."[41]

But the Administration's capacity to take advantage of the popular mood was limited by its ideas concerning the war, by political considerations, and by the prejudices prevalent in Northern society. As James McPherson has observed, the Civil War was a "conflict where political leadership and public opinion weighed heavily in the formation of strategy."[42] In this environment, politics and strategy interacted in what was basically "a political war, a war of peoples rather than of professional armies."[43] Pressures from political parties and state power groups were carefully taken into consideration by the administration in all aspects of its planning for the war effort, from the designation of the officers' corps to the selection of the racial groups that could be admitted in the army.[44]

An important area in which the limitations of prejudice conflicted with strategy involved the enlistment of African Americans. From the beginning of hostilities, black leaders such as Frederick Douglass, J. Stella Martin, J. W. C. Pennington, William Wells Brown, Martin Delany, Henry Highland Garnet, and John Mercer Langston, backed by white abolitionist and black publications, asked for the enrollment of African Americans. These leaders saw the restoration of territorial integrity and black enrollment as related tasks. In May 1861, Frederick Douglass summarized such feelings: "The simple way . . . to put an end to the savage and desolating [war] now waged by slaveholders, is to strike down slavery itself, the primal cause of that war . . . let the slaves and free colored people be . . . formed into a liberating army, to march into the South and raise the banner of Emancipation among the slaves."[45]

But the federal government did not accept such pleas, and initial offers by African Americans to enlist were dismissed as unnecessary and undesirable. Racial prejudice was especially strong among foreign immigrants and those recently arrived from the South, an important part of the Midwest's population. Many people in midwestern states were dependent on the Mississippi River and the Southern port of New Orleans for much of their trade and transportation. Three states—Illinois, Indiana, and Iowa—had enacted laws to bar blacks from their states. The war heightened fears that hordes of black laborers would descend on the region and displace the original settlers from their jobs.[46] As put by a Massachusetts corporal in a letter to the president, "When the war trumpet sounded . . . the Black man laid his life at the Altar of the Nation,—and he was refused."[47]

During the first year of the war, many Northern leaders saw the conflict as a war for the Union, which should be fought only by white men. Demography seemed to be on their side, because the North had 3–5 times as many white men of military age as the Confederacy and a total ratio of about 2.5 to 1 among those actually willing to serve. Consequently, they took for granted Northern superiority in all kinds of resources and imagined that this imbalance would bring a rapid resolution to a conflict of limited duration. Major General George B. McClellan defined the essence of this kind of warfare in a letter to Lincoln in August 1861 when he explained his strategy for campaigning in Virginia: "We have not only to defeat their armed and organized forces in the field, but to display such an overwhelming strength as will convince all our antagonists, especially those of the governing, aristocratic class, of the utter impossibility of resistance."[48]

The same McClellan was eager to assure Southern aristocrats that their property would not be taken by Northern invading armies. In a pamphlet addressed to "The Union Men of Western Virginia," this high-ranking officer assured them that: "Your homes, your families & your property are safe under our protection. All your rights shall be religiously respected. Notwithstanding all that has been said by the traitors to induce you to believe that our advent among you will be signalized by interference with your slaves, understanding one thing clearly—not only will we abstain from all such interference but we will on the contrary with an iron hand, crush any attempt at insurrection at their part."[49]

Northern efforts to reunite the country did not initially lead to a changed view of racial stereotypes in the Union. Even those who considered recruitment of blacks and Indians to be reasonable feared the likely reaction of the conservative branches of the Union coalition. Some feared that arming free blacks and runaway slaves could bring "fatal and dangerous dissatisfaction in the army"; thus "it would do more injury than good."[50] These circumstances have been confirmed by empirical research conducted by professional historians. James McPherson noticed in his sample of Civil War soldiers' letters that "relatively few Union volunteers mentioned the slavery issue [as a relevant motivation] when they enlisted."[51] In his study of Northern soldiers, Bell Willey pointed that scarcely one in ten Union soldiers "had any real interest in emancipation per se."[52] Costa and Kahn observed that "with rare exceptions, the free black men who sought to enlist as soldiers in the Union army [at the beginning of operations] were turned way."[53]

Other sectors of Northern public opinion, less concerned about African American destiny, believed the war should reunite the country, not create an additional focus of social tension. Important as the conquest of the

Confederacy might be, it should never interfere with property rights or assumed racial hierarchies. Thus, while there was agreement on the main goal of keeping the Union together, other questions, such as emancipation or the status of the Southern states after reunion, were conveniently kept out of the political debate. On July 4, 1861, Lincoln still envisioned a war of limited goals, explaining that he had "no purpose, directly or indirectly, to interfere with slavery in the states where it exists."[54] At this time, Northern leaders believed secession could be reversed through the use of limited measures. The "Anaconda Plan" presented by Major General Winfield Scott was such a strategy. To end the war with as little bloodshed as possible, Scott hoped to divide the area in rebellion and, in conjunction with a naval blockade, envelop the insurgent states. The aim was to have the army occupy as much Confederate territory as possible without engaging in long, bloody campaigns. A war of movement, not of permanent attrition, was the preferred option. Given this limited conception of warfare, expropriation of any form of property as punishment or revenge was rejected by the administration. The *New York Times* reflected the sentiments of most Northerners in May 1861 when it editorialized: "The war on the part of the people of the North is not against the States or the institutions of any State. It is against treason and in defense of the best government in the world."[55] A rapid war with volunteer soldiers would not put stress on communities nor would it bring the threat of a draft. Assuming that few troops would be needed, Republican leaders did not expect to call a draft.

## The Dynamics of the Civil War

During the first year of campaign, President Lincoln and his military leaders aimed for a decisive victory (possibly in a major battle), which, they believed, would bring back the Southern states.[56] What they soon learned, however, was that major battles, even if won, failed to break the back of the rebellion, however frequent or costly these battles might be.

The presidential call for volunteers led to the second and final wave of secession involving the states in the upper South, including the painful loss of Virginia. In addition to being the most important state in the Confederacy, Virginia was the home of many military leaders, and it was closely identified with the nation's heritage. In spite of this loss, and that of North Carolina, Arkansas, and Tennessee, the upper Border States of Maryland, Delaware, Kentucky, and Missouri remained in the Union. Together, the Border States had a combined population of approximately 3,137,000 and an area of 152,000 square miles. They constituted a pivotal asset for the Union during the first inconclusive months of the war. In these states slaves were still considered property and subject to the Fugitive Slave Law. The states' allegiance to the Union was far from complete, as a large proportion of their population supported the Confederacy and viewed the Union army as an occupation force.

The enforcement of federal authority in those states was elusive. Union border policy was extremely cautious and formed a major obstacle to a quick radicalization of the war. In particular, to maintain the allegiance of Border States, the administration moderated racial and recruitment policies during the first year. In the Border States, as in other loyal states, the war effort was based on cooperation between local and federal authorities. But such cooperation would work as only long as the interests of local and federal politics coincided.[57] As a Border State leader put it: "Our course in Delaware, owing to her feebleness politically, ought to be to watch the progress of events, which we can neither control nor retard in the slightest degree."[58]

## Second Phase: Tension

When operations began, few if any Union policymakers foresaw the consequences of the war effort for relations between the center and the periphery of American society. Although enthusiasm for the war alone fueled support for initial Northern mobilization, it did not give leaders a clear vision of the tasks that lay ahead. The military strategists of the Lincoln administration underestimated both the force of Confederate nationalism and the level of cooperation its non-slaveholder groups would offer to secession.[59] By the spring of 1862, the head of the Army of the Potomac, preparing for battle in Yorktown, expressed "the conviction that here is to be fought the great battle that is to decide the existing contest."[60] As in the initial surge to take Humayta fortress in Paraguay (1866), expectations of a quick and glorious conclusion clouded military judgment.

In addition to enthusiasm, the Confederacy had an enormous territory rich in natural resources. It was equipped with good military leadership and was inhabited by a population highly motivated to fight. During the Revolutionary War, similar conditions helped the weaker army prevail.

Technological developments in modern weaponry also reinforced the superiority of the defense. Consequently, the war required a more formidable effort to defeat rebel armies, occupy the land, establish lines of communication, and force into submission an entire country than Northerners imagined. Men and resources would have to be multiplied far beyond initial estimates.[61]

After a year of war, however, there was growing awareness that the South might succeed in winning independence. In April 1862, the Confederate government passed its own Conscription Act, aimed at enrolling most of the able-bodied male population to serve, showing the country's willingness to defend itself from Northern invasion. Soon it became clear that the country could be reunited only through a complete defeat of the Confederate armies. As the last prospects of compromise vanished, the hopes for friendly reunion increasingly became associated with Copperheadism and treason, a stigma that became attached to peace Democrats in the North during the last two years of the conflict.[62]

While the Confederacy was taking firm steps to build its army, both the federal administration and the military bureaucracy lacked the skills needed for stronger mobilization. In 1860, the office of the secretary of war and the military bureaus employed 93 people, including 14 clerks. In the Department of War things were not much better: this pivotal department employed 248 people nationwide, not counting troops. Although this organization was able to manage the procurement system, it proved incompetent at supplying new recruits to an army in permanent need of fresh soldiers.[63]

The difficulties in raising an army became apparent as soon as regiments were gathered in the camps. American military tradition, political factionalism, the lack of infrastructure, the scarcity of adequate military equipment, and bad management quickly contributed to deteriorating conditions in the field. Many troops were poorly dressed and fed. Constant delays in soldiers' pay contributed to growing dissatisfaction, intensifying the demands for bounties and other local incentives. As demand for men grew, some recruits were left to fend for themselves in the cities and camps where they gathered. Word came from Philadelphia that "Ohio troops now here have been on our streets as beggars for food," and in Connecticut payments could be delayed as much as seven months for some troops.[64] Andrew Knox, a lieutenant in the First Connecticut Artillery, complained to his wife, "We have been mustered again for payment and inspection. But the pay does not seem to come. It is going on seven months since I was paid before."[65]

Many of these problems were worsened by the dynamics of the conflict. After the first battles, romantic assumptions about glory and heroism vanished. The Civil War introduced weapons technologies that made the idea of a decisive battle obsolete. Long-range weapons such as the minié ball enhanced defensive capabilities and helped the Confederates maintain strategic positions at a great cost to Union troops. But after the South was invaded, Southerners suffered the worst effects of battle.[66] Prolonged warfare transformed the nature of the conflict, leading to long periods of violence often directed against civilians and infrastructure. Rufus Kinsley, an officer serving in the Mississippi theater, captured the effects of total war on the Confederate populations: "The South is being burned with fire, and drowned in blood. Her villages are desolate, her lands, the richest in the world, laid waste, the wings of commerce idle, all her interests, material, social, political, tied to the hideous monster—Slavery—which is marching with rapid strides to its death."[67]

Pictures and sketches taken on site and published by illustrated magazines, such as *Frank Leslie's Illustrated* and *Harper's Weekly*, exposed the war's realities to populations far behind the battlefields. The Civil War was among the first conflicts that received immediate press coverage. Consequently, communities were well informed about the risks and perspectives faced by volunteers. Enthusiasm for enlistment also decreased with the circulation of casualty lists, which showed an increasing number of soldiers dying from infectious diseases spread by poor sanitation in camps.[68]

During the winter of 1862, recruitment in the North ground to a halt. Men were less and less willing to enlist for long periods of time to the detriment of their personal activities. Most potential recruits were afraid of suffering the consequences of military mismanagement and lack of medical care, common during the first months. They also feared missing the harvest and a chance to help relatives and friends with collective tasks at home. With rising inflation and frozen military salaries, the discrepancies between what soldiers received in the army and market-based salaries grew larger. As campaigns became longer, serving in the army meant more and more sacrifices for families and relatives in the rearguard. It also prevented enlisted soldiers from sharing in the economic boom that increased opportunities in many parts of the North as a consequence of war demand.

In the spring of 1862, successes at the front brought a new wave of enthusiasm to the Northern population. Opinions began to change for the
better when a new secretary of war took charge. Edwin McMasters Stanton, a Democrat committed to the war effort, became secretary of war
with the promise to better organize the Northern armies.[69] With Stanton
in Washington and the energetic George B. McClellan at the head of the
Army of the Potomac, both the training and supply of the Union army
were reorganized. Improvements also came through nationalizing the procurement system. One of the first new national bureaucracies to develop
during this period, national procurement ended the influence of state governors and regional contractors over lucrative military supply contracts.

Special attention was given to the Army of the Potomac and to the spring
campaigns on the eastern front.[70] McClellan's obsession with every detail
and his strong administrative capacity convinced soldiers, politicians, and
civilians that Lincoln had finally found his general. Preparations looked toward a short campaign, to be followed by the occupation of Richmond, the
Confederate capital, during the spring.[71] But confidence was undermined
when Secretary Stanton discontinued recruitment through General Order
33, in April 1862, following the capture of Fort Henry and Fort Donelson
in the west. His order reflected rising optimism and the administration's
overconfidence in McClellan's leadership. It proved to be a major mistake.
Halting recruitment amazed some Republican leaders, among them Thurlow Weed, advisor to Secretary of State William Seward, who critically reg-
istered in his memoirs:

> When we stopped recruiting in the midst of our successes, we dealt a fatal
> blow to our army, and it is really a wonder to me that our commanding
> generals consented to submit to such a measure, which crippled them
> at a time when an overwhelming force became necessary to finish up
> the good work. It was a policy hardly less suicidal than if we had stopped
> sending supplies and ammunition to our men in the field. Where we
> would have found last winter ten men eager to enlist, anxious to share in
> our triumphs, we will scarcely now find one, so deep is the gloom and dis-
> trust which has taken hold of our people. I think ours is the first instance
> in history where a government shut off supplies of men in the midst of a
> gigantic war . . . [72]

From May to July, General McClellan continually demanded more
troops to support his long-delayed and ultimately thwarted attacks against
Richmond. The Northern manpower shortage intensified during the

spring campaigns because of a combination of war reversals and renewed economic opportunities in the North. In the Shenandoah Valley as well as in the western theater, progress was slow and costly.[73] As long as Vicksburg resisted, it was impossible to make the Mississippi River a conduit for Union troops and supplies. On the home front, the combined effects of an improving economy and the agricultural work cycle also discouraged many potential recruits.

Many of the above features were also common to Brazil during the Paraguayan War. But citizenship was much more widespread in America. Opposition political parties could elect state governments in the United States, whereas in Brazil, provincial presidents were appointed by the emperor. This constituted an important asset in the hands of local communities around the Union, as voters could pressure representatives and governors to negotiate more advantageous quotas with Washington. Brazilian recruiting agents, on the other hand, targeted the poor or clients of political bosses temporarily out of power.

### Third Phase: Federal Reaction

Public dismay in the North rose during the spring of 1862 when news came of the failure of the Peninsular campaign, McClellan's attempt to take Richmond. Patriotic feelings began wearing thin, and volunteers became increasingly hard to find. The period from June 1862 to July 1863 can be considered the watershed of Northern war efforts. The conflict turned from a campaign to preserve territorial unity into a total war against Confederate society. Months of failure and relentless resistance by the enemy reinforced the perception that changes were needed if Washington was to win the war. Members of the coalition in power became more convinced than ever of the need to undertake stronger measures to reinforce national power. As Lincoln explained to the New York financier August Belmont during the summer of 1862: "This government cannot much longer play the game in which it stakes all, and its enemies stake nothing. Those enemies must understand that they cannot experiment for ten years trying to destroy the government, and if they fail still come back into the Union unhurt."[74] Even Thurlow Weed, a conservative Republican, agreed that the war's conduct must change, asserting: "It may appear almost hopeless to attempt to bring the South back to the Union by negotiation. Men and women alike, in that distracted portion of our country, have become frantic and exasperated by the teachings of unprincipled leaders and the miseries of civil war."[75]

During the course of the next two years, a war between armies would turn into a war of societies, involving the destruction of Southern slavery and the annihilation of the Confederate army. This strategic shift encompassed enormous transformations in the organization of the army, as well as in the structure of American government, especially in the scope of the federal capacity to recruit, interfering with traditions and practices of large and small communities around the country.[76]

The federal government centralized decisions to an unprecedented level and extended the range of recruitment to encompass a larger number of citizens who would not have enlisted voluntarily. In his war memories, Silas Wright Burt, an assistant to Governor Oliver P. Morton of Indiana, expressed the shift in thinking of those directly connected to the war efforts: "We had learned . . . that war was such a barbarous institution that it could not be conducted upon democratic principles of our civil authority."[77] At the same time, the dynamics of the war created a new and more radical vision of its objectives and main targets. As James McPherson has argued, Robert E. Lee's victories in Virginia provided the stimulus that would bring about the destruction of his own social environment. Senator Fessenden from Maine voiced such feelings in July 1862: "The war must be fought on 'different principles'; for the 'white kid-glove warfare' was past."[78] Part of the problem lay in the failure of volunteerism. While war enthusiasm could serve as a strong element in support of mobilization, it alone could not provide the additional numbers needed. Most of those who had enlisted for patriotic reasons were already in the ranks, and additional manpower was becoming scarce. In the face of a progressive decline in recruitment, and alarmed by the range of tasks lying ahead, authorities began to look for strategies to keep a permanent inflow of new recruits. To accomplish this, the federal government would need a central structure with the power to overrule local objections and enforce compliance. That brings us to the problem of mobilizing the militia, an old puzzle in American military history.

### The Militia Act

In order to recover from the unfortunate consequences of General Order 33, the Republican administration decided to coordinate a "governors' call" for new troops in June 1862. Secretary of State William Seward persuaded all governors to unite in supporting the president and to call for 150,000 more volunteers. This call helped replenish the army, which had been reduced by reversals resulting from administrative mistakes and a sequence of battlefield losses. But the Republican governors conveniently issued the call as a decentralized and local request, not as a centralized presidential order. Although general perception acknowledged the urgent need to increase the Union's military power, many Republicans feared that a direct presidential request could be interpreted as a sign of desperation, and likely increase the impression of failure associated with the delicate status of the war.

To the "governors' call" of June 28, Lincoln responded with a presidential request for an additional 300,000 troops on July 2. The men who responded to the July 2 call were mustered in for three years' service. All sides profited from this strategy: the federal government avoided a public demonstration of weakness, governors kept the initiative in the eyes of their constituents, and the army received reinforcements to support its summer campaign in Confederate territory.[79]

Meanwhile, Congress discussed and approved the Militia Act, a measure that represented the first real incursion of federal power into the realm of the states. The bill authorized the president to call out the states' militia whenever needed and allowed him to issue quotas for each state, thus extending presidential power. It also empowered the federal government to order a draft in states with deficient or nonexistent conscription laws. Should a state be unable to fill its designated quota, the governor was expected to coordinate a draft, calling for federal help when necessary.[80]

The Militia Act extended the federal recruiting base, but it also limited the term of enlistment to nine months, clearly different from the terms of the July volunteers.[81] It allowed each township to claim credit for all the men enlisted, regardless of whether they actually resided there or not. This provision opened the window to searching for substitutes from other places. If states did not achieve their July quota by August 15, they were to fill incomplete regiments through a draft. Although most states avoided the draft, the prospect of one stimulated local recruitment, breaking through the lethargy that had prevailed during most of the spring.[82]

The Militia Act marked the awakening of the federal government to the magnitude of the war, overthrowing traditional assumptions about the adequacy of a volunteer force. It was the initial step toward transforming a fragmented and multiform combat force into a uniform national army. Signed into law by President Lincoln on July 17, 1862, after a very brief discussion in Congress, the measure was supported by both political parties and the partisan press. It signaled the advent of national conscription in the North.[83]

Although the Militia Act used a carrot-and-stick approach in order to get the states to recruit more men, it did not relieve the states of the work of raising troops, nor did it question the power of governors and local authorities in this particular area. Many features of the former, decentralized system were kept in place. For example, governors remained in charge of recruitment procedures, and the formation of regiments was predominantly local. Communities held meetings to encourage men to enlist or to engage a substitute, and they also raised money to pay for higher enlistment bounties. Militiamen and volunteers stayed in local units that continued to elect their own officers. "Volunteers" also had the privilege of entering newly formed regiments, if they desired. Consequently, the range of the act was limited: the national government abdicated the power to directly compel citizens to enlist or to appoint junior officers. Governors retained the power to coerce local authorities to raise the troops, thus avoiding the controversies of a federal draft in their jurisdiction.[84]

While states retained control over officer appointments, governors failed to provide positive leadership in the unpopular area of recruiting. Localism remained strong and delayed the draft in some states for months. Sometimes local authorities were able to extend the range of exemptions, temporarily shielding political allies and dependents. Many men avoided enlistment through medical exemptions or because they worked as railroad employees, state clerks, telegraph operators, post office employees, firemen, or other strategically important jobs. Yet one newspaper declared, "Medical ethics in Connecticut at this time were of the most casual sort," due to the number of medical exemptions granted.[85] A growing number of potential recruits also applied for ideological and moral exemptions, such as "conscientious objection."[86]

One of the more effective ways to increase compliance was by offering bounties. The bounty system originated in the colonial period and was reinstituted, with great success, during the first year of the war. The federal government instituted a bounty of one hundred dollars to be paid to those who enlisted for a three-year term of service. Originally the bounty was paid at the time of discharge, but under pressure from the states, the government decided to give twenty-five dollars in advance to those who presented themselves voluntarily. States, local communities, and private individuals soon expanded the bounty system in their anxiety to fill quotas with volunteers, thereby avoiding the stigma and disgrace of conscription. Many towns created additional bounties. Cape Elizabeth, Maine, duplicated the hundred dollars offered by the federal government.[87] As the threat of the draft increased, bounties multiplied, especially in affluent communities where resources abounded.[88] Bounties distinguished post-1862 volunteering from that of 1861. As enthusiasm decreased, the force of "selective incentives" was pivotal in keeping up recruitment. The richer a community was, the more easily could it get volunteers. Such regional imbalances worked against the poorest areas, which lacked the means to pay for substitutes. In the long run, the multiplication of bounties would break the links between soldiers and their communities, as a growing number of recruits were no longer connected to the places where they enlisted. But in the middle of 1862, these unintended effects were not clear to most, and they appeared avoidable if the armies of the Union achieved rapid progress on the battlefields.

Fear of the draft and incentives of increasing bounties caused a new cycle of volunteerism in the North. The August 4 troop call, which was directly linked to the Militia Act, was met with enthusiasm by many states and the District of Columbia. Overall, the number of recruits surpassed the original demand, and thousands were enlisted in new corps of volunteers. Such success was partly due to the excellent results of the July 2 call, which furnished a surplus for the rest of the year.[89]

Although most areas exceeded their assigned quotas, the states of Indiana, Ohio, Wisconsin, and the Border States fell behind. When these states were unable to draft, their populations suffered repressive measures, generally undertaken by state agents, sometimes with the support of the militia. These included the suspension of the writ of habeas corpus; the institution of a passport system; and, occasionally, a draft. Selectmen and state-appointed sheriffs organized local drafts when needed. But overall, drafts were scattered, popular resistance was limited, and authorities viewed the results as very positive. As a Maryland reformer observed, "the fear of being drafted [would] compel every loyal man to foster recruiting."[90]

According to Robert Sterling, the Militia Act was the halfway point between state recruitment and national conscription. Although it advanced the power of the national government, it did not challenge local prerogatives, nor did it energize a more organized movement of anti-draft resistance. Consequently, the regulations established in the Militia Act were a curious composite of national guidelines superimposed on antiquated state militia statutes. The act could work well as long as both the center and the periphery cooperated, but its efficiency also depended on battle results.[91]

In spite of great enthusiasm throughout the North during early summer 1862, failure on the battlefield undermined the Union's war efforts. Advances were made in the Gulf States by extending the naval blockade. In August, however, the Union army was defeated in the Second Battle of Bull Run, and in September it failed to achieve a decisive victory at Antietam. In November, after months of indecision, George McClellan was removed from his command. His replacement, General Ambrose Everett Burnside, led the Army of the Potomac into disastrous defeat at Fredericksburg in December, and Union troops retired to winter quarters without having achieved the dreamed-of decisive victory in the eastern theater. A great wave of depression fell over the North in the aftermath of Fredericksburg. Confidence in the war effort was severely shaken at the same time that internal problems and political dissension damaged the administration's continuous endeavors to reorganize its armies. Politically, the Emancipation Proclamation in January 1863 temporarily weakened the war coalition.

After Lincoln's preliminary Emancipation Proclamation, issued in September 1862, a great uproar arose from people who felt they could not support a war to end black slavery in the Confederacy. The combined effects of war reversals and the Emancipation Proclamation roused "peace Democrats" or "Copperheads" from initial resignation to more aggressive opposition to the war and to the Republican administration. Other less radical Democratic groups continued to support the war while demanding a return to the war's original, limited goals. These "war Democrats" believed that the Union should be preserved, not that slavery should be destroyed, and they had strong reservations about the temporary suspension of civil liberties in certain areas.[92] The Democratic Congressman Daniel Vorhees of Indiana voiced the position of this group, complaining that war enthusiasm would decrease due to the abolitionist agenda: "I am showing up this abolitionist policy as a reason why the loyal enthusiasm which impelled men at first to the field, under a mistaken confidence and reliance upon the good faith of this Administration, can no longer be relied on."[93]

The commitment of the Democratic Party to the war effort was still connected to the antebellum local and individualist vision of America, representing "the great pre-modern cultures within American society."[94] In line with such views, Democrats opposed confiscation of "rebel property," including slaves. George C. McClellan voiced this view in a letter to Lincoln, predicting, "A declaration of radical views, especially upon slavery, will rapidly disintegrate our present armies."[95]

Democratic electoral successes in the 1862 state and Congressional elections sparked the reemergence of the partisan spirit and the possibility of a presidential shift in the next elections. In practice, control of state government meant control of recruitment, so that Democratic governors could become major obstacles to Republican war efforts. Moreover, out of office Democrats could become noisy minorities, as they did in Indiana, Ohio, Connecticut, and Pennsylvania.[96]

Among the many structural problems that plagued the army in early 1863 was the urgent need to replenish veteran regiments. Since the beginning of the war, different troops had enlisted for different terms of service, varying from three months to three years. Under the volunteer system, recruiting led to the constant creation of new regiments, while veteran regiments shrank as a result of deaths, casualties, furloughs, and desertion. Multiplying calls for volunteers and concessions to local needs turned the lack of uniform terms of enlistment into a major problem. If permitted to choose, volunteers would prefer to enlist in new regiments that maintained links to friends and comrades. The nine-month terms of soldiers who enlisted under the Militia Act were set to expire in May 1863. With most of the two-year terms set to expire at the same time, the army's manpower crisis turned for the worse.[97]

Another difficulty for the army was the different levels of pay soldiers received, as the normal wage of thirteen dollars per month, established in the beginning of the war, was increasingly supplemented by federal, state, and local bounties. Such incentives acted as an enticement for new enlistment, but they also increased resentment among veterans who had not received bounties, and they increased federal and state budgets.[98] Volunteers from the beginning of the war resented being paid less, despite greater sacrifices, than newly arrived recruits, who were better paid simply because they had enlisted later. This resentment disrupted reenlistment and risked depriving the Union army of its most skilled combatants.

Until spring 1863, the army relied on popular enthusiasm and local goodwill to replace soldiers and keep recruitment at full strength. But as communities faced increasing sacrifices, their disposition to cooperate with federal authorities dropped throughout the North. By fall 1862, Union leaders faced a dilemma similar to the one that imperial bureaucrats in Brazil would face four years later: either change their strategy or give up the war effort. Their decision made the war still more violent, and required a greater degree of compliance from civilian populations in the North.[99]

Although there were many similarities between the dilemmas confronting governments in the United States and Brazil, Lincoln had a much more sophisticated organization in place to deal with social and political dissenters: the Republican Party. From the beginning of the war, the party's primary objective had been the reunification of the nation. But it soon became clear that, to subdue the rebellion, it would be necessary to resort to extreme measures, including the development of centralized authority. Given their political position, the fate of the Republicans became tied to the military defeat of the Confederacy. Consequently, the Republican Party worked to cement the alliance between state governors and the federal government. Without such a working agreement, it would have been impossible to extend federal authority over the states. In the absence of a bureaucratic structure, the party furnished the best alternative to strengthen the central government's capabilities, restraining the centrifugal impulses in the states and transforming the war into what one author has defined as "an enterprise in modernization."[100]

On February 16, 1863, Republican legislators introduced a single bill that would provide for stronger control by the federal government over the process of recruiting. Senator Henry Wilson, head of the Committee on Military Affairs, presented Senate Bill 511, a conscription measure aimed at providing the federal government with the supplementary powers it needed to enroll troops. The bill was the subject of extensive debate, with Republicans and Unionist Democrats in support, and Peace Democrats in opposition. Senator Wilson's speech on the Senate floor revealed a new radicalization of the Republican attitude: "The needs of the nation demand that we should rely not upon volunteering, nor upon calling forth the militia, but that we should fill the regiments now in the field, worn and wasted by disease and death, by enrolling and drafting the population of the country under the constitutional authority 'to raise and support armies.'"[101]

Peace Democrats opposed national conscription as a matter of principle. They saw the bill as undue intervention of the federal government in the lives of the states. They denounced such interference as a violation of America's fundamental beliefs in the primacy of the individual and the right of choice. As asserted by Democratic Representative John Steele, from New York, "I think it is unjust to the States. I think it is one of a series of measures tending to centralize power unnecessarily, and I think it will alarm and distress the people."[102] A minister denounced the new situation as an "immorality," noting that "this doctrine is rank and treason. It seems like a spontaneous conspiracy of a mighty faction, inflamed with selfish passion to overthrow the government of our Fathers, and destroy our constitutional liberties."[103]

In spite of the objections from the opposition, the Republican majority in both houses succeeded in passing the bill. On February 28, 1863, Congress approved what was called "An Act for Enrolling and Calling out the National Forces," commonly known as the Enrollment Act. It was signed by President Lincoln on March 3. The measure granted the president full power to raise and support armies without state assistance. Under the new law, all men between the ages of twenty and thirty-five and all unmarried men between thirty-five and forty-five were liable for military duty. In a more radical step, the bill absorbed state militias into the national forces. This statute centralized and militarized the draft by replacing local selectmen and sheriffs with uniformed, national provost marshals and federal enrolling officers. The federal government redefined exemptions at the same time that it extended the draft's reach to state officials and other previously exempt groups. The election of officers and other democratic links between soldiers and their communities were severely reduced or suspended. Soldiers also lost the capacity to choose their units, as military service became compulsory, national, and bureaucratic.[104] Francis Lieber, the chairman of the National Loyal League, connected these changes to a new kind of nationalism, one that appealed to the nationalization of civic virtue: "We pledge ourselves as National men, devoted to the Nationality of this great people. No government can wholly dispense with loyalty except the fiercest despotism ruling by naked intimidation; but a republic stands in greater need of it than any other government, and most of all a republic beset by open rebellion and insidious treason. Loyalty is pre-eminently a civic virtue in a free country. It is patriotism cast in the graceful mould of candid devotion to the harmless government of an unshackled nation."[105]

The most significant change that came with the new law was the designation of federal provost marshals subject to a provost marshal-general in Washington, D.C. These agents had special military powers and could call a draft in districts that had not reached their quota. They reduced the ability of local functionaries to mediate between military needs and parochial pressures, and they eliminated the role of local power in recruitment. Through the Enrollment Act, provost marshals were empowered to ignore hostile Democratic state and local governments and to enforce authority as they pleased, overruling local opposition and controlling it by threatening dissenters with a charge of treason. According to Iver Bernstein, the Enrollment Act, more than any other Civil War legislation, "brought the presence of the federal government into the community, into the waged workplace, and into the household—into nearly every corner of working-class life."[106]

In spite of its centralizing character, the Enrollment Act failed to provide a "fair tool" for recruitment. Fairness was lost from the beginning as a series of exemptions and opportunities for commutation and substitution were negotiated in the Congress. For those with enough money to pay, it was just a matter of negotiating a substitute in the informal markets for men that spread throughout the North. For those who could not find a substitute, commutation clauses and community efforts furnished a palliative. The more affluent communities raised money to commute the services of local inhabitants, and hired outsiders to fill their quotas. A woman from Rochester, New York, commented, "The city is making an effort to pay 600 dollars bounty and I guess we shall get our quota filled before the draft."[107] The system spawned factious competition for recruits and produced the twin evils of bounty jumpers and brokers. Free riders took advantage of the rules and profited from the situation. Frequently "selective incentives" competed with each other, and substitutes responded to increasing bonuses by enlisting in towns that offered the highest payments.

As the year 1863 advanced and war needs grew, the cost of substitutes rose. The enforcement of the draft during the summer and the fall of 1863 coincided with the development of insurance clubs and efforts by factory owners and political machines to aid those unable to pay for exemptions and unwilling to be conscripted. Commutation costs were fixed at three hundred dollars, about two-thirds of a workingman's annual income. The Democratic Senator James W. Nesmith of Oregon, a member of the Military Affairs Committee, remarked that permitting draftees to "commute their patriotism" would lead to the nation's death. He ironically suggested an appropriate epitaph: "Died of Commutation."[108]

Northern communities reacted in different ways to increasing demands for manpower. Some communities raised funds for substitutions or commutations. In Cape Elizabeth, Maine, the town's quota was increasingly supplied by outsiders. The proportion of enlisted soldiers born in town fell from 51.7 percent during the first year of the war to only 6 percent after the draft. Such an influx of outsiders can be explained by the high bonuses this affluent community provided.[109]

This strategy, however, was not available to all communities; it depended on each town's capacity to raise sufficient funds. Evidence points to a situation in which the richest communities benefited from the disadvantages of the poorest. As a result, there was increasing resentment among poorer groups. In the summer of 1863, the act was answered by a wave of resistance; riots broke out in major eastern cities and in the Midwest. There was no planned opposition to the draft, because most people agreed that something should be done to put down the rebellion. Catholic and Democratic authorities urged their constituents to find a way to comply with increasing war demands. But many less affluent communities saw commutation as an instrument that reinforced the political hegemony of the Republican Party and the economic power of industrialists and merchants, penalizing Democrats, immigrants, and the poor. Charges of incompetence, dishonesty, political immorality, and political partisanship were thrown at many officials who worked for the new recruitment machine. A parody of a popular song mocked the growing interference of the federal government in citizens' personal lives: "We're coming, ancient Abraham, several hundred strong[;] We hadn't no 300 dollars and so we come along. We hadn't no rich parents to pony up the tin. So we went unto the provost and there were mustered in."[110]

Robert Sterling's work on the Midwest shows a strong correlation between anti-draft resistance and class, partisan affiliation, and religion. Democratic counties with smaller incomes and higher percentages of foreign immigrants, especially Irish and German Catholics, were more likely to have riots than more-affluent Midwestern communities. Sometimes draft dodgers, deserters, and resisters used every device and artifice imaginable, including outright violence, to escape what they perceived as the injustice and inequity of the draft.[111]

In the Midwest, enrollment resistance was most widespread in Wisconsin, Illinois, and Indiana. In these states popular reaction went from complaints in the Democratic press to open insubordination, including attacks on the property and persons of provost marshals. Sometimes resisters targeted federal agents or local appointees responsible for draft enforcement. Rioters usually targeted books and lists of eligible draftees, but some riots were more violent; thirty-eight enrollment officers were murdered in ambush, or by crowds. As a result, many enrollment officers and district provost marshals had to be protected by army units.[112]

Popular revolts raised two specters for government authorities: Copperheadism, treason, and internal dissension on the one hand, and irrational disorder on the other. Both fears were clearly stated in the final report of Provost Marshal General Peter Fry. Fry called acts of resistance crimes perpetrated by the poorest of lower-class immigrants, who were unconnected to American patriotic heritage. To Fry, the actions of the crowds were not rational but responded to propaganda from opportunistic Democratic politicians opposed to the war for partisan reasons. New York Congressman Abram B. Olin voiced such fears when he defended the use of force by federal authorities during debates on the draft, emphasizing that: "the Government [should] arm itself with every power that lies in the strong arms and loyal hearts of the people."[113]

Similar perceptions of anti-draft motivation can be observed in the pioneering historical analyses made by Eugene C. Murdock and Fred A. Shannon, who studied information presented in the *Official Records of the Civil War*. They focused attention on the political-engineering of the war, especially on the role of the federal government as an enforcer in modern society during modern warfare, rather than on the particular justifications of groups negatively affected by modernization. Both argued that draft resistance could best be explained as opposition to the Lincoln administration's determination to win the war for the Union.[114] More recent, multilayered, approaches emphasize the diversity of interests involved in the resistance to the draft, as well as the connections between Republican efforts and the cultural backgrounds of some resisting groups. These groups did not necessarily oppose recruitment or the Union cause, but they resisted what they perceived to be unjust features of the process. Taking into account previously existing local conflicts, analysis reveals that popular resistance reflected a plurality of grievances and local complaints, aggravated by the transformation in the nature of the recruitment.

As demonstrated by the classic studies of collective action developed by George Rudé, Eric Hobsbawm, and E. P. Thompson, it is possible to identify in the crowd's apparent disorder organizational forms and coherent logics of action.[115] Further studies by Robert Sterling, Grace Palladino, and Iver Bernstein of local communities show that popular violence did not result from mere "copperhead manipulation." Resisters interpreted factionalism and political partisanship as part of a Republican attempt to subdue long-established institutions connected to local autonomy. The military occupation of such areas reinforced the fears of "political despotism" denounced by local Democratic newspapers and strengthened by people's beliefs in the virtue of local government, by racism, and by class antagonism.[116]

In the anthracite region of Pennsylvania, local provost marshals cooperated directly with the bosses of the largest coal companies, linking the draft to the suppression of unions and repression of labor leaders. In Illinois, martial law was declared in many districts where Democrats predominated, temporarily subverting long-established local institutions. These actions were perceived as illegal interference by the national government into local business, interference that reinforced the position of industrialists and merchants long connected to the transformations taking place in the structure of American markets. In the special case of immigrants, the threat of a draft revived memories of one of the most hated institutions of European politics, the draconian laws that regulated recruitment in their former homelands. Consequently it is not surprising that immigrants stood out among early resisters.[117]

## The Draft and Republican Dilemmas

One of the most dramatic episodes of resistance to federal recruitment occurred in New York City in July 1863. For five days, armed mobs interrupted the first enforcement of federal conscription, challenging national authority in the most important American city of the day. The riots had their origin in New York's political and social environment, but they were exacerbated by the circumstances of the war, especially by the grievances resulting from the threat of an imminent draft whose burden would weigh heaviest on the poorest white inhabitants of the city. For some, the riots signaled a struggle for political power between Democratic immigrants and reformist Republicans. But for many observers, the riots were a challenge to the new rules that had emerged from the war.[118] To Republican authorities in New York City, the draft brought fear and astonishment.

According to Iver Bernstein, the draft riots must be seen in the context of an ongoing process of urban change, with ramifications at the regional and national levels. An important issue was the dispute over control of the labor market. Written in the aftermath of the 1863 New York City draft riots, a *New York Tribune* editorial gives an indication of how deeply threatened some whites felt by black labor: "The mob exults in the belief that if it failed in its other objects, it has at least secured possession of the labor of the city, and has driven the blacks to seek work elsewhere."[119]

Some Republicans saw the riots as a political maneuver orchestrated by New York Peace Democrats. Lincoln's private secretary, John Hay, a critic of Governor Horace Seymour, saw in the episode a chance to subdue the city´s insubordination. In his diary entry for August 14, 1863, Hay observed: "The Govt. was never intended by the Constitution to be left helpless to the attacks of discontented State officers. I thank God for the riot if as one of its results we set a great authoritative precedent of the absolute supremacy of the National power, military and civil, over the State. Every nail that enters the coffin of the dead-and-gone humbug of State's Rights is a promise of future & enduring peace and power."[120]

At the national level, the main fuel was provided by the implementation of the Enrollment Act in the city. The provisions of the act touched three explosive issues in New York social life: relations between the wealthy and the poor, between blacks and whites, and between the city and the nation.[121] What began as a protest against the draft turned into a direct attack on the wealthy and on Republican Party institutions, as well as a grotesque racial pogrom as shown in a father's letter to his soldier son: "We have indeed had fearful times in N.Y. . . . a week yesterday 10 men attacked Lew Lacksman's father house and broke with stones at the parlor windows . . . the most wicked & fearful part was their ill treatment of the poor colored people several of whom were murdered by hanging."[122]

As a consequence of the five-day riot, the federal government prudently postponed the draft in New York, thus avoiding declaring a state of emergency.[123] The federal administration avoided more serious interference in local New York issues, recognizing Democratic hegemony in the country's biggest city in exchange for its tacit loyalty. New York's quotas were filled through the increase of recruitment in other states in a process that would bring renewed episodes of political and social tension during the months to come.

New York's experience with the draft riots tells us much about the ambiguous results of the draft policy during 1862–1863. If the draft exemplified a push toward centralization, its failure was clear by the fall of 1863.

It revealed the limits of radical legislation to expand the powers of the federal government. If the Republican government was forced to compromise on conscription, however, it left unresolved the problem of how to raise an army adequate to the task of winning the war. The anti-draft riots were only the most visible aspect of the problem. As Peter Levine has shown, protest took many forms and turned into a widespread phenomenon during the spring of 1863. Resistance crossed the barriers of class and ethnicity, involving a decline of compliance even in the most loyal areas. The combined effects of illegal and legal avoidance strategies were more harmful to recruitment than active resistance. Of 292,441 individuals originally drawn in the 1863 draft, only 9,881, or 3.4 percent, effectively served themselves. Discharges, commutations, and substitutions severely undermined the efficacy of the draft, and 83 percent of those liable for conscription found legal means to avoid the military.[124]

To resolve the dilemma posed by these limits to national power, it became necessary to fill the ranks with other groups, challenging old prejudices and opening the army to racial minorities that had previously been excluded. European immigrants became the easiest and most common target of recruiting agents. They had less protection and fewer rights since many were not yet citizens. African Americans provided another solution to the Republican dilemma because from the beginning of the war it had been clear that a large number of men in the South were available to substitute for Northern volunteers. Blacks comprised less than 1 percent of the Northern population, but they formed a large portion of the population in the Confederate states.[125] Such an option offered a much smaller financial and social cost to the government and lowered the costs for substitutes. The boom of black enlistment during the second half of 1863 was one of many possible responses to the North's difficulties. It would assume a pivotal role in the enormous expansion of the army in the last two years of the conflict. If prejudice had prevented the federal government from using African Americans before, the realities of war had, by 1863, provided enough reason to change. Therefore, the shock of war led to one of the biggest transformations in the history of racial relations in America.

The unexpected direction taken by events during the American Civil War parallels some of the developments in Brazil years later. War aims changed. In the United States, a war over states' right to secede versus the determination to preserve territorial integrity became a war to emancipate slaves and preserve democratic government. Ironically, those transformations were propelled through increasing government intervention in the affairs of the states and increasing control over the activities of citizens. In Brazil, a war to preserve territorial integrity against a foreign invasion became a complicated dispute over the limits of Imperial intervention over the provinces, where some eventually saw the Imperial government as a foreign invader.

Waging war placed enormous burdens on the poor and unprotected in both countries. The Union army was initially composed of citizens, but gaps in the ranks were increasingly filled by immigrants and former slaves fighting to have their rights recognized. In order to end traditional conscription of the unprotected poor, the Brazilian Army tried to enlarge its ranks with volunteers by appealing to their patriotism. But patriotism could not overcome social stigmas. Service in the ranks of the regular army failed to become an acceptable business of citizenship.

# THREE

# From Inertia to Insurgence

## The Crisis in Brazilian Recruitment, 1865–1868

In the early morning hours of August 22, 1865, a gang of about thirty armed men assaulted the jail in Ingá, a village in the Northeastern cotton province of Paraíba. The gang released all fifteen prisoners. Some of these men were undoubtedly criminals, but others had been conscripted into the Imperial army and were being held in the jail before being sent to the front. Among the conscripts were two sons of the landowner Francisco Antônio de Arruda Câmara. Intoxicated with success, the gang and the prisoners, now close to fifty strong, marched to the recruitment officer's home, brazenly shouting insults and curses. Cornered by the angry crowd, the official hid inside, in fear for his life.

A few hours later, a new gang arrived, commanded by the National Guard Lieutenant Colonel Eufrazio Arruda Câmara, Francisco Antônio´s brother. Eufrazio had learned of his nephews' imprisonment and had rushed from his command fifteen miles away to free them. According to provincial records, Eufrazio publicly lamented that he had missed the earlier action, declaring with belligerence that he would have tied the sub-delegate up and locked him in jail in place of the freed prisoners. Moreover, he was sorry the attack had happened at night because during the day everyone in town could have watched! There was no immediate imperial retaliation. The angry crowd dispersed unmolested.[1]

An administrative investigation swiftly followed. As important as the mob attack on the jail was the fact that a National Guard lieutenant colonel had publicly humiliated a sub-delegate (deputy), an imperial official representing the chief of police in this village, and this constituted an offense to national authority. Imperial, provincial, and local authorities were supposed to cooperate to fill provincial recruitment quotas. In Ingá, however, cooperation over recruitment had broken down, and the simmering conflicts between local and Imperial authorities finally boiled over.[2]

Concerned about the crisis, the president of Paraíba appointed Judge Felinto Henrique de Almeida to head the inquiry. Provincial presidents were appointed by the Cabinet in Rio de Janeiro and reported directly to the Imperial ministry. In early September, Judge Almeida submitted a report that sharply contrasted the bold actions of the liberators with the lack of resistance by guards, local officials, and members of the community. His narrative touched on a delicate issue: the growing unpopularity of military recruitment for the war against Paraguay. After describing the sorry state of public security in the region, Almeida observed that "the facility [with] which [the population] accepts the idea of resisting prison" was connected to "the repugnancy felt by the people for the service of war."[3]

The unrest in Ingá was a preview of greater unrest to come. As recruitment quotas increased, popular repugnance for the war grew stronger and increasing numbers of recruits had to be held in jails, lest they flee before they could be shipped to the front in Paraguay. Expanded military recruitment, now targeting individuals who had hitherto been safe from impressments, led to increasing resistance by the inhabitants in the countryside. Attacks against jails became more and more common as villagers defied Imperial authority and as local authorities sided with them.

This recalls what happened to Provost Marshal William Pors in Illinois, discussed at the opening of chapter 2. In the United States, however, military service was still viewed as an emblem of citizenship until the Enrollment Act of 1863 brought the threat of a draft close to home and American attitudes towards military campaigns began to sour. While recruitment was traditionally directed toward social undesirables in Brazil, conflicts on the home front eventually arose when men previously immune from impressments were targeted by Imperial agents. Consequently, patriotism was a casualty of war in both countries.

From August 1865 to December 1868, the Paraguayan campaign was crippled by the Empire's inability to transform Brazilian civilians into soldiers. The root of the problem lay in the unexpected dimensions of the war. Its long duration and the strategic dilemmas faced by the military command made it bloodier than anyone had foreseen. The Brazilian army of 18,000 professional troops was insufficient for a prolonged war, and, as a result, the monarchy had to enlarge its army quickly.[4]

Many sectors of Brazilian society rebelled against the increasing war demands. Local patrons opposed the transfer of workers under their protection to distant battlefields, seeing in it an affront to personal prestige and also the loss of valuable labor. Poor free workers fought conscription because it temporally erased differences of class and status, reducing them to the level of the worst social scum, a stigma in a society with many distinctions in rank, even among the poor.[5] The crisis underlined the nation's inability to extract local resources, in particular human resources, for military service. Since 1850, proposals to create a national census and adopt the metric system had met with no success, setting a precedent of opposition to standardization. During the Triple Alliance War, however, conflicts of interest between the Imperial bureaucracy and local bosses became much more intense. State power circumvented traditional arenas of private patronage by recruiting clients and protégés out from under these bosses, forcing large contingents of the free population into the army and increasing demands to liberate slaves for army service.[6] As the campaign against Paraguay continued, growing popular resistance against military service created great tension between the monarchy and land barons in all regions of the country.[7]

## The Paraguayan Campaign

The first wave of recruitment for the Brazilian army occurred from December 1864 to May 1865. It furnished a contingent of soldiers large enough to help drive Paraguayan forces out of Rio Grande do Sul and liberate Uruguay from the Blancos. Now headed by former rebel leader Venancio Flores, the Uruguayan Allied government abandoned Paraguay in support of the Triple Alliance. The Alliance victory at the naval battle of Riachuelo (June 11, 1865) less than a month later destroyed the Paraguayan fleet and cut off contact between Paraguay's government and foreign nations.[8]

During this first phase of operations, volunteer enthusiasm impressed Imperial authorities, who were used to a population extremely resistant to recruitment.[9] In this case, however, the population responded to Paraguay's sudden invasion of Brazilian territory without a declaration of war. This insult inflamed patriotic sentiments and encouraged spontaneous demonstrations and enlistment across Brazil. Popular support and a feeling of general enthusiasm underscored the early campaigns, although patronage still played an important role in the way people volunteered. Army reports from 1865 and 1866 give a clear picture of this patriotic spirit, and provincial reports present additional evidence of widespread enthusiasm for the war.

Volunteers poured in from provinces very far away from the theater of operations. More than three thousand miles from the front in the northeastern province of Alagoas, the patriotic citizen José Severiano de Mello petitioned the provincial president to accept six of his children, three sons and three daughters, for the war effort. In his petition, dated April 4, 1865, Mr. Mello attributed his generous zeal to "the true love for the fatherland that has always inflamed my heart; its flood of electric fire pushes me to the battlefields, to take my part in this glorious campaign of my fellow countrymen against the Paraguayans!"[10]

To the west, similar expressions of support appeared. In a private letter to the minister of war, José Caetano de Vaz Junior, Maranhão's provincial president, listed many individual initiatives supporting national war efforts. Influential citizens and political bosses brought relatives, protégés, and clients to enlist in the newly created Corps of Volunteers. Others signed up themselves, along with friends, sons, and brothers.

As Ricardo Salles noted, monetary donations supporting the war were not limited to the rich. Public employees, small tenants, tailors, and other petty functionaries donated funds. In the small village of São José da Penha, Luís Antônio Rodrigues, an elementary school teacher exempt from recruitment offered to contribute 10 percent of his salary until the end of the campaign. A coast pilot (prático mor) in São Marcos Bay, Domingos da Silva Ribeiro, offered 10 percent of his profits (gratificação) to help in the war efforts.[11]

In Pitanguy, a small town in the interior of the province of Minas Gerais, fifty-two volunteers simultaneously presented themselves for enlistment. On the day of their departure, the entire population came out to bid them farewell. Mass was said; the town council met. A band played the national anthem, and a young woman dressed like an Indian delivered a flag to the volunteers. Those remaining behind created a "Society for the Love of the Fatherland" (Sociedade Amor da Pátria) to collect money for the campaign. Similar demonstrations took place in villages along route to the capital of Minas Gerais, Ouro Preto. Patriotic feelings ascended to a new height. The war highlighted the significance of the fatherland as an important source of social identity for everyone.[12]

Because recruitment went so well during these early months, the provincial president of Bahia complained that "the only limit [to enlistment] was due to the orders of the Imperial government, included in its notice from October 21, 1865, stopping the organization of new corps and stating that only one more should depart for the front. Otherwise, the movement would have no other limit but the unfailing feeling that inspires it."[13] In view of the wave of enlistments, the flood of donations, and the initial victories against Paraguay, Brazil's governing Progressive League cabinet became optimistic. The somewhat precariously organized Empire appeared to be poised for quick victory. In all likelihood, the Paraguayans would surrender after a decisive battle and the war would be won—without a standing army. José Tavares Bastos, the president of Rio de Janeiro, Brazil's richest province, expressed such optimism when he wrote, "Deeply inspired, the [Liberal] Cabinet, relying on the national enthusiasm and through the creation of the Corps of Volunteers saw them coming from every corner of the Empire to take their part in this Holy War. It became an acknowledged truth that Brazil does not need a large permanent army to maintain its integrity and its rights."[14]

But the Imperial government did not rely on popular patriotism alone to increase the army's size. Initial recruitment success was also rooted in administrative innovations put into place after the earliest skirmishes. Anticipating difficult obstacles ahead, the Empire preemptively worked to improve Brazil's military capacity in the event of a prolonged conflict. Since wholesale reform was impossible, the ministry tried to create pockets of efficiency inside the army.

The first measure, Decree 3371 of January 7, 1865, created the Battalions of Voluntários da Pátria (Volunteers of the Fatherland; henceforth, Volunteers), which were organized in many provinces. As Peter Beattie showed, the creation of "Volunteers" was part of a strategy to make service in the army honorable for Brazilians of all classes. Volunteers obtained advantages unavailable to ordinary recruits, such as higher pay, shorter enlistments, discharge bonuses, land grants, preference for public service positions, pensions, and support for their families in the event of their death.[15]

The program's goal was not only faster recruitment but also the enlistment of men of high social standing and avoidance of difficulties that could result from impressments. Some Volunteers petitioned to have a commander of their choice. A group of volunteers raised in the province of Ceará requested that General Sampaio be appointed their commander, since "being from Ceará, [he] will mitigate the sacrifices we are willing to undertake so far away from our homeland."[16]

The war against Paraguay temporarily reinforced an integrative notion of fatherland, which had never been achieved before. The government appealed to all kinds of people across all of Brazil, not just those directly linked to vulnerable frontier areas in the south. Through the creation of the Volunteers Corps, the government tried to improve the status of soldiers by enrolling all ranks of men. In fact, the name of Emperor Pedro II appeared first on the list of Volunteers. Thus Brazil simultaneously nationalized enlistment across both class and geographical barriers, although impressment still provided a great number of troops.

Paradoxically, the great influx of volunteers disclosed a serious weakness in the Imperial government. When hostilities began, Brazil lacked the bureaucratic infrastructure necessary to quickly enlist great numbers of volunteers. Similar to what had happened with Union Army recruitment four years before, local institutions had to fill the organizational gap. But the connection between national and local interests in Brazil was weaker than in the United States, and the Imperial government lacked a war party like the Republicans. Consequently, the government had to appeal to groups of notables more interested in immediate reward than in the long-term results of foreign policy.

Recruiters had to rely on the cooperation of local barons and bosses, normally planters with considerable prestige and influence, for the logistical support necessary to raise a strong army. These men normally commanded National Guard militias in the interior, and their cooperation was critical to the success of any national recruitment initiative.

During the first months of mobilization, Imperial authorities relentlessly appealed to their goodwill and patriotism to gain the cooperation it needed to recruit at full scale. This letter from the Marquis of Olinda, president of the Ministerial Council, to a prominent planter reveals how raising new corps of Volunteers depended on such support.[17]

> The manifest deficiency of our army and the urgent need to increase and support it in a convenient way . . . obliges the Imperial government

to address the farmers and landowners to demand their consenting for the recruitment of Volunteers for the Army . . . Your Excellency is one of these planters whose patriotism is necessary to the Imperial government. By yourself or, in association with other farmers, you can make the complaints of the outraged and unrevenged fatherland felt, filling the glorious commission the Imperial government entrusted to you.[18]

Provincial presidents recognized their dependence on local bosses. They appealed to their influence and prestige to facilitate enlistment and recruitment. Recruitment was a private form of impressment controlled by the same local autocrats who promoted volunteerism, a "privatization of civic responsibility" similar to what happened in the United States through the agency of different institutions and methods. In a dispatch to the minister of war, the president of São Paulo, João Crispiano Soares, described conversations with Paulista boss Nicolau José de Campos Vergueiro that emphasized the advantages of Volunteers over conscripts in an Army with many different modes of enlistment: "I also told [Vergueiro] that, as the provincial police authorities were taking care of the recruitment for the army, he should be smart and emphasize [to them] that the listed Volunteers are not subject to it [Army recruitment] and that he should certify them [the Volunteers] in the government's name that, on the occasion of recruitment, we will fulfill all the warranties and promises presented in the Decree 2271 of March 7."[19]

Despite the successful recruitment of more soldiers and the advantages they enjoyed, Volunteers did not solve chronic problems of logistics and infrastructure. Most pressing among these was the army's inability to provide adequate housing and training for the new soldiers. In three letters that barely disguised his irritation, the São Paulo provincial president complained to the minister of war about the precarious supply of guns and uniforms: "The Corps of Volunteers we are organizing in [São Paulo] is composed of 235 soldiers that are being housed at the penitentiary due to the lack of available installation in the barracks. This corps lacks discipline. There is no discipline without the constitution of commands. I will need instructions. Unhappily, I do not have instructors. [Soldiers] have neither guns nor uniforms. I told the Ministry that I had ordered some linen shirts to give to this corps a military appearance. My procedures have not been approved to this date."[20]

Because the Empire lacked means of mobilizing ordinary citizens, troop organization depended initially on support services provided by local bosses cooperating with the Imperial Army. Planter and politician Nicolau José de Campos Vergueiro gives a good example of the services these men provided. In January 1865, Vergueiro visited the towns of Rio Claro and Limeira in the new coffee-growing regions of São Paulo to form a second corps of Volunteers, the Provincial President "authorized [Vergueiro] to give military instruction to this corps and also to house them, as it is necessary."[21]

Yet there were limits to cooperation. The power to recruit and the capacity to exempt were often combined in the same person, and when this was the case, it strengthened bargaining power when dealing with Imperial authorities. Describing the behavior of an indolent local boss, the president of São Paulo implicitly acknowledged the limits to his own ability to recruit soldiers: "It is relevant to note that the president of one of these towns is also the Lieutenant Colonel of the National Guard's Battalion of the district! It is clear that very little should be expected from this person."[22]

The government's dependence on the goodwill of both the bosses and the populace reveal its inability to extract resources directly from society on its own initiative. Under favorable conditions, planters supported the war effort. But conditions depended on the duration of the war: the shorter, the better for everybody. As the campaign dragged on and continued to drain resources, enthusiasm waned. Senator Nabuco de Araújo, a leading Imperial politician, lamented that Brazil became despondent because "its main feature was enthusiasm, not perseverance."[23]

This situation raises the question of internal cohesion, a subject central to the social effects of war and national military mobilization. It has often been suggested that war increases the internal cohesion of the warring state. Some analysts, such as Arthur A. Stein and Bruce M. Russet, however, have pointed out that the relationship is more complex. War may increase internal cohesion, but only under a variety of specific conditions, including the perception of an external threat to the society. If this perception decreases, as was the case during the Paraguayan campaign, cohesion may actually decline.[24]

In the case of Brazil during the Paraguayan War, social cohesion vanished as the long campaign and the drain on the workforce became less compatible with the interests of planters and others for whom prosperity was linked to the labor supply. While vagrants, migrants, and beggars were easily impressed, planters protected fieldworkers as much as possible. Transferring free laborers and slaves to the front lines was viewed with suspicion, sometimes with indignation. This reveals the importance of patron-client relations in the social history of Brazil. Local bosses released some workers to serve as volunteers, but their willingness to contribute was limited by their labor needs. Labor needs would eventually conflict with war demands.[25]

## Designating National Guards

A second, more controversial measure to increase the size of the army came under Decree 3383 of January 21, 1865. This edict legalized the transfer of National Guard soldiers to the regular army, and as such they could be deployed out of the country. These National Guard troops were "designated" for the army. Initially, more than 14,000 troops were designated for the front, but these numbers would eventually increase. Because Brazilian law was unclear about the conditions under which these transfers could take place, Decree 3383 created a legal crisis.

The Guard was responsible for internal security and subject to the minister of justice, not to the Army. In the United States, national guard units fit in well-defined state hierarchies commanded by state governors, but in Brazil, autonomous local units were led by local strongmen, who recruited, organized, and trained these militiamen. Some of the commanders had been around a lot longer than the provincial presidents. Each enjoyed a large degree of autonomy in his own province. Thus, the Brazilian National Guard was the traditional bastion of landowners and other powerful local citizens. Membership was the best excuse a free man could offer to escape impressment. Under its umbrella, guardsmen loyal to local bosses avoided recruitment, and the bosses gained prestige through the protection they provided their followers. By transferring National Guard units to the front, the Imperial government directly undermined the traditional authority of local leaders.

Decree 3383 violated the longstanding cooperation between central and local authorities, destroyed the notion of the Guard as a sanctuary from conventional recruitment, and undermined Imperial capacity to arbitrate conflicts between planters. Moreover, it abrogated customary power-sharing arrangements sanctioned by tradition, arrangements that had helped to legitimate centralization during Brazil's first turbulent decades of independence.

To make matters worse, provincial presidents had authority over local police forces, and could order their members to join the Corps of Volunteers. Once in the Volunteers, these men could be sent to the front lines. Strictly speaking, this was not impressment, since the police had "volunteered." But the loss of regular police units had ramifications for the National Guard. National Guard units not designated to go to the front performed additional military surveillance and police patrolling at home. The president of Rio de Janeiro emphasized the burden on National Guard soldiers serving in the province: "It is not only the service of designation that weighs on the National Guard, but also the offer of the police force to march voluntarily to the campaign. . . . The [army] have been substituted for the National Guard even in the surveillance of the province fortresses that was usually made by the Army but has been done, since 1865, by this Guard."[26]

Even more importantly, the loss of police forces left towns and plantations unprotected against slave rebellions. The Province of Rio de Janeiro had a large slave population. Transferring local police to the war effort spread feelings of insecurity and anxiety throughout the countryside. When the government demanded more troops, the National Guard commander in Vassouras, an important coffee-growing center in the Paraíba Valley, complained that "the force already ready to march is so thin that it is barely fit for the normal services. These services have been made with much sacrifice and we can't provide the necessary number even to guard the town's jail."[27]

Clearly, problems related to the transfer of troops illustrated the inadequacy of the bureaucratic structure. But more serious challenges lay ahead. By the second half of 1865, Paraguayan forces had been expelled from Brazil's southern territory and the Uruguayan Blanco government had been defeated, but the precarious structure of military recruitment had become evident. When Imperial authorities began to organize the Second Army Corp, they noticed a sullen mood in the population. As the theater of war moved out of Brazil into northern Argentinean provinces, popular enthusiasm for the war vanished and resistance became endemic. The situation deteriorated further with the first significant defeat of the Triple Alliance at the battle of Curupayty in September 1866.

### The War Dynamics and Recruitment Amplification

From April 16, 1866, when Alliance forces crossed the Paraguayan borders, through September 1866, the invasion of Paraguay was a series of victo-

ries. The Paraguayan army had suffered serious losses during its failed offensive. Now weakened, it was defeated and suffered heavy casualties at
Tuyuti on May 24, 1866, and Curuzú, September 1–3, 1866, when it tried
and failed to regain the initiative.[28] As a result, the Paraguayans retreated
to the margins of the Paraguayan River, concentrating their forces in the
fortified trenches around Humayta fortress. These were months of intense
skirmishes, and peace initiatives made no progress.

The unexpected defeat of Allied forces at the Battle of Curupayty, on
September 22, 1866, accompanied by the loss of four thousand troops,
exposed the fragility of the Brazilian military organization.[29] This defeat
paralyzed the campaign and perplexed the Brazilian military command.
Politicians and military officers slowly came to understand that they faced
a united enemy and a cohesive army recruited through universal conscription, which, in spite of its technological limitations, was well disciplined
and loyal. Now that Paraguayans were fighting to defend their country,
they offered a much more determined resistance than the Brazilians had
faced in any previous opponent.[30]

Brazilian military superiority was not sufficient to convince Solano
López to concede, and Emperor Pedro II insisted that only unconditional
surrender would be acceptable: "The war should be concluded as honor
demands, cost what it cost."[31] Four years later, the British ambassador acknowledged "the general feeling, that the persistence of Brazil in carrying
on the war to its close, was due to the determination of the Emperor."[32]

The Paraguayan retreat did not signal a failure of national will. But to
the Brazilian government, it was counterintuitive and confusing, and it
made the outcome of the war unpredictable.[33] Military operations were
interrupted for seventeen months. During this hiatus, internal troubles
prompted the Argentineans and Uruguayans to retreat from the front lines,
and the erosion of the Alliance reduced troop strength. The loss of enormous numbers of soldiers due to desertion, disease, terrible sanitary conditions, and the lack of adequate food intensified the need for more troops
and an extended campaign.

As in the North during the U.S. Civil War after 1862, familiarity with
the reality of the war sobered the most ardent saber-rattlers and voices fa-
voring an armistice could be heard. But antiwar movements were not organized in Brazil as they had been in the United States, nor were there strong
ideological motivations for peace. Brazilians were tired of the war. Peace
initiatives sounded more like criticisms of the Liberal-Progressive Cabinet

than an ideological agenda, even though they came from Conservative sectors who would return to power with changing public sentiment.

The Brazilian government worked desperately on the home front to reinforce the army and rebuild momentum. Loans from British banks paid for new battleships and modern weaponry. Local arsenals in Rio de Janeiro and Porto Alegre worked at full strength to rearm the army. But few initiatives improved existing infrastructure. Unlike the enormous transformations the Civil War brought to the American economy, manufacturing capacity, and transportation industries, the Triple Alliance War generated no new industries in Brazil, and no railroads were extended to the front.[34]

According to testimony from Menenio Agrippa (pseudonym of José Fernandes Pereira Jr.), of the 51 battalions that invaded Paraguay, only 14 were still organized when the conflict resumed in 1867. Of 45,000 men, only half were ready for combat. It would be naive to ascribe these problems to the interruption of the campaign; the lull in fighting had only accentuated circumstances that had been building since the second half of 1865. Although genuine enthusiasm surrounded Brazil's initial recruitment programs, individual and collective resistance was always present, and it grew as the war dragged on. In many respects, internal resistance was as serious a threat to a Brazilian victory as Paraguay's military efforts.

Hierarchical differences among the Volunteers, the Designated National Guards, and the impressed soldiers or recruits reveal interactions between the external crisis and the internal crisis, which were generated by the war. At the top of the hierarchy, Volunteers entered the army of their own will. Considered more altruistic than any other group, they were rewarded for their sacrifices both symbolically and materially. Powerful patrons gave Designated National Guard troops political consideration and a degree of negotiating power. At the bottom rung of free society were the impressed, or recruits who normally belonged to socially undesirable groups. These differences in civilian status were carried over to the military, determining one's place in the military strata. As the war against Paraguay progressed, however, hierarchical differences were increasingly erased as socialization within units equalized the status of soldiers. Fear of the consequences of the leveling effect of serving made resistance common among all parts of the population. Thus, internal responses to the changing fortunes of war were not related solely to historical deficiencies in the enlistment of recruits, which were accentuated in wartime by a lack of manpower. They were also related to unprecedented changes in patterns of selection. As enlistment became more universal, more-acute protests followed. A confidential letter from the Ministry of War called attention to the fact that: "officers and soldiers returning from the army, bring . . . evils to the provinces, spreading terrible news, in such a way that as soon recruiting begins, most of the prospective soldiers hide into the wilderness, and organize to resist being arrested."[35]

Delays at each step of the war made regrouping the existing army impossible and increased the demand for new soldiers. The Empire demanded more manpower from its hinterlands to fill the lacuna, but the people were no longer willing to comply. Slowly and steadily, Brazilians of all classes and in all regions turned against recruitment and resisted intimidation. Acts of insubordination and resistance, both individual and collective, sought to physically isolate recruits and National Guard units in local barracks and residences. Tensions between center and periphery were more acute than at any time since the 1840s.

## The Micropolitics of Desertion

In 1867, the president of Minas Gerais, Vicente Pires da Mota, complained vehemently about the many problems he faced in preparing for a new offensive against Humayta Fortress and detailed the obstacles he faced in recruiting more soldiers to the Imperial Army. Trying to justify his poor record in acquiring new recruits in a confidential letter to the minister of war, he enumerated the difficulties of transporting recruits from the hinterlands to the Court, the capital of the Empire, and accused physicians, priests, parish judges, and other important elements of Minas Gerais society of conspiring against him: "Your Excellency has no idea of the efforts I have been making to capture and send recruits. While in prison they receive visits of (important) people who counsel them to resist the guards, force the doors, and run away."[36]

Conservative opponents of the war obstructed the policy of the Progressive League, undermining recruiters by convincing soldiers to desert. This web of opposition included most sectors of the Minas society, which opposed the increasing impressment of individuals whose status and connections should have left them exempt from service.

Public lack of confidence in the government was bad enough, but the conditions recruits experienced as they marched through the hinterlands were shocking. In discussing this subject with the minister of war, the president of Minas Gerais offered sharp images of deteriorating public enthusiasm for war, violent recruitment methods, and increasing popular sympathy for desertion. Describing the risks of mutiny during the forced march, he justified using handcuffs and irons on dragooned soldiers marching against their will, despite the revulsion such a view could inspire in civilians:"I gave orders for the handcuffs, with which the recruits march, to be taken off in [the city of] Petropólis, to avoid making them arrive at the Court in chains, as they depart from the diverse points from which they are sent."[37]

The minister suggested that appearances should be maintained by unchaining recruits as they passed through each village, but the president countered by writing: "Every time we [needed] to unchain them, we would need a blacksmith . . . [but] where to find them? In any case, in these villages escapes would be unavoidable. Each inhabitant, each farmer, and even . . . each authority would hide those they could. Believe me this is the entire truth."[38]

Though regrettable, he recognized that delivering recruits without such safeguards would be virtually impossible. Fourteen months later, General James Watson Webb, the American ambassador in Brazil, reported similar situations while describing the departure of volunteers from Petrópolis:

> I have seen at least fifty bands of these voluntary soldiers, either passing through Petropolis or coming on board the train at the Railway station and they invariably are "brought in," as follows: the parties numbering from 30 to 70 or 80. Each "Voluntario" has an iron collar round his neck; which opposite to the lock, has an Iron ring, about two and a half inches in diameter. Through this ring is passed a heavy ring chain, known to us as a "Log chain," extending from the front to the rear file, and of course, there is no possibility of escape. In this condition the Volunteer soldier goes a board the transport and sails for the River. Formerly at West-Point, the cadet who was "found" and turned away, was called "a forced volunteer." So Brazil has a precedent for calling these men "Voluntários."[39]

Why did the initial patriotic fervor give way to widespread demonstrations of resistance? Even at the beginning of the war, desertion was a significant factor in many provinces. In one of the few comparisons made between rates of enlistment and desertion, the president of Alagoas noticed a huge difference between the numbers of individuals enlisted and those who went to war. Table 1 permits a comparison between the number of recruits Presented and those effectively sent to the Court to

TABLE 1. Recruitment and evasion in Alagoas Province, 1865

|  | Presented | Sent to the Court | Rate of evasion (%) |
|---|---|---|---|
| Volunteers | 134 | 129 | 3.73 |
| Transferred National Guards | 101 | 73 | 27.72 |
| Recruits | 680 | 422 | 38.08 |
| Freed Slaves | 26 | 26 | 0 |
| Total | 941 | 650 | 30.92 |

Source: Provincial Report of Alagoas Province, May 1865

proceed directly to the theater of war. At the beginning of the campaign, when provincial reports showed the best possible picture, the total rate of evasion in Alagoas was above 30 percent. The highest desertion rates were among transferred National Guards and recruits. Recruits were conscripted through coercion or force, and National Guards were designated for the front through arbitrary bureaucratic acts. Involuntary soldiers were concentrated in these two categories, and almost 37 percent of them never arrived at the capital. This rate of loss contrasts sharply with the volunteerism and other patriotic activities at the beginning of the war.

Alagoas does not seem to be unusual when compared to other provinces. The progress of desertion can be followed in a report from the president of Maranhão, a province on the border of the Amazon basin. In April 1865, twelve guardsmen left from the village of Tutoia, but only one arrived in the provincial capital, São Luís. During their passage through São Luís before boarding the vessels that should have taken them to the Court, 66 soldiers deserted, 71 failed to show up, 94 were dismissed by the previous president, and 67 fell ill at the hospital. Of those qualified to embark for the capital, 26 were dismissed for disability and 40 more for legal exemptions. Thus, of a total of 910 Maranhense guards designated for transfer, only 546 (60 percent) left the province. Desertion, exemption, and pretended illness, common in all regions, severely undermined recruitment.[40]

No province presented a stronger contrast between the two initial waves of recruitment than Rio de Janeiro. The Empire's richest province, at the heart of the coffee-growing region, the province of Rio was also close to the Court.[41] These circumstances should have made the province sensitive to Imperial needs.[42] And, indeed, the first wave of Volunteers from December 1864 to May 1865 showed that most enlistment was spontaneous (82 percent) rather than coercive. Confident about the supply of recruits, the provincial government dispensed with the services of 1,384 designated National Guards. But this decision proved to be foolish, because in the second wave of recruitment (May to September 1865) there was a 43.1 percent drop in the total number and an 80.1 percent drop in Volunteers. By that time, coercion, including rounding up deserters from the first call, provided 72.3 percent of the troops.[43] (See table 2.)

In Minas Gerais, a province well known for resistance to recruitment, the provincial report also shows a preponderance of conscripts and designated guardsmen, but in contrast to Alagoas and Rio, coerced groups were a majority from the very beginning. Minas had a population of 1.6 million—16 percent of the total population of the Empire at the time.[44] The Imperial government requested an initial quota of just 1,200 (0.075 percent of its total request). In spite of the proportionally small requisition, only 21 percent went to the front during the campaign's first months. Of these 251 men, only 5 (1.9 percent) were Volunteers; recruits and designates comprised 216 (86.4 percent). The remaining 30 (8.3 percent) were freed slaves, whose enlistment was not considered a question of public concern at this time.[45]

Dom Viçoso, the bishop of Mariana, a mining center closer to the capital, was very concerned about the shortage of recruits and voiced his official disappointment in his proclamation of November 1866. At the request of the provincial president, Saldanha Marinho, the bishop proclaimed the church's official support for the war. The bishop also expressed govern-

TABLE 2. Sources of recruits in Rio de Janeiro, Dec. 1864–Sept. 1865

| Source | Dec. 1864–May 1865 (% of total recruitment) | May–Sept. 1865 (% of total recruitment) |
|---|---|---|
| Provincial police corps | 510 (17) | 0 (0) |
| Volunteers | 2,458 (82) | 473 (27.7) |
| Recruits for the army and the navy | 32 (1) | 644 (37.7) |
| Designated National Guards | 0 (0) | 459 (27) |
| Deserters imprisoned and sent to the Headquarters | 0 (0) | 130 (7.6) |
| Total | 3,000 (100) | 1,706 (100) |

Source: Provincial Reports of Rio de Janeiro, 05.1865.

ment chagrin at the province's low level of cooperation: "When the fatherland demands your assistance to your brothers [and] when they call for
your help to obtain the victory [you] run to the forests or pretend illnesses
so as to be dismissed! So many cowardly acts do not seem proper of serious
people. . . . If we have always to be ready to appear in front of the lord's
tribunal, why not in the middle of bullets, bayonets and torpedoes!"[46]

Yet fear of death was stronger than religious appeals. A year later, the
new president complained that even priests were campaigning in the interior against the draft:

> There are preachers everywhere who infuse fear in the population who
> are ready for the war. In [the city of] Queluz, Dr. Lafayete and his brothers
> and relatives are permanent missionaries of this propaganda. . . . Just now
> I am suing a vicar from Diamantina . . . because [he] spent his Sundays
> counseling (from the pulpit)! that [the people should] resist, run, but not
> go to the war because this is like a plague created by a corrupt govern-
> ment to destroy all Conservatives and peace lovers.[47]

Statistics from the province of São Paulo indicate how impressments
progressed during the third wave of recruitment, October 1866 to May
1867 (see table 3).

More than 80 percent of all men sent to the front were nonvolunteers.
These numbers confirm contemporary reports describing the increasing
role of impressments. During the time frame of table 3, coffee plantations
flourished in São Paulo. Slaves were sent down from northwest provinces
in huge numbers, but the provision of the labor force was still affected by
the interruption of international slave traffic. As a result, the use of free
laborers was absolutely necessary on the plantations. Under these circumstances, with a great demand for workers and few available, it seems logical that voluntary enlistment would be low. Large planters protected their
workforce from impressments, and this partially explains why important
provinces like São Paulo and Minas Gerais contributed few recruits. But
resistance was endemic and increasingly spread throughout the country.
Later in 1867, the president of Minas Gerais testified about the heightened
tension provoked by recruitment. Complaining about scarce recruits and
uncooperative National Guards, he painted a terrible picture, emphasizing that, "almost all active National Guards who were ready to march took
refuge in scattered places that offered the resources they needed to survive
and where the response of the authorities was slow. [They] formed large

TABLE 3. Sources of recruitment in São Paulo, Oct. 1866–May 1867

| Source | Number (% of total recruitment) |
|---|---|
| Volunteers | 87 (6.5) |
| Volunteers for the army | 81 (6.1) |
| Volunteers for the navy | 51 (3.8) |
| Recruits | 693 (52) |
| National Guards | 419 (31.6) |
| Total | 1,331 (100) |

Source: Provincial Report from São Paulo, 1867

groups of deserters, both designated and recruits, that could not be captured due to the [recruiter's] lack of material supplies."[48]

Many causes contributed to the decrease in the number of volunteers during the second and third waves of recruitment. According to the president of Alagoas, this was due to "the natural decline of the early shows of patriotism, the sedentary character of the [provincial] population, the traditional existing horror in relation to the wars in the south of the Empire, and, above all, to the exaggerated and terrifying news coming from the theater of operations concerning the mortality of enlisted men, resulting from weather conditions, the fatigue caused by the marches, and epidemics."[49]

The president of Maranhão complained that recruits evaded service by running away, hiding, or using legal exemptions. These remarks should be seen in the context of a popular Brazilian saying, "God is great but the wilderness is greater!," which clearly captures the popular wisdom of the poor in Brazil. At first, many poor or marginalized men who could not count on protection from patrons or others hid in the forests to evade impressment. Soon they were joined by the less vulnerable, made anxious by terrifying news coming from the south that increased collective resistance to military service. Serving in the army became identified with the worst forms of slavery. As soon as the war lost its initial romantic glamour, resistance became the order of the day.

News and rumors spread quickly, crystallizing into a hostile recruiting environment. But some individuals had more difficulty avoiding service than others. Men without protection, the preferred targets of recruiters in all provinces, responded with individual acts of rebellion. In the small town of Rio Bonito, in the province of Rio de Janeiro, a superior commander described for National Guard commanders the criteria used to designate substitutes, that is, culling troublemakers from the ranks in favor of obedient guards. As an example he described a soldier from the Seventh Infantry Battalion, João Batista Pereira Jr. Pereira had been designated as a substitute for guardsman, who had evaded service through legal exemption.[50] The commander's description included many characteristics of a socially undesirable person:

> His behavior as a Guard and individual is terrible. Married around two years ago to evade recruitment, [he] abandoned his wife after eight days. . . . During this time he has been making a living through robbery [while] seeking refuge in the forests. [Because he knew] he would be captured sooner or later he has been so obnoxious as to self-mutilate the index finger of his right hand. This wound is completely cured and [he] is now completely ready for the service he has been designated for. This command asks your Excellency, in the name of discipline, and also to make him an example to those that take advantage of mutilations and amputations, to give him the fate that his cowardice deserves in order to not have imitators.[51]

There is no doubt that recruits tried to evade service by running away and hiding or by more dramatic actions, such as impromptu weddings or even self-mutilation.

Guardsmen who were designated to go to the front looked to traditional social networks of relationships to avoid obstacles to recruitment. Legal exemptions, substitution, or political influence commonly helped individuals evade service. These exemptions grew out of personal relationships that linked National Guard commanders to their men, and they offered much more formidable protection than individual resistance could provide. When these methods failed, designated guardsmen were still able to "buy substitutes." These strategies had been used in previous conflicts with relative success, and it was natural that terrified men looked to their bosses in order to receive exemptions.[52]

The transferring of members of the National Guard to the front led to a variety of conflicts. From the beginning of the war, provincial reports had described conflicts between recruiting agents and designated guards. During the war, the political will of the Imperial government became heavily focused on the transfer of these guards. Pressure on the Guards mounted as imperial officials insisted that preserving national integrity was more important than maintaining local relationships based on custom, tradition, and personal influence. The extent of private negotiations between bosses and officers narrowed sharply in the face of a seemingly permanent shortage of ordinary soldiers to undertake a long campaign. Provincial presidents were compelled to pressure National Guard commanders to send the largest possible number of recruits to the respective provincial capital. Some of the political officials, such as the vice president of Maranhão, tried to justify poor results by blaming ordinary soldiers while exempting commanders of responsibility. In his provincial report of August 1865, the president stated that although "there is no doubt about the National Guard commander's goodwill," guardsmen on their way to the front used every means to avoid marching. "When all else failed, they ran for the forests, and it was necessary to escort them to the capital as recruits."[53] This vice president appropriately called organizing the new corps "an insane task."[54]

Other presidents were less tolerant of the partiality shown by National Guard commanders when designating men for the army. When confronted with a choice between loyalty to the Empire or local relationships, local bosses did not hesitate to protect their clients. In a letter to the minister of war, the president of São Paulo confessed that, despite his recruitment efforts, "I do not count on the cooperation of the commanders of the National Guard [because] they began to send me complaint that constantly remind me of the evils brought about by the designation of the National Guard troops."[55] In Minas Gerais as well, the president blamed Guard commanders for the lack of recruits: "The designations, generally irregular, were not even made at some superior commands."[56]

Occasionally legal exemptions could be obtained by recruits with important jobs. Workers in strategic areas, such as railroads and post offices, were able to avoid service. For instance, a National Guardsman of the Third Battalion of Infantry was designated for the war, but he was also an employee of the Dom Pedro II Railroad. In a report of October 6, 1866, the minister of war argued that, "in spite of the fact that the railroad became [recently] state-owned, all the employees still have legal exemption from National Guard service, because the exemption was conceded not in favor of the company, but in favor of their employees, because of the nature of their service."[57]

Even in Rio Grande do Sul, a traditional source of troops and horses for the army, recruitment went poorly. In a private letter to the minister of war, the most prestigious military leader of the Liberal Party, General Manuel Luís Osório, described the precarious situation in November 1866.

> The delay in the mustering [of troops] comes from circumstances very difficult to modify: "Many people have hidden in the wilderness, and many others have taken refuge in the Oriental (eastern) State (Uruguay). It is very difficult to reunite such dispersed elements. Speaking of the Oriental State, I should mention to you that I asked General Flores permission to take [our] soldiers there and send them for the service of war."[58]

Ennobled as the "Marquis of Herval," Osório was an experienced Brazilian general and one of Rio Grande do Sul's most prestigious military chiefs. His correspondence reveals the problems associated with recruitment in a province traditionally important to war mobilization. One problem was the high degree of partisanship in politics, which increased tensions during the election period: "The difficulties are many and they come from everywhere and I try to make everybody forget about such political hostilities and just hear the voice of the nation."[59]

Osório's testimony also shows how political competition inside the army affected the loyalty not only of the gaucho militias but also of cattle ranchers and saladeros (salted-beef businessmen), many of whom had lands in Uruguay. In 1867, Osório calculated that around eight thousand gauchos had deserted into the Uruguayan frontier. As the gaucho elite had land on both sides of the border, it's likely that they encouraged mass desertions to preserve the loyalty of their men. Thus, the province that precipitated the war and the leaders who had stressed Rio Grande do Sul's swift cooperation with the Imperial Army could no longer contribute soldiers.[60]

One way to satisfy the army's demand for soldiers while maintaining local prestige was to recruit the followers of political opponents or to take the command of battalions away from them. In Maranhão, the vice president described how "amidst all these problems the Superior Commanders [of the National Guard] and Battalion Commanders are unenthusiastic toward everyone's recruitment and send the sick, the elderly, the underaged, the widow's only sons, every man who has the more positive legal exemptions."[61]

The president of Minas Gerais complained: "The works of the qualification (designation) councils were very irregular. Many iniquitous designations were made [because] the spirit of party dictated them."[62] In the province of São Paulo, the president also remarked, "after recruiting the single and able for the service, the designations have fallen on many that had exemptions, and those that do not have it hide in the trees."[63] Joaquim Manoel de Macedo, an influential advisor at the Imperial court, viewed recruitment as a weapon to intimidate the poor at election time: "No party or faction that calls itself a party can throw stones at any other. They all employ or have employed forced recruiting with the ultimate immoral end of the blatant oppression of the poor people."[64]

Complications from partisanship were unending and affected military procedure and command structure on the battlefields. In October 1866, intense disputes erupted between the Conservative commander, Polidoro da Fonseca, and the Liberal one, Porto Alegre. When Porto Alegre learned that the Conservative leader, the Marquis de Caxias, could be nominated to command all Triple Alliance troops, he asked to be dismissed. The rivalry continued, although with less intensity, after Caxias assumed command.

In the rearguard, partisan disputes destabilized command positions and affected local power structures. It was a common strategy to conscript political adversaries or to deprive them of command over their own forces. In the district of São Miguel, in the province of Rio Grande do Norte, the province president removed a National Guard officer from his position as district sub-delegate. The officer's political enemies "rejoiced publicly in their happiness, going to the extreme of provocation." According to the Justice Report, the offended officer tried to avenge his honor by attacking his opponents with a cane. What in normal conditions would have been a mild conflict escalated to include partisans on both sides. Two slaves and one Indian were killed, and six more people injured. Fifty soldiers were needed to reestablish order.[65]

The Marquis of Caxias, named to the command of all Triple Alliance forces after the Argentinean commandant Bartolomé Mitre retired in September 1866, was a legend in the Imperial Brazilian tradition, and his nomination was an attempt to standardize practices in the command forces. But Caxias was also a Conservative politician, and his nomination intensified internal disputes in the provinces by depriving many Liberal and Progressive provincial presidents of their recruiting prerogatives.[66] Rivalries between factions led to administrative discontinuity. The removal of commanders and the reorganization of their regiments encouraged more desertions. In a private letter to the minister of war, a gaucho commander complained that "these facts indicate to me that my command will be taken from me very soon and this is the reason why I am telling you about all these circumstances just to emphasize that: I've never refused to give my weak services in these times, as neither I nor my friends have chosen this situation to . . . speculate in politics; and far from preparing a new army [there is] only personal politics, to prepare the terrain for electoral victories, neutralizing supposed adversaries."[67]

To secure additional southern troops, the Imperial government suspended congressional elections in Rio Grande do Sul during the second semester of 1866. In a special meeting of the Council of State on August 23, many councilors agreed that elections and the violence inherent in the electoral process were not compatible with recruitment. The councilor Pimenta Bueno declared that "those would not be free elections because the voters would not go to the polls or they could be recruited while entering or exiting the churches.[68] The government would not be able to keep the law because arbitrary [local] police authorities would do as they wished in defense of party interests."[69]

In the early months of 1867, while the organization of the Third Army Corps was still in progress, the president of Rio Grande do Sul saw more problems on the horizon: "Many desertions have been taking place at . . . different points of this province, even in the camp of general Baron of Herval. I keep sending to the first corps all deserters who have been caught, including those coming from the Third Corps. . . . I beg your Excellency to provide a monthly supply of two hundred contos to help with the urgent expenses required for formation of the Third Corps."[70]

Since the second half of 1865, desertion had become a national phenomenon. Members of the opposition and marginal social groups saw recruitment as just another source of power exercised against them. As a consequence, disputes over who would be designated for the army eroded the National Guard's solidarity. It also revealed the Guard's inability to protect the homeland in the event of a major conflict. The president of Rio Grande do Norte observed, "The National Guard is a legal embarrassment to the police, an electoral machine, and a cadet factory."[71] The Report from the Ministry of Justice from 1867 clearly recognized such deficiencies, emphasizing that the current war experience "confirmed the need to reform the National Guard. This militia created to defend order and public liberty is very far from its final goal."[72]

Individual or collective desertion was a serious challenge, but it did not undermine the whole recruiting process. The resistance was neither life threatening nor well organized, but it did inhibit efforts to enforce recruitment and expressed contempt for the law. The large number of rebellions against recruitment posed a much graver threat to the Empire's internal peace. Some rebellions were supported by Guard commanders or other important local authorities, such as judges, priests, or planters. Through these revolts, various social groups expressed their dissatisfaction with the interference of national agents in their private lives. In their eyes, the interference lacked legitimacy because it disrupted the local and regional balance of power. Under the impact of external forces, the resistance of inertia gave way to violent manifestations of collective action.

Union recruiters faced similar local opposition in Northern states as outsiders trying to assert national authority against a background of localism and suspicion. While Brazilian provincial presidents had much more real power, they, too had little authority to advance national political goals. The Imperial appointees had to depend on local elites and institutions to advance agendas. Because they lacked a local constituency, using coercive measures to obtain new levees of recruits exposed Imperial authority to mounting violence.

During the Triple Alliance War, the expansion of government prerogatives in Brazil interfered with established loyalties, that is, the private agreements between planters and their clients. State interference with traditional rituals of social control led provincial populations, especially those living in small villages and districts far in the interior, to appeal to local sources of power for protection against what they saw as unreasonable demands by the state.

An explosion of local rebellions sought to push recruitment agents out of villages and districts and restore previously existing conditions. No rebellion achieved the level of earlier secessionist movements, but some of them seriously challenged the execution of governmental power. In this sense, Imperial demands on the people made the Crown vulnerable to popular resistance through a movement that rejected progress through rationalization in the name of tradition. Populations in cities and towns reacted as if Imperial agents, not the Paraguayans, were the real invaders. There was no uniform strategy in these revolts. Some actions expressed individual resistance through personal confrontation. In the city of Penedo in Alagoas, on October 13, 1866, designated National Guard Albino Vieira de Castro stabbed to death Manoel Leandro do Nascimento, the second lieutenant in charge of the recruitment. The assassination took place in a public square when the lieutenant gave Albino an "order of imprison-ment." In the town of Pioca, in the same province, another designated National Guard was killed fighting two recruiter escorts. In the village of Imperatriz, Alagoas, a recruit shot the bloc inspector as he was recruiting. In the locality of Maióba, Maranhão, a boy was killed by a stray bullet fired by a man defending his nephew from a recruit escort.[73]

Many such conflicts divided neighbors along partisan lines. Some peo-ple tried to execute government orders, but others resisted, sometimes uniting an entire community against the government. Spontaneous acts of individuals escalated into open, collective rebellion, involving an entire community. This happened in the city of Pacatuba, in the province of Ser-gipe. Many deserters were hiding in the forests around the town, and an escort was sent by the provincial president to recapture them "by reason or force." A "fierce struggle" followed, during which three people died, in-cluding the mother of a refugee.[74] Sometimes captive recruits mutinied on their way to prison. In the town of São João del-Rei, Minas Gerais, a group of seventeen recruits and deserters rioted against their escorts, resulting in one death and three serious injuries.[75]

No actions undermined Imperial authority as much as attacks on es-corts and jails, many of which are recorded in the Reports of the Ministry of Justice from 1866 to 1868.[76] They multiplied as recruitment dropped. Some were due to misunderstandings, as in an incident that occurred in the little town of Mar de Espanha, Minas Gerais. Portuguese immigrants were employed working on the "União e Indústria road." Mistakenly be-lieving that some of their compatriots were "imprisoned for recruitment," these immigrants assaulted the jail to free them from being marched to the provincial capital. The delegate and many escort soldiers were severely injured in this attack.[77]

At other times, attacks came from the deserters themselves, organized into gangs in the forests. In the district of Cruz do Espírito Santo, Rio Grande do Norte, "a group of deserters and criminals" attacked recruit-ment escorts and the town jail, releasing all prisoners.[78] In the Parish of Águas Belas, Province of Pernambuco, a group of "armed persons" attacked the recruitment patrols, killing one soldier and releasing one recruit.[79]

Occasionally, relatives commanded attacks, as in the city of Icó, Ceará, where "a large group of relatives and friends" released a designated Na-tional Guard. "Happy with their success the crowd paraded through the city streets carrying in triumph the released man." At other times, attacks

84

were led or supported by local authorities, who disagreed with national policy. Usually, however, the involvement of authorities was indirect, as in the village of Pau D'Alho, Pernambuco, where a group of armed men attacked the prison, liberating thirty-four recruits. According to the Justice Report, four prisoners had been previously convicted as murderers, and seven had been accused of other crimes. In spite of that, all were released by the assailants, who killed three sentries during the struggle and hurt many others. The deserters then looked for refuge in forests owned by Lieutenant Colonel Luiz Albuquerque Maranhão, a sugar cane planter and National Guard officer who was indicted as the mob's main supporter. Records do not reveal what happened to Maranhão. In all likelihood, no juridical action took place because of his important position in local politics.[80]

In other cases, direct involvement was touched off by actions perceived as abusive to local interests. In Aguas-Belas, Pernambuco, a second lieutenant of the National Guard, Manoel Cavalcanti de Albuquerque Barão, and his followers attacked the town jail to liberate a recruit. Similar actions took place in the parishes of Canelada, Correty, Capoeiral, and Bonito. In Imperatriz, Alagoas, an armed group commanded by a bloc inspector attacked a patrol and rescued some recruits.[81]

Sometimes authorities became involved after the collective action by families. At the district of São Caetano da Raposa, Pernambuco, relatives of National Guardsman Joaquim Manoel Outeiró attacked the jail to release him from the hands of recruiters. In the struggle Manoel was released, but a relative who commanded the action, Antonio Leite de Lima, was imprisoned. Immediately, two groups appeared in front of the police chief's house demanding his freedom. According to the Justice Report, "one was commanded by the parish judge and the other by a second lieutenant." After this "reunion," which failed to obtain Lima's freedom by peaceful means, the men rescued their friend by force. In Imperatriz, Pernambuco, Lieutenant-Colonel Joaquim da Silva Corrêa appealed for the release of a soldier in his battalion who had been designated for the war. Failing in his request, the lieutenant-colonel gathered 150 men and, in conjunction with the sub-delegate, attacked the jail with the intent to release "his recruit" and the other convicts. But nineteen loyal guards repelled the attackers. Invoking the "prestige of his social position," Silva Corrêa, joined by an entourage that included family and friends, attacked again. This time the attack was successful, and they went on to perform "a series of depredations." It is unknown if they finally rescued the recruit, but, according to the Justice Report, "such vertiginous spirit did not fit the pacific nature of the Brazilians and could not endure."[82]

After analyzing all the problems brought about by designations, the president of São Paulo bitterly acknowledged the inefficacy of the National Guard. "Since it was directed to its present finality [external war] it became very oppressive for most of the population. Today it became necessary to proscribe all the hopes associated with the expression 'nation in arms.' The experience of the current war has erased all illusions. . . . The resistance offered by inertia is worse than that offered by violence."[83]

In spite of this turmoil, neither the time nor the political will existed to advance substantive reforms. The Report of the Ministry of War of 1867 highlighted these deficiencies as causing an enormous waste of men and resources. According to Minister João Lustosa da Cunha Paranaguá:

> The current war made still clearer our need to have a permanent army, if not numerically big, at least disciplined and well armed. It should provide for our internal security and tranquility, [and] at the same time will become the support of our national integrity. If the Empire had (one), when its honor was offended by the Paraguayan government, our territory would not have been invaded; the war, against all modern principles of military science, would not have continued for such a long time; the number of immolated victims would have been much smaller; the public money would not have been wasted on such a vast scale; in short, the fatherland's sacrifices would have been much smaller.[84]

## Dealing with Slaves and Criminals

The greatest fear among slaveholding societies was the possibility of slave uprisings. After events in Santo Domingo, where a slave rebellion led to national independence, the only such war successfully waged by slaves, even the smallest sign of discontent was viewed as a threat to the public order. In Brazil and the United States, it was immaterial that most revolts involved small groups of slaves or encompassed limited geographical areas and failed to spread. The threat was perceived as real, and fear of uprisings contributed to the latent conflict between masters and slaves.[85] As Stuart Schwartz notes, the long chain of slave revolts marking the passage of slavery into the nineteenth century "made the dangers and costs of slavery clearer than they had ever been."[86]

With most coercive forces located far from the provinces, the risk of slave rebellions was taken seriously by Imperial elites of all political persuasions. The Brazilian rearguard was left weaker by the designation of National Guard troops and the mobilization of the police corps for the war, with a lessened capacity for dealing with runaways, rebellions, and other disruptions of bonded labor. Perceiving such fragility, the chief of police of Rio de Janeiro requested the use of disabled soldiers to keep the peace, because he was "convinced of the public utility of such a measure to maintain the public order and tranquility, which is constantly challenged . . . I appeal to your Excellency to obtain the necessary authorization to permit the engagement of disabled soldiers of the army as members of the provisory police corps."[87]

Slaves took advantage of the shift in focus of the Imperial coercive apparatus toward foreign enemies during the Paraguayan War and occasionally rebelled. At the Carmo Convent in the province of Pará, on July 8, 1865, slaves expelled a new overseer and assumed control of the convent. The substitution of an overseer suggests that what was involved was a vigorous negotiation, over working conditions, not an insurrection. In spite of that, some detected the influence of international events behind the slaves' movements.[88] Lamenting the awful situation faced by his province, the president of Pará believed that the institution of slavery in that area was threatened because, among other reasons, "with [the end] of the war in the United States, there is rooted among [the slaves] a belief that all will be freed soon."[89]

Other revolts brought more serious consequences. In Maranhão—a province with a history of rebellions by slaves, Indians, and runaways—slaves organized a quilombo, a maroon village, close to the parish of Vianna in the district of São Bento.[90] From this camp, runaways began to raid neighboring farms. Because of the serious threat they posed, designation of National Guards was temporally suspended until after a group of forty soldiers put an end to the rebellion.[91]

In Rio Grande do Sul, slave revolts were frequent during wartime. On February 14, 1866, the sub-delegate of São Francisco de Paula mobilized the free inhabitants of the region to defend against a group of runaways joined by National Guard deserters who had refused to march to the front. Planters panicked at every rumor and were very concerned about the departure of the Sixth Corps of the National Guard because "many of the same farmers have a great number of slaves, and when [they lose] their supervisors or administrators or overseers, [they] do not know which means to use to prevent an attack [from the runaways]."[92]

According to the police authority, some slaves were imprisoned and "moderately punished without proof," but no evidence was found to positively incriminate the slaves. According to the sub-delegate, in view of the permanent risk of slave rebellion, overseers should be exempt from recruitment. Yet the succession of false alarms opened the door for another possibility: cattle ranchers might manipulate insurrection fears to obtain the release of their overseers. Still, fears could not be totally ignored.

According to Paulo Moreira, an expert on gaucho slave history, the war against Paraguay added to the fear of insurrection the suspicion that insurrection could be supported by foreign elements. In March 1865, the sub-delegate of Bagé communicated the formation of a militia of ten soldiers to avert a slave insurrection encouraged by "the Barbarian assassins from Montevideo's government." In a secret letter dated February 2, 1865, the police delegate of Jaguarão described the invasion of the province by 1,500 men under Blanco General Basilio Muñoz. Along with considerable property damage, the invaders took the slaves they found, with "the promise of being freed." In another letter of February 7 the same authority declared:

> Eight slaves were sent to me from the district of Arroio Grande. They had been imprisoned as suspects of convenience in the slaves' insurrection that was planned in the time when our frontier would be invaded by the forces of Montevideo. According to the testimony of colored Florêncio, slave of Marcos José da Porciúncula, . . . [he] declares that he had been invited by oriental [Uruguayan] José Benito Varela that . . . had attracted [him] to go to the Oriental side, telling him that this would be the way to enjoy freedom. It seems to me that some plan was accorded and due to unknown circumstances was aborted. I am performing a thorough investigation to see if it is possible to discover the agents of such plotting because I have news that some slaves in this city were accomplices in this assault.[93]

Gaúcho slaves and deserters understood the use of arms and could ride like skilled cavalry. They could provide important information to Brazil's enemies concerning the organization of gaucho defenses in Rio Grande do Sul. Even without a general rebellion, it seemed impossible to ignore the potential damage that slave revolts could cause to everyday frontier life.

## The Meaning of the War for Brazilian Civic Culture

The war against Paraguay propelled civic, political, and social mobilization that affected Brazilian society and government institutions in ways previous conflicts had not. The long campaign with its permanent demand for men and supplies constituted a challenge to a bureaucratic structure based on personal links, party patronage, and local cooperation. Thousands of civilians from many distant Brazilian provinces were incorporated into the army, and long supply lines had to be established to provide for soldiers serving in foreign countries. Mobilization became a national phenomenon.

The conflict against Paraguay involved every major institution in Imperial society: government, provincial presidents, National Guard commanders, the church, parliament, police, and civic associations. However, the degree of commitment varied according to individual circumstances. Political polarization strongly determined the amount of patriotism each group showed, but, unlike in the United States, these institutions could not protect the Monarchy from the war's growing unpopularity.

The war mobilized people of every region, race, and class, although enrollment of the unprotected poor and powerless individuals outstripped those of higher origins. Military mobilization was based on forced as well as on volunteer recruitment. National budget priorities were reoriented in order to feed and supply growing military forces until the war ended with the total defeat of the Paraguayan army.[94]

As in the American Civil War, the conflict against Paraguay interfered in state–society relations and the transformation of those relations was slow and hard won. In Brazil, however, few changes in the economic infrastructure or the bureaucratic machine were lasting. War efforts did not favor creating powerful industries; neither did it lead to building roads and railroads in order to more efficiently transport supplies. Consequently, the Paraguayan War engendered widespread unpopularity and general resistance without achieving economic and institutional modernization.

The challenges brought about by mobilization were important because they reminded Brazilian leaders of structural deficiencies in the state-building process. These deficiencies reinforced old fears about the precariousness of the social order and the relative weakness of the central state with respect to its peripheral territories. Wartime challenges revealed an underdeveloped national bureaucracy and an inept military, which hindered state organization and squandered early popular support. Finally, the war against Paraguay created new tensions involving the control of internal social order, exposed by disputes over the control of local recruitment and the politicization of military service. These problems had always challenged the army's capacity to obtain soldiers, but the grueling international campaign revealed acute limitations in effectiveness and alarmed to an unprecedented degree those responsible for Brazil's defense. Provisioning the army and levying troops became the Achilles' heel of the Brazilian government during these crucial years of institutional development.

In the United States, the Civil War was the moment of an economic take-off that included industrial standardization, increasing levels of production, the growth of rail transportation, and the creation of an environment in favor of national development.

Demands for the War of the Triple Alliance created opportunities for innovation, but ultimately the war efforts failed to strengthen national loyalty. Traditional patronage remained virtually intact. Miguel Angel Centeno observed that "state capability is not an absolute phenomenon but a relational one." The Brazilian recruitment crisis showed that war and patriotism were incapable of generating enough popular unity to sustain a national movement when social cohesion was minimal and state bureaucracy weak and inconsistent.[95]

The Imperial government failed to gain strong, permanent, popular support for its war efforts. Victory against Paraguay was a foreign policy goal that had little permanent appeal for planters and slaveholders after the initial invasions of Mato Grosso and Rio Grande do Sul were beaten back. This is the main difference between the enormous appeal the Civil War had to Northerners and the meager results for Brazilian recruitment. The mobilization to fight in Paraguay was not propelled by new national demands or a consistent project of state building. While the Civil War evolved after years of debate concerning different visions about the future of the United States, the Triple Alliance War was an unintended consequence of foreign policies, and its outbreak was unexpected.

Military recruitment was increasingly unpopular among all social classes, and the long campaign, fought on foreign soil and under miserable conditions, only exacerbated public resentment and distrust.

At best, Brazil fought a "limited war" according to Miguel Centeno's definition, that is, a war in which the nation-state showed a limited ability to inspire loyalty, ask for sacrifices, or command obedience from its leading citizenry.[96] In the end, the Monarchy acted with remarkable prudence by maintaining links with the social elites who were traditional supporters: landlords, slaveholders, and merchants. As a consequence, the Imperial government incurred greater war expenses, paid for with international borrowing and by stimulating inflation. This aggravated the country's precarious financial situation and eroded the Emperor's position among political cadres.

The American Civil War had the exact opposite effect on U.S. history. It transformed American society as though by yanking it up by the roots and transplanting it in new soil. Change affecting all regions of the country was swift, permanent, and so deep that it cannot be measured simply in terms of state capacity or government control.

The War of the Triple Alliance and the demand it created for a steady supply of troops caused problems in Brazil as the government sought to extract recruits from provincial society to fill the ranks of the Imperial Army. Imperial agents faced enormous difficulties in recruiting men and resources to conduct the military campaign from an unwilling populace. Such problems were not new, but the pressure of an unprecedented international campaign exposed powerful limitations in the state's ability to increase its army. Slavery was clearly at the base of the problem. It limited the enlistment of a significant proportion of adult males, thus preventing the formation of a large, strong army. It also destabilized the countryside by reducing the workforce in cities and fields and leaving them vulnerable to insurrection.

From the beginning of the war, individual or collective donations of slaves had taken place in many parts of the country. But these limited initiatives were not enough to solve chronic manpower problems related to recruitment. By the middle of 1866, the emancipation of slaves for enlistment had become a question of state and a priority for Imperial leaders. Yet, the recruitment of freed slaves offered another acute challenge for Brazilian authorities, as it implied an expansion of the state's capacity to extract resources from citizens in times of emergency.[97] No question troubled the center–periphery relationship as much, and no other crisis so clearly indicated the urgent need for reforms.

There were no racial restrictions for army enlistment as there were initially in the Army of the Potomac. But slaves and recruits came from the most productive areas of the country. This posed a very different challenge from that faced by Union officers acting on Southern battlefields, where freed slaves were obtained from their enemies.

# FOUR

# Forged in Inequality

## The Recruitment of Black Soldiers in the United States, September 1862–April 1865

On February 6, 1864, Senator Orville Hickman Browning of Illinois, a long-time acquaintance of Abraham Lincoln, visited the White House. In the course of conversation, as was customary among political allies, Browning asked the president if he could help a friend in trouble. The friend, Mrs. Fitz, was a loyal widow from Mississippi, where she owned a cotton plantation and its labor force. During its advance through Confederate territory, the Union army expropriated her forty-seven slaves and ten thousand bushels of her corn. This conformed to the Emancipation Proclamation, which declared free all the slaves living in rebel territory after January 1, 1863. Browning emphasized that Mrs. Fitz, who was living as a refugee in St. Louis, was nearly indigent and that some of her slaves had been taken in 1862, before the Proclamation, "and put upon our gun boats." She did not seek compensation; instead Mrs. Fitz asked if the government could provide freedmen to work her farm during the next planting season, enabling her to raise a crop of cotton. She proposed "to pay them [the freedmen] out of the proceeds the same wages which the government pays those it employs." She referred to the hundreds of thousands of refugee slaves living at military encampments, who were normally designated as "contrabands." By employing contrabands with government acquiescence, Mrs. Fitz intended to make her farm productive once more and thus resolve her financial difficulties. She hoped that Senator Browning's political connections would lead to swift government approval of her plan.

After hearing Browning's proposal, the president "became very excited" and said with great vehemence that "he had rather take a rope and hang himself than to do it. That there were great many poor women who had never had any property at all who were suffering as much as Mrs. Fitz— that her condition was a necessary consequence of the rebellion, and that the government could not make good the losses occasioned by rebels."

Browning reminded the president that Mrs. Fitz was loyal to the Union, that her property had been taken from her by her own government, that it was not being used, and that he "thought it a case eminently proper for some sort of remuneration and her demand reasonable, and certainly entitled to respectful consideration." Lincoln replied, "she had lost no property—that her slaves were free when they were taken, and that she was entitled to no compensation." Browning left the White House "in no very good humor."[1]

This story illustrates the enormous changes that took place in the status of free and bound individuals during the Civil War, as well as the contentious, contradictory relations between the occupation forces and the former slaves, who were considered simultaneously free men and federal wards. Even more confusing is the story of how people of African descent came to be enrolled in the Union army.

Although African American military service was not exactly novel at the time, the Civil War period presented circumstances different from previous American experiences recruiting this population, as well as from the Brazilian situation during the War of the Triple Alliance. In Brazil, race and slavery were not the same thing. Slaves could not be recruited into the army as slaves—only as freed men. The Imperial army had officially accepted blacks since the 1830s. Unofficially, blacks had been impressed into service long before that time. Slavery remained an important institution integrated into the fabric of Brazilian society, and changes in the institution were slow and initiated from the top. During the Triple Alliance War no working relations were uprooted, and expropriation of slaves was not used to increase the size of the Imperial Army. Black enrollment had little effect on government centralization or changes in the Imperial modus operandi.

In the United States, however, the Republican administration's decision to recruit African-Americans was immediately controversial. The centralization and bureaucratization of the government in response to war needs were fundamental factors in black enlistment and also sources of political debate and conflict. The incorporation of blacks into the Union army related to the crisis in volunteer recruitment, but also to changes in the nature of the war and the treatment of Confederate populations. Consequently, army occupation in the South brought irreversible transformations to the status of African Americans that were fast and permanent.

## Background

The enlistment of black men in the Army of the United States was authorized under the provisions of the Second Confiscation Act (July 1862), the Militia Act (July 1862), and the Emancipation Proclamation (January 1863). These three pieces of legislation were conceived in the spring of 1862, when the recruitment crisis threatened the supply of new troops for the Union army.[2] The Militia Act emancipated slaves who worked for the army or the navy, stating that the enrollment of militias should include all able-bodied male citizens between the ages of eighteen and forty-five, permitting, in some interpretations, the recruitment of black men.[3] The Second Confiscation Act extended freedom to slaves coming from areas under Union control whose owners were disloyal. The Emancipation Proclamation declared free all slaves in the Confederacy, except those in the Border States and in the Union-occupied regions. This progressive legislation resulted from congressional as well as presidential initiatives and was part of a more determined pursuit of military victory that captured the nation's imagination during the spring and summer of 1862. The transformation resulted from unexpected developments in the conflict and the capacity of Republican leaders to learn from experience, one of many qualities displayed by the Civil War generation.[4]

Public debates that involved public opinion to a degree unimaginable for Brazilians mediated these developments. In Brazil, debates were restricted to Imperial bureaucrats, Cabinet members, and landowners, whereas, in America, debates embraced the full complexity of Northern society: immigrants, industrial workers, the press, politicians, abolitionist activists, and the Northern African American population. Emancipation and recruitment were among the most important developments in the political discourse concerning the conduct of the war, bringing questions of social and ethnic diversity to center stage.[5]

The progressive legislation accompanied a transformation in the ideological justification of the war, as it evolved from the goal of preserving the Union to an effort to destroy the basis of Southern power. Emancipation and recruitment of blacks in the United States were not preordained projects; instead, they evolved out of necessity. The Union army's insatiable demand for soldiers, a changing attitude in the North's policy toward black troops, and increasing recognition of slavery as the central issue of the conflict pushed the Lincoln administration to take steps toward black enlistment. The president calibrated his conduct of military operations according to the interplay of military and political considerations, moving forward from his initial goals and embracing emancipation as being essential for victory. This evolution played a crucial role in the growth of the central government's authority through the creation and maintenance of a large army. It also brought ordinary Americans into contact with the government as never before.[6]

There is now a consensus among historians that African American enlistment, as well as the contribution of black laborers, transformed the status of black Americans. This point has been highlighted in post-1945 analyses of black Civil War soldiers. Most of these writings focused on the federal government's slow acceptance of black enlistment, the subsequent recruitment of black troops into the Union army, the efforts made by a few Northerners to raise black units, and the battlefield experiences of notable black regiments. Taking as their departure point Joseph T. Wilson's *The Black Phalanx*,[7] historians have challenged the traditional historiographic approach that viewed the conflict as a white man's war by showing that blacks were not passive observers of the destruction of slavery.[8] These works, however, did not connect black recruitment with the draft crisis. By filling state quotas, accepting blacks into the army lessened the effects of the draft on white American citizens.[9]

The relation between legislation and black recruitment has been developed in more recent studies on wartime recruitment and social control. These works demonstrate that integration, democratization, and bureaucratization did not necessarily reinforce each other in American military organization, emphasizing that access was extended to blacks just when the army reduced the degree of democratic participation by ordinary soldiers.[10]

There is much to be learned about the impact of black recruiting on the centralization and nationalization of the Union army. Black recruitment contrasts with decentralized strategies prevalent at the beginning of the conflict, just as partial military desegregation is connected with the failure of volunteerism in the American military tradition. In sharp contrast with Brazil, where the enrollment of free blacks and freed slaves in the Army was not considered a threat, African American recruitment advanced the destruction of Southern slavery during the final years of the Civil War despite the fact that blacks served in segregated units commanded by white officers.

## African Americans and the American Military Tradition

White Americans had always been ambivalent about the recruitment of blacks. It was generally assumed that black soldiers were rare before the Civil War, a situation that differed from that of Brazil. There, the use of blacks in the army was supposedly more common and more widespread.[11] As Carl Degler pointed out some decades ago, however, these different scenarios cannot be explained by fundamentally diverse racial attitudes but, rather, arose from the particular strategic and political circumstances that confronted responsible authorities in Brazil and in the United States.[12]

During the colonial period, demographic and cultural factors restrained the recruitment of blacks in British North America.[13] In the thirteen colonies, the use of black soldiers was hindered by a predominant white population from which soldiers were drawn, a small military establishment, and the close connection between military service and citizenship.[14] Consequently, the right to use arms or to be enlisted in the militia did not exist for blacks, either free or enslaved, in colonial America. In Brazil, however, both law and custom tolerated the service of blacks, even though legal desegregation became law only in 1837. In America, military service was a privilege of race, whereas in Brazil, it was often a punishment for social undesirables.[15]

The armed militia was a civic foundation of the American nation, but membership was open only to citizens, that is, to white free males. Nevertheless, although blacks were not officially permitted to fight, they were enrolled on special occasions. Necessity often led to the recruitment of racially segregated minorities in colonial societies, and British North America was no exception. Men of African descent were always present during times of trouble, filling the ranks to fight the enemies of white colonists.[16] Although demographic conditions reinforced racial segregation in the militias, military exclusion was temporarily suspended when emergency demanded it. As recent scholarship has shown, such emergencies were more common than the traditional view allows, with blacks being called to fight during colonial revolts, such as Bacon's Rebellion (Virginia, 1676), and in the campaigns against the native Americans, such as the Tuscarora War (1711–12) and the Yamasee War

(South Carolina, 1715).[17] According to Peter Voelz, "desperation was thus a mark of raising and arming slaves and free blacks on a colony wide basis. It took an emergency to overcome the habitual fears of the planters and masters, fears not only that the slaves might turn their weapons against their masters but also that they might join an enemy to destroy the colony."[18]

There were discussions on a national level about the enlistment of blacks in the army as early as the struggle for Independence.[19] Unlike the Brazilian experience, revolutionary leaders in the thirteen colonies faced a long struggle to defeat the British and their Tory allies.[20] As in other colonial revolts, the Patriots faced chronic shortages of troops, a permanent nightmare for military leaders on long campaigns, which lead to the recruitment of blacks. Of the 300,000 American troops that took part in the Revolutionary War, an estimated 5,000 (1.6 percent) were blacks.[21] Blacks substituted for affluent whites in nonsegregated battalions and served in most theaters and campaigns. Some of these individuals were free men of color who enlisted voluntarily.[22] Others were slaves who saw the Revolution as an opportunity to gain freedom on the battlefield.[23] Southern blacks, for obvious reasons, did not participate significantly, although many enlisted on the British side. The vulnerable position of the Southern colonies was well expressed some years later in a letter sent from the planter-dominated "Louisiana Committee of Defense" to General Andrew Jackson, describing their country as "strong by Nature, but extremely weak from the nature of its population."[24]

In 1792, Congress passed the Federal Militia Act, which defined the national militia as "free able-bodied white male citizen[s] of the respective states."[25] The Federal Militia Act maintained state control over the militias, incorporating racial restrictions and excluding blacks and Indians from military service. These restrictions also affected the regular army, with the exception of occasional black or Indian scouts who were not considered regular soldiers.[26]

Despite official segregation, blacks continued to be called up when emergency demanded a shift away from dominant racial patterns. During the War of 1812, free blacks were accepted into the Louisiana troops organized under the leadership of General Andrew Jackson. Two battalions of blacks, 180 soldiers each, faced British forces, which also included between 1,000 and 1,500 black soldiers coming mostly from the British West Indies. For their efforts, particularly during the fighting at New Orleans in 1814 and 1815, African Americans earned the praise of General Jackson, but were soon stripped of their arms.[27]

Segregated militias continued to be the norm, even in a progressive state like Massachusetts. In 1859, Governor Nathaniel P. Banks vetoed legislation that would have allowed blacks into the state militia, on the grounds that it violated the whites-only provision of the 1792 Federal Militia Act.[28] In 1857, the U.S. Supreme Court made its own symbolic declaration of black inferiority when it issued the Dred Scott Decision. In his opinion, Chief Justice Roger B. Taney reaffirmed the importance of racial exclusion in the army in terms that sounded familiar to many white Northerners: "Nothing could more strongly mark the entire repudiation of the African race . . . [than] not being permitted to share in one of the highest duties of the citizens. . . . He forms no part of the sovereignty of the State, and is not therefore called on to uphold and defend it."[29]

## The Sectional Crisis and Racial Issues

When the Civil War began, the question of black recruitment resurfaced for the federal government, the logical agency for handling this issue because states were legally prevented from enrolling blacks in their militias. Black communities in the North and their allies in the abolitionist movement demanded the inclusion of African descendants in Northern military efforts. Black leaders understood the opportunity the crisis offered and engaged in a campaign to recruit freed African Americans. They expected that black contributions to the military would be rewarded, helping African Americans achieve both emancipation and citizenship. Fighting for the Union, blacks could at the same time strike a blow against slavery and demonstrate their worth as citizens. The "colored citizens of Cleveland" who declared in October 1861 that "we will pray for the Union, will give our money for the Union, and will fight for the Union" publicly expressed the civic virtue demanded of citizens. But most white Northerners agreed with the decision of the Lincoln administration to enlist only whites. Prejudice in the Northern states was powerful, and few whites outside abolitionist circles believed that blacks had the character to endure combat. Frederick Douglass lamented such arguments in an editorial published in May 1861: "We are ready and would go, counting ourselves happy in being permitted to serve and suffer for the cause of freedom and free institutions. But you won't let us go."[30]

Many Republican leaders supported racial military restrictions as long as they aided the primary objective of preventing Southern secession. A restrictive policy satisfied both federal and state legislation and fit with the racist traditions of American military service. It was also consistent with Lincoln's devotion to the Constitution. One of Lincoln's favorite themes was the uniqueness of the American experience. During the first months of the war, the president struggled to preserve the Constitution as living proof of American exceptionalism.[31] Noninterference with slavery was one of the pillars of his administration's official policies, as outlined in his Annual Message to Congress in December 1861: "In considering the policy to be adopted for suppressing the insurrection, I have been anxious and careful that the inevitable conflict for this purpose shall not degenerate into a violent and remorseless revolutionary struggle. I have, therefore, in every case, thought it proper to keep the integrity of the Union prominent as the primary object of the contest on our part, leaving all questions, which are not of vital military importance to the more deliberate action of the legislature."[32]

No major slave revolt developed before or after Lincoln issued the Emancipation Proclamation. When Thomas Wentworth Higginson questioned his soldiers about this after taking charge of his "colored regiment" in spring 1863, the former slaves invariably answered that they never openly revolted because "they had neither the knowledge, nor the weapons, nor the mutual confidence to make any such attempt successful."[33] White Southerners, however, could not prevent small, local revolts, involving individuals or handfuls of slaves. Neither could the Confederate army prevent slaves from running away to Union lines, a fact of vital importance for the evolution of the war. Clearly, slaves voted with their feet, leaving plantations and moving to meet invading Northern troops.[34]

## Blacks in the Confederate War Effort

While Northerners denied blacks the right to serve, Southerners tried to optimize the use of slaves and free blacks in the war effort. In the Confederacy, the large black population was viewed by many as an important military resource in the rearguard. At the beginning of the war, freed blacks throughout the Confederacy offered their services to the cause of secession. Southern leaders rejected these proposals, invoking moral and ideological principles that conflicted with black mobilization. As the prominent Georgian slaveholder and Confederate General Howell Cobb stated at the end of the war, reliance on black military power would be equal to the destruction of the movement: "The day you make soldiers of them [blacks] is the beginning of the end of the revolution. If slaves make good soldiers our whole theory of slavery is wrong."[35]

Confederate racial fears did not prevent Confederate leaders from using the heavy labor of blacks (free or slave) in support of the fighting armies. Slaves built much of the infrastructure of the Southern war effort. Hundreds of thousands worked on fortifications, breastworks, trenches, and other defensive works that were built in nearly every city and town in the South. Indeed, one of the persistent themes in Confederate politics was how black labor should be used. What compensation, in other words, should be given to owners of slaves who were used for national projects?[36]

Blacks staffed Southern hospitals and worked in weapons manufacturing plants in Virginia and Georgia. They also followed their masters in the field, working as cooks or assistants and eventually taking up arms. If, for ideological and political reasons, Southerners rejected the drafting of slaves, they could not dispense with their work on the home front. A Virginian slaveholder summarized the sacrifices planters made to support their army with black laborers: "In this section of the country a heavy draught has been made upon the farmers (half of the available working force) to work on the fortifications. I, for one, rendered this tribute cheerfully to a cause which is dear to my heart, though that, together with the excessive rains will materially shorten my crop."[37]

While portions of the slave population worked on the Confederate defenses, some individuals began to run for Union lines. With the advance of Union troops, the picture begun to change, and so did the position of slaves in the Confederacy.


## Runaways and the Union Army

When Union troops moved into the South, commanders had to choose how to deal with the runaways that began to cross their lines. Early in the war, troop units constituted microcosms of communities, reflecting the customs and prejudices existing in different parts of the North. For many soldiers, seeing the South for the first time convinced them that it was indeed a backward society in need of fundamental changes. As one soldier observed, "They [Southerners] are certainly the most primitive ignorant people I ever came across."[38]

The behavior of Northern soldiers and their attitudes toward the slaves have been subjected to extensive historiographical debate. Most analyses agree that Northern condemnation of slavery did not necessarily reinforce ideas of racial justice, nor did it lead to the acceptance of blacks as equal citizens.[39] Many soldiers condemned slavery while holding reservations about the slaves themselves. With the exception of some abolitionists and of Northern blacks, neither Northern society as a whole nor the newly formed Republican Party supported full citizenship for blacks (although some Republicans did). The "Black Codes" that existed in most Northern states, with the exception of New England, demonstrate this.[40] Many officers reflected this behavior, including the provost marshal of occupation forces in Norfolk, Virginia, who told President Lincoln that "the decided majority of our officers of all grades have no sympathy with your policy. . . . They hate the Negro, more than they love the Union."[41] Such attitudes, as George Fredrickson has pointed out, "suggest the tragic limitation of the white racial imagination of the nineteenth century, namely its characteristic inability to visualize an egalitarian biracial society."[42]

There was no uniform response to runaways. Because immediate communication with Washington was difficult, many commanders exercised considerable discretion in their treatment of runaways. Neither the military nor the Lincoln administration had a comprehensive plan to deal with the torrent of African Americans who approached Union lines. Responses depended on a commander's moral beliefs, as well as on the relations among Union troops, slaveholders, and slaves in each area. In this environment, individual Union commanders established their own policies regarding runaways.

Some immediately understood the importance of the slaves to the Confederate war effort, but others preferred to return fugitives, expecting some cooperation from loyal slaveholders. During the Peninsular Campaign (spring 1862), Major General John A. Dix worked to exclude blacks from his lines, assuring local slaveholders that "special directions have been given not to interfere with the condition of any person held to domestic service."[43] This position was criticized by some Republicans, for example, Congressman Owen Lovejoy from Illinois, who declared, "It is no part of the duty of the soldiers of the United States to capture and return fugitive slaves."[44]

The situation of each group of runaways varied according to circumstances. In some cases, slaves fled their masters; in others, masters evacuated, leaving their slaves behind; in still others, masters stayed and declared their loyalty to the Union cause. The first situation involved personal or collective decisions on the part of the slaves. From the outset of the war, many slaves sensed that the conflict would ultimately destroy slavery and that, if they could escape behind Union lines, they would find freedom. Susie King Taylor, a young slave girl from South Carolina, described the excitement at the time of her family's escape: "I wanted to see these wonderful Yankees so much, as I heard my parents say the Yankee was going to set all the slaves free."[45] Another fugitive informed by a Union general that he could not enlist into the army because "it wasn't a black man's war," answered that "it would be a black man's war before they got through."[46]

During the first months of the war, the Virginia tidewater was the Confederate theater where Union troops most often met with runaway slaves. General Benjamin Butler, then in command of the Union forces at Fort Monroe, refused to return runaways on the grounds that they should be considered "contrabands of war." Butler's justification was useful for the North's war efforts because it associated black labor with military needs.[47]

Slaves looking to Northern troops for protection often faced difficulties. Runaways who came into contact with Federal forces needed to be fed, clothed, and provided with shelter. They also had to be put to work as soon as possible, or they would soon become an impediment by consuming Union supplies and slowing down troop movements.[48] In part to alleviate this problem, Congress passed the Second Confiscation Act on August 6, 1862. This law allowed Union commanders to confiscate and employ slaves who had labored for the Confederate military or worked for disloyal masters. The act basically confirmed Butler's policy at Fort Monroe. A slaveholder who permitted his slaves to be used against the government "forfeit[ed] his claim" to his slaves' labor. However, the act did nothing for slaves who had not served the Confederacy.[49] An editorial in *Frank Leslie's Illustrated Newspaper* portrayed the derogatory way in which runaways were viewed in the Northern press during these first months. Under the title "Morning Mustering of the Contrabands," the magazine stated that "doubtless the nigger band have never had so pleasant an existence as under their new state of contraband existence."[50]

The problem of caring for and governing large slave populations was a new issue for the Union army. When South Carolina's Sea Islands were occupied in November 1861, masters and their families fled the region, leaving a significant black population of ten thousand persons behind. The former slaves as well as the plantations were subject to the supervision of the Treasury Department. The Port Royal Experiment, as it became known, united a particular set of Northern expectations to an experiment in "free labor" applied directly to the Confederate landscape. The best of

New England abolitionists came to the Sea Islands as teachers. Military and civilian administrators also came, including businessman less interested in the well-being of freed slaves than in profiting from wartime circumstances. Conflicts involving Northern officers, former slaves, commercial agents, and religious missionaries soon emerged, showing the limits of reform ideals. In retrospect, the Port Royal experience was atypical when compared to Northern management of slave labor elsewhere in the conquered South.[51]

The relations between soldiers and runaways became more complex as Union forces advanced into the Confederate heartland, assuming command of plantations and dealing with black populations whose labor was potentially useful. The Union invasion of heavily populated areas in Louisiana and the Mississippi Valley did not assure complete control of the territory or its people. Taking advantage of this precarious distribution of power, many masters declared loyalty to the Union and pressured the army to enforce labor discipline. The Union Army on the Mississippi River initially shored up its fragile military situation with a labor program that maintained the dominance of the planter class. As work conditions had deteriorated, many slaves had run away from the plantations. The army's main concern, therefore, was control of the labor force, especially the runaways whom they classified as "vagrant blacks."[52] General Nathaniel P. Banks assured Louisiana's white population that "the well being of this people [blacks] requires that they should labor, and be preserved from vagrancy and idle, vicious habits."[53]

Former slaveholders in these areas kept a high degree of control over the African American workforce and enjoyed the cooperation of Union occupiers until late in the war. They were supported by a free-labor ideology that blamed the slaves' lack of initiative for their economic plight. Late in the war, a Northern editorial expressed the concerns of many in the Northern white community about the rupture of the South's social hierarchy: "The slaves with the idea of freedom had not imbibed the idea of labor, and were in a state of perfect bewilderment. Many wandered around the streets, so many in fact to become a growing evil."[54]

The difficult problem of defining the status of black refugees beset Northern commanders during the war and continued after its end. The Second Confiscation Act solved part of the problem by giving commanders full power to employ them, pay them for their work, and, eventually, demand their cooperation for military purposes, but it did not give commanders a clear blueprint for dealing with recently emancipated slaves. The ambiguous policies of federal authorities could not block the deterioration of slavery, which was an inevitable result of the war. Dislocation, migration, and the introduction of wage labor impelled the destruction of slavery, but military recruitment was the decisive factor in preventing a return to the antebellum status quo.[55] An officer serving with General Butler in Louisiana wrote in his diary in September 1862: "Negroes still coming, on foot and in carts, drawn by oxen and mules, bringing poultry and pigs, and the little furniture they possess. Most of them as ignorant of letters as the mules they drive; but as keen and shrewd as a live Yankee. From them the key to knowledge has been taken away, and the fact has a wonderful tendency to quicken as many as two of the senses, at least."[56]

### Early Experiences with Black Soldiers

As Union troops occupied plantation states, unauthorized recruitment of black soldiers began to take place. Initially, Union officers recruited blacks largely on their own initiative and without official sanction. The federal government tolerated some of this, but several officers were subject to strong censure. During the spring of 1862, David Hunter in South Carolina, Benjamin Butler in Louisiana, and James Lane in Kansas seized the chance to arm former slaves against their masters before the Lincoln administration had taken steps to authorize such action. Although these unauthorized actions by officers in the field met with a rebuke from the Lincoln administration, they paved the way for a shift in federal military policy once manpower demands became pressing and white induction declined. In each of these cases, the officers' initiative responded to a perceived emergency in a region considered vulnerable to Confederate guerrillas. The president remained "averse to arming negroes," but he agreed to allow local commanders "to arm, for purely defensive purposes, slaves coming within their lines."[57]

Facing a military shortage and a Confederate threat in occupied Louisiana, General Butler recruited the 1,400-man Louisiana State Guard in 1862, a force of free blacks that had earlier served as an auxiliary militia with the Confederates.[58] Butler thus became the first Union general to successfully organize a black regiment, although his regiment, the Louisiana Native Guards, would not see combat until the spring 1863.[59] The ranks of the Native Guards were filled by free blacks, most light-skinned mulattos, who had been previously enrolled under the Confederacy (although their service was refused in

1861). With their enrollment, Butler helped to co-opt an important minority that possessed some property and influence in New Orleans.[60] "The Darkest of them," said General Butler, "were about the complexion of the late Mr. Webster."[61]

Louisiana's nonwhite community was heavily stratified; differences between free people of color and slaves were stronger there than in any other part of the South. Consequently, the early recruitment of Louisiana's black soldiers did not lead to an emancipation policy. This made Butler's regiments more palatable to white public opinion in the North and to loyal slaveholders in the state. Even so, Butler's successor, Nathaniel P. Banks, did what he could to dismiss black officers.[62]

In May 1862, while Butler's efforts in Louisiana were proceeding, General David Hunter, the military commander of South Carolina, ordered the enlistment of all able-bodied African Americans.[63] Recruitment in the Port Royal area was complicated because it threatened economic gains made by the recently liberated slaves. Many were employed as wage laborers, earning an income on the cotton plantations for the first time in their lives and improving their standard of living. They felt no desire to become soldiers and risk their precarious status on an uncertain enterprise. Hunter's decision instituted the first African American draft of the Civil War, a practice that later spread to other parts of the South. With the implementation of the draft, panic ensued on the plantations, with black men fleeing to the woods and being hunted down by the soldiers. Those who were caught were marched off under guard, as if they were still slaves. Almost six hundred men were dispatched to Hunter's headquarters to be drilled.[64]

The regiment did not last long. President Lincoln refused to sanction the recruitment of black troops and never authorized Hunter to pay or to equip them properly. By August 1862, Hunter's regiment was disbanded, to the joy of its would-be soldiers, and General Rufus Saxton replaced Hunter as the military commander of the Sea Islands. Probably the worst effect of Hunter's attempted conscription was the bad impression it left on the black population around Port Royal. As a result of these draconian impressments, many former slaves remained deeply distrustful of the Union army. Colonel Thomas Wentworth Higginson, commanding officer of the First South Carolina Volunteers, later complained that Hunter's actions were detrimental to his own recruiting efforts: "The trouble is in the legacy of bitter distrust bequeathed by the abortive regiment of General Hunter— into which they were driven like cattle, kept for several months in camp and then turned off without a shilling, by order of the War Department. The formation of the regiment, was on the whole, a great injury to this one . . . those who now refuse to enlist have great influence in deterring others."[65]

In Kansas, Senator James Lane, a veteran of the border wars, undertook a different strategy for black enlistment. In July 1862, Lane introduced a recruiting system whereby black agents were authorized to enroll former slaves with the promise that they might become officers. The system worked very well, although gaps in the ranks were filled by impressments. By October 1862, the First Kansas Colored Volunteers was formed, with many volunteers responding to the promises of equal pay and equal promotion with white soldiers. But because Lane acted without Federal authority, his regiments were not paid, and his black officers did not receive commissions until 1864.[66]

## The Emancipation Proclamation

An important difference between the recruitment experience in Brazil and that in the United States lies in the direct consequences the Civil War had for emancipation in the South, in contrast to Brazil, where emancipation did not immediately follow the Paraguayan War. By 1863, Northern Republicans saw themselves as attacking the enemy by emancipating slaves and enlisting them in the army; in Brazil, emancipation would not have aided the Brazilian cause but rather would have inflicted damage on the regime's supporters. While Brazilian leaders compromised with slaveholders, Republicans formulated a policy of emancipation.

During the spring and summer of 1862, opinion in the North began to shift in favor of stronger measures to deal with slaves and abandoned property in the rebel areas. Another important difference between military emancipation in Brazil and the United States was the role of public debate. In America, debates were not restricted to the presidential cabinet. Although Lincoln's decision for emancipation was essential, there were simultaneous discussions taking place in Congress and the press. Senators and representatives were tuned in to public opinion, which reflected changing attitudes in the North. These debates disclose the gradual steps taken toward abolition during the Thirty-seventh Congress.[67] On April 16, 1862, President Lincoln signed a bill abolishing slavery in the District of Columbia. By July 1862, the Republican leadership clearly favored emancipation as a war aim. The continuing drop in the enlistment of white volunteers and the lack of success on the battlefield convinced Lincoln that emancipation was necessary as a weapon to defeat the Confederacy. In March 1863, Henry H. Halleck, the general-in chief of the army, summarized for Ulysses S. Grant, the military commander of the Department of Tennessee, the administration's new understanding: "The character of the war has very much changed within the last year. There is now no possible hope of a reconciliation with the rebels. The union party in the South is virtually destroyed. There can be no peace but that which is enforced by the sword. We must conquer the rebels or be conquered by them. The north must either destroy the slave oligarchy or become slaves themselves."[68]

The preliminary Emancipation Proclamation was issued on September 22, 1862. It asserted that unless the rebels relinquish their arms by January 1, 1863, their slaves would be considered free. The Border States and other areas with a population of "loyal masters" were excluded from the proclamation. The *New York Times* of November 21, 1862, pragmatically expressed support for the presidential decision: "Slavery is a prodigious element of the strength of the rebellion. It multiplies its military power,—for it releases every white man from labor and sends him to the field. It is a tremendous weapon in the hands of the rebels. . . . Why have not our military authorities precisely the same to deprive the rebellion of that weapon which they have to deprive of any other?"[69]

Lincoln's stated purpose in issuing the proclamation as a war measure was no subterfuge. The North was desperate for manpower. In addition to defeating Confederate armies, the Union army had to occupy and administer large areas of Southern territory. The army had to protect long supply and communication lines from Confederate cavalry and guerrillas. Union forces often had to attack entrenched Confederate positions, and this proved costly in lives.

Mounting casualty lists caused many citizens and the government to look favorably on black enlistment. Many Northern and Southern blacks were willing to join the war because of the promise of emancipation, which encouraged slaves to flee the South in still larger numbers, thereby depriving the Confederacy of its labor. In turn, blacks serving as laborers strengthened Union armies, liberating white troops from fatigue duties. The final Emancipation Proclamation, on New Year's Day 1863, authorized freed slaves to "be received into the armed services of the United States" for garrison duty. Within days, President Lincoln took further action allowing black men, whether freed slaves or free born, to become full-scale Union soldiers.[70]

The federal administration acted more cautiously in the Border States. Strong resistance still existed in some Northern areas where the political controversy over the recruitment and organization of black soldiers was significant. There, government officials confronted what Eric Foner called "the inner Civil War."[71] Northern Democrats had great influence until very late in the conflict. Peace Democrats opposed emancipation and black enlistment, positions very popular among immigrants and midwesterners.[72] Many of these sectors feared that freedom would bring a flood of black immigrants to the North, competing for the most menial jobs in the cities.[73]

The Democratic press, politicians, and soldiers complained bitterly against what they perceived as a subversion of the war's objectives. On receiving the nomination for governor at the New York State Democratic convention on September 10, 1862, Horatio Seymour expressed common Northern reservations about the Emancipation Proclamation: "The scheme for an immediate emancipation and general arming of the slaves throughout the South is a proposal for the butchery of women and children for scenes of lust and rapine, of arson and murder unparalleled in the history of the world." In November, he swept to victory in the polls, one of many electoral defeats for the Republicans.[74] New York's was the only state government in the North that did not raise a black regiment. Recruitment in New York was directly promoted by federal authorities in connection with a group of affluent citizens organized around the Union League, an association of entrepreneurs connected to the Republican Party that supported war efforts in the state.[75]

## From Contraband to Soldiers

When Congress began to discuss the possibility of recruiting black soldiers, it was moved by public willingness to sacrifice closely held values in exchange for a more effective mobilization strategy. The relentless shortage of troops was only partially relieved by a conscription policy that was incomplete and difficult to implement.[76] Something had to be done. Senator John Sherman, a conservative Republican, captured this reversal in a letter to his brother General William T. Sherman: "You can form no conception at the change of opinion here on the negro question. Men of all parties who now appreciate the magnitude of the contest and who are determined to preserve the unity of the government at all hazards, agree that we must seek and make it the interests of the Negroes to help us."[77]

By the spring of 1863 the perception of the war had changed substantially in the North. Many soldiers had died; others were disabled or out of combat. The number of desertions was growing, especially along immigrants, substitutes, and recruits coming from less homogeneous communities.[78] After approval of the Enrollment Act in March 1863, pressure on the free male population increased substantially, and soon there were clear signals of increasing resistance to the conscription lottery.

"Partyism" seemed stronger than "patriotism" in most Northern states, remarked Secretary of the Navy Gideon Welles in January 1863.[79] Federal law enforcement could adopt extreme measures to cope with public emergencies, as in the temporary suspension of the writ of habeas corpus, but elections were not suspended, and politicians had to take into account the opinions of the voting public.[80] A group of Boston businessmen expressed a common belief that recruitment of black soldiers in the South would ease the recruitment crisis in the North:

In the free States the great numbers already drawn from the workshops and fields have seriously embarrassed many branches of the industry upon which the production of the country depends, and it is desirable to reduce the call upon such resources to the lowest point which is consistent with the vigorous prosecution of the War. . . . For these and other reasons we earnestly recommend that permission should be immediately given to the loyal states to recruit soldiers (against their Quotas) in those parts of the Rebel States within our control, both to fill up the white regiments now there and to create such black regiments as you may deem it expedient to authorize.[81]

Official recruitment of black troops began in the wake of the Emancipation Proclamation, in the winter and spring of 1863. At that time, the effects of the Enrollment Act were most deeply felt. The process that permitted Northern states to recruit slaves in fulfillment of quota obligations involved steps taken by the federal government. The Enrollment Act of March 1863, by subjecting the mass of white Northerners to the draft, encouraged the use of black soldiers; that blacks could "stop a bullet as well as any white man" became a common currency in the North as the war in Virginia and Tennessee became ever more costly. Massachusetts Senator Henry Wilson, a Republican and a leading proponent of using black troops, noted with enthusiasm the impact of the draft on Northern white attitudes: "When the [Enrollment] act was passed, you had a wild, unreasoning prejudice against using a black man to fight the battles of our country. But when people who were filled with these prejudices saw that they must go themselves, and bare their bosoms to the shot and shell of the enemy, they learned that the black man's blood was no more sacred than their own, and that they would as soon have a black man stand up and fight the battles of the country as to do it themselves."[82]

By May 1863, the Bureau of Colored Troops had been created to organize black troops and standardize procedures. Creation of the bureau also completed the process of military centralization, as most regiments would be directly linked to the federal government, not to the states.[83] By the middle of 1863, Secretary of War Stanton permitted all Northern states to recruit freed slaves in the South. The Union had reached the end of a long transformation through which it became committed to recruiting black troops in the North, the South, and the Border States.[84]

## The Parameters of Change

By the fall of 1863, war weariness made Northern whites increasingly willing to accept the revolutionary impact of emancipation and black enlistment. At the same time, many conservatives in both parties understood that the African American population offered a possible solution to the troop crisis.

The federal administration soon realized that the relatively small number of free blacks of military age in the North would not suffice to supply manpower for the Union army.[85] The number of free black males between the ages of eighteen and forty-five, excluding those in the Border States, totaled 46,150. An impressive 32,671, or 71 percent, of these black men served in Union armies. Because the proportion of African Americans in any one locality was very small, these regiments were filled with people from many areas.

The Union's greatest manpower reserve was Southern blacks, who were finding their way to Union lines. They were the "yet unavailed" resource that Lincoln wanted to tap. Editorials in *Frank Leslie's Illustrated* reveal how much white attitudes could change when confronted by the draft. After months of fighting, with thousands of casualties, and enlistment reduced to a trickle, the newspaper reconsidered its conservative position on black troops. In its 1862 Christmas editorial, it surrendered to the war needs: "Whatever may be the abstract opinion of the community as to the policy of forming contraband regiments, there can be no doubt as to the great interest with which the public must regard the first hostile collision between the slaves and their former masters."[86]

With the threat of a draft quite near, many white Northerners began to see the enrollment of black volunteers as preferable to the drafting of relatives and friends. An Illinois soldier expressed this opinion clearly in early 1863: "For my part I would like to see all the negroes we could raise armed and put under military discipline. . . . I think if a negro could save their [white] lives by sacrificing theirs, they [the whites] would be willing."[87] Against a background of mounting casualties, desertion, and growing sacrifices, this soldier came to see African American recruitment as a "lesser evil." A letter from the governor of Iowa to the general-in-chief of the army illustrates the same attitude, if more crudely. "When this war is over," he wrote, "and we have summed up the entire loss of life it has imposed on this country I shall not have any regrets if it is found that a part of the dead are niggers and that all are not white men."[88]

## Mobilizing Black Regiments in the North

The final Emancipation Proclamation called for the enrollment of blacks in the Union army and navy. During the winter of 1863, few black units were recruited. One of the few was in South Carolina, where General Rufus Saxton nominated Thomas Wentworth Higginson, an abolitionist minister from Massachusetts, to reorganize the unit disbanded by General David Hunter, now renamed the First South Carolina Volunteers.[89] The regiment was composed mainly of men from the South Carolina Sea Islands, together with refugees from the coastal areas of Florida, Georgia, and North Carolina. In spite of the importance normally associated with this initiative, the regiment saw little action during its first year, except for occasional raids on the Gulf coastal areas.[90]

Initial steps toward recruitment in the North followed the traditional American pattern, with the governors of states undertaking the organization and designating officers. In Massachusetts and Rhode Island, governors John Andrew and William Sprague received federal authorization to raise the first black regiments in New England. Abolitionist governor Andrew of Massachusetts immediately nominated prominent black leaders, such as Frederick Douglass, Martin Delany, and John M. Langston, along with several clergymen to recruit in diverse parts of the North. From February to May 1863, two regiments were raised and trained, the Fifty-fourth and Fifty-fifth Massachusetts Colored Infantry.[91] Soon, following the examples of Massachusetts and Rhode Island, most Northern states requested authorization to raise their own black regiments.[92] The Fifty-fourth Massachusetts soon achieved fame through its heroic attack on Fort Wagner in South Carolina. Although it was repulsed, the high number of casualties helped the regiment to acquire a reputation of courage that made black recruitment more acceptable to whites in the North.[93]

## Recruitment, Emancipation, and the States

The experience of black soldiers illustrates the importance of state power in the shaping of African American citizenship. During the American Civil War, the army emerged as the most important sector of the federal bureaucracy, its functions far surpassing the straightforward military sphere in which it was constitutionally designated to perform.[94] Unlike the national system of parties or the courts, the post-1863 army had a centralized command and a nationalized bureaucracy.[95]

As a force of occupation, the army became the organizing branch of the federal government in the South. It implemented policies that disrupted traditional labor relations, countermanding the interests of Southern oligarchs when the necessities of war demanded. In its quest to enhance national authority, the army interfered in local affairs in ways not previously permitted in the United States by any branch of the federal government. Through its actions, the army altered the fundamental relationship between citizens and the federal government; black rights basically became federalized.

Many military commanders assumed positions as military governors of occupied Confederate territory, becoming arbiters of the social conflict that followed conquest and emancipation. In the Border States, their authority sometimes surpassed that exercised by loyal governors, especially where it affected the structure of the labor market. After the Emancipation Proclamation, military successes magnified the immediate power of generals and their local allies among non-slaveholding whites.[96] William H. Johnson, a free black soldier from Connecticut, passionately described the connections between the army's success and emancipation: "The abolition of slavery is rapidly progressing South—it is the natural course of events, and must be; for wherever the Federal Army goes, the so-called master dies, and the slaves, once chattels, are transformed into men!"[97]

In the recruitment of black soldiers, the national government confronted Southern sensibilities more intensely than in any other area. This precipitated a series of crises between federal and state authorities. Loyal slaveholders in the Border States were gradually forced to recognize that the real breakthrough in recruiting black regiments occurred in the occupied South and border region. Some fought these changes. From Kentucky, Congressman William H. Wadsworth protested administration policy, arguing, correctly, "If they . . . arm the negro they are logically bound to recognize his freedom and equality."[98] Kentucky provided the most extreme case of slaveholder resistance, but the situation was far from exceptional.[99] Some Tennessee slaveholders submitted more easily, recognizing their powerlessness: "It matters not what may have been our opinions upon this subject," one wrote; "or whether we prefer a different state of things, the destruction of negro slavery in this country, is an accomplished and immutable fact, and we are willing to accept it as such."[100]

Most blacks recruited for the Union army came from areas that stood on the periphery of the Northern industrial economy.[101] Thus, the reaction faced by Union Army officers who confiscated agricultural slave labor was qualitatively different from that faced by Imperial agents in Brazil. Brazilian Imperial policy was deeply constrained by the interests of powerful slaveholders, especially the coffee producers, who constituted the pillars of Brazil's agrarian economy.

Black recruitment in Brazil was limited by the willingness of planters to cooperate and by the need to defend the stability of the Imperial state. In the American South, the conflict over the recruitment of black soldiers took place in a very different political environment: it mainly affected the region of slave labor. Recruiting from the Confederacy meant depriving the enemy of valuable resources. Moreover, disruptions in the plantation economy did not directly affect the Northern economy. Only in the Border States and in southern Louisiana and the Mississippi Valley did conflicts similar to those in Brazil arise. There, some loyal masters were able to keep a modicum of prewar power and press the government for concessions. Nonetheless, as soon as these areas lost their strategic importance for the

Union war effort, guaranteed exemptions previously given to slaveholders vanished.[102] (See figure 1 for the proportion by region of black soldiers recruited into the Union army.)

In early 1864, the adjutant general of the army informed the secretary of war about the disruption of slavery in Kentucky: "Being informed at this place that the slaves of Kentucky on the borders of Ohio, Indiana, Illinois and Tennessee, were constantly crossing the lines and quite a number of them enlisting in organizations were for the distant states of Massachusetts and Michigan, I . . . suggest [to the governor] the organization of regiments within its limits, and thus obtain a credit for the Negroes in the States quota."[103] Massachusetts Governor John Andrew clearly correlated the recruitment of Southern blacks with the maintenance of an active labor force in his home state:

> I think it not improper . . . to recruit wasted [Massachusetts] regiments on the very fields where those regiments have borne the National flag with honor, and in the very States they have helped to grasp from rebel usurpation. Every man she might thus induce to join her ranks, would be one civilian saved to the National industry, one soldier added to the army of the Union, one less possible victim of rebel conscription, one Union man of the South enjoying, in the form of a Massachusetts bounty, some compensation for the waste and want with which the rebellion had visited him. Now, whether white men or black men, why should we not be permitted to invite them to come?[104]

Throughout the South, black recruitment was inseparable from the politics of emancipation. Although President Lincoln proclaimed respect for loyal property owners, there was no strategy for containing the disruption brought by emancipation, recruitment, and the social forces they unleashed. Recruitment made emancipation inevitable even in those regions originally exempt from it, overcoming the limits originally established by Lincoln's proclamation. Union officers and agents increasingly interfered with plantation work throughout the South and Border States. By spring 1864, the enrollment of African Americans was conducted on a large scale in most Southern and border regions. The right of emancipation granted to any conscripted slave (and his family), authorized through the act of Congress of March 3, 1865, became one of the last measures taken against slaveowners' rights in these states.[105]

Although the federal government played a crucial role in dismantling

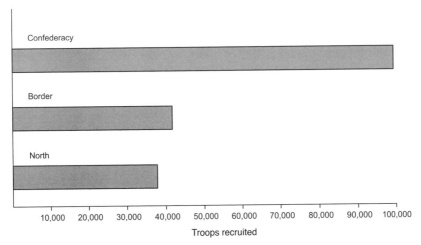

FIGURE 1. Sources of recruitment of black soldiers in the Union army, 1862–1865. From *War of the Rebellion*, 3rd series, 5:138.

slavery, the slaves themselves made the strongest contribution. Slaves moved quickly to take advantage of the opportunities opened by Northern invasion. During 1863 and 1864, a vast number of slaves left plantations and headed for army camps, dissolving the bonds of servitude. The process was spurred by credits given for black soldiers against state draft quotas.[106] Consequently, in 1863 and 1864, the nation watched the practical destruction of slavery and the development of freedom on a scale unknown to any other slave society in the Americas, with the possible exception of Haiti. Augustin L. Taveau, a Southern master from Charleston, commented on the realities of the post-emancipation South and the lack of attachment of former slaves to the old social order: "I believed that these people [slaves] were content, happy, and attached to their masters. . . . If they were content, happy and attached to their masters, why did they desert him in the moment of his need and flock to an enemy whom they did not know, and thus left their, perhaps really good masters whom they did know from infancy?"[107]

## Blacks and the Nationalization of the Army

By April 1865, around 10 percent of the Union army, or 178,000 men, was composed of black troops, many of them former slaves.[108] During the last two years of campaigning, blacks comprised 13.1 percent of the 1,261,571 estimated soldiers recruited after the passage of the Enrollment Act.[109] Approximately 144,000 (78.5 percent) of the African American troops who entered Union ranks came from the slave states. They were largely illiterate and overwhelmingly suspicious of white motives, but they were inexorably drawn by the guarantee of freedom offered by enlistment. Many of their families were still enslaved or living in refugee camps, and they faced an uncertain fate if captured. Confederate behavior toward captured black soldiers was ambiguous. As the well-known episodes at Port Hudson, Fort Pillow, and Poison Springs showed, the fate of those captured could be worse than reenslavement.[110]

It should be noted that these men were not considered to be citizens at the time of their enlistment, and they could be subjected to severe treatment more easily than white soldiers, even post-1863 white draftees. Disparate treatment was manifested in less pay, worse living conditions, harsher discipline, and other forms of discrimination.[111] Harsh military discipline broke with the established patterns of voluntarism. Yet it was more compatible with the needs of a modern army in campaign than the democratic relations between officers and soldiers sanctioned by American military tradition.[112] It suited the modern strategy of "friction," in which Northern demographic superiority was used to degrade Southern manpower in a sequence of bloody battles that forced Confederates to spend their reserves defending their heartland.[113] As the secretary of the navy confided to his diary: "all of our increased military strength now comes from Negroes."[114]

African American soldiers were approximately one-fifth of the country's eligible black population (17 percent). They fought in 449 battles, leaving 37,000 dead in the service of the Union, 10,000 on battlefields (or 10 percent of Northern casualties).[115] When we add the 200,000 blacks, men and women, whose labor supported the soldiers in the field, their work can be seen as absolutely essential to the Northern war effort. Black soldiers fought bravely and honorably in spite of the enormous discrimination suffered in the ranks.[116]

## Centralization

In clear contrast to the local character of white recruitment before 1863, the Department of War and the Bureau of Colored Troops directly recruited most African Americans for service in the Union army.[117] Only a few of the 144 regiments of United States Colored Troops carried a state designation.[118] After May 1863, these regiments were mustered directly into federal service, organized and led by officers acting under the authority of the United States. The War Department decreed that henceforth all new black regiments would be regulated together and labeled "United States Colored Troops" (USCT), even though they might be recruited and sponsored by Northern states. One-third of the regiments it administered were organized from units mustered early by state and regional military administrations. Eventually, all black regiments, with the exception of those from Massachusetts and Connecticut, were designated "USCT." Most were infantry regiments (USCI), some were in the cavalry (USCCO), and a few were in the heavy artillery (USCHA). No regiments composed of black troops elected their officers, and very few of them had black officers.[119]

The recruitment of African Americans continued the gradual subversion of local-volunteer practices that prevailed when the war began, what Ira Berlin called a "minor revolution." The old system was based on the traditional primacy of states' rights and on the assumption that the primary allegiance of the body of citizens was to state and local sources of power.[120] With conscription threatening volunteerism and blacks being regularly enrolled, the usual system was temporarily modified.

## Impressments

Black enlistment in the army advanced the African American struggle for citizenship, yet the military experience was not necessarily good for the soldiers who served in the USCTs. One problem facing Union recruiters in enlisting emancipated slaves was the reluctance of freedmen to leave their families without support. Jane Walls of York County, Virginia, complained that her husband was kidnapped and forced to join the Union army in 1863, leaving her and their three children without means of support.[121] Thousands were enlisted against their will by ambitious agents or army patrols. John Banks of Virginia testified in January 1864 that while cutting wood he was seized by about ten black soldiers and threatened with death if he did not enlist.[122] The precise number of black men drafted or impressed against their will and sent to distant camps will never be known. It is clear, however, that blacks in the South could be more easily targeted because there was no public opinion to defend them against these attacks. The Southern African American population was also forbidden to bear arms, so their capacity for self-defense was much more limited than that of their white counterparts, who could also count on Democratic Party support.[123]

Opinion about black impressment was divided. Some, for example Senator Andrew Johnson from Tennessee and Adjutant General Lorenzo Thomas, strongly supported it, and others, such as Governor John Andrew, John Murray Forbes, and George Stearns, opposed it, preferring volunteer solutions and a transformation of the South's racial relations, reshaping them on a Northern free-labor model. Resistance to impressments also came from some military commanders more interested in using blacks as laborers than as soldiers. General William Tecumseh Sherman protested against the depletion of his work force. Benjamin Butler, commander of the Department of Virginia and North Carolina in 1864, also banned recruiting agents, reporting to the secretary of war that African Americans were sold at fifty to one hundred dollars to become substitutes to white draftees.[124]

The fact that Southern blacks were more easily subjected to the draft than whites expanded the reach of conscription but also brought problems to recruiters. Some African Americans protested against being treated as able-bodied citizens for purposes of a draft while state laws denied them the rights of citizenship. As Robert Sterling noted, several petitions to the War Department asserted the argument that blacks should be exempted from the draft on the grounds that they had never been granted citizenship. A black draftee from Wisconsin, who previously had been rejected as a volunteer, underlined the contradictions presented by the draft of African Americans: "Now will you permit a poor fugitive from Bondage to ask you Some questions, Am I by the Laws of Wis. A citizen of the State[?] And if not and am not allowed to inlist in the Army to fight for our Country which you know was my wish to do when I saw you. Am I by the Laws of the United States Subject to be Drafted—the same as the white Man who has rights under the Constitution[?]."[125]

## Blacks Substituting for Whites

Despite the progressive nationalization of black recruitment, states continued to receive credits for their quotas on the basis of the regiments raised. Republican governors in the North faced the dilemma of being loyal both to the Lincoln administration in its efforts to reunite the country through a military victory, and to constituencies who increasingly reacted against military service. With local resistance increasing, the recruitment of black substitutes became an important element in reducing local tensions, enhancing its appeal to the white community. On July 4, 1864, an amendment to the Enrollment Act extended black recruitment to all the rebellious states except Arkansas, Tennessee, and Louisiana. Although no more than 5,050 substitutes were enlisted in the Southern states, a growing number of Confederate-born African Americans went north and enlisted as substitutes for whites. Section 13 of the Enrollment Act, which provided for substitution and commutation, represented the most controversial provision of the draft. Under this section, draftees could pay other men to serve in their places, or they could escape military service completely by paying the federal government a $300 commutation fee. Substitution was legal throughout the four federal drafts; commutation was in effect for just the first two. In theory, substitution would enable only draftees with a civilian station or occupation crucial to the war effort to remain at work, but in practice it allowed any citizen with sufficient financial resources to avoid military service.[126]

By mid-1864, black soldiers had become eligible for federal bounties, and state competition for their services grew relentlessly during the final months of the war.[127] There were increasing opportunities for substitution after the commutation clause was eliminated in summer 1864, and substitutes became a significant portion of the enlistment in the North.[128] According to Taylor Cornish, the practice of substitution was so widely accepted that even Lincoln's secretary, John G. Nicolay, furnished a replacement when he was drafted in New York in 1864.[129] A cartoon published in *Frank Leslie's Illustrated Newspaper* on February 13, 1864 (see figure 2) shows the growing visibility of black substitutes as a consequence of decreasing white patriotism. Two recruitment agents struggle to enroll a black man under a poster offering a bounty of three hundred dollars.

Many communities in the North contributed toward the purchase of a substitute for each of their draft-eligible men, eliminating white men from the state's draft quota. According to James D. Geary, the highest proportion of substitutes was provided by the state of New Hampshire, with 75 substitutes for every 100 drafted men.[130] But the average was high throughout the North.[131] Data from the New Hampshire Colored Troops confirms the significance of substitutes. Of a total of 393 black soldiers recruited from 1862 to 1865, 75 percent (295) came from out of the state.[132] Confederates and foreign soldiers provided around 58 percent of the total, the Border States about 4 percent, and other Northern states about 12 percent. The high percentage of Southern-born people illustrates the correlation be-

RECRUITING.

1ST BROKER—" *Now, then, yer know I spoke to yer first.*"
2ND DITTO—" *Can't you let the gentleman decide for himself.*"
BEWILDERED MAN AND BROTHER—" *You bofe very kind gemmin, but I'se afraid dey's waiting up dere for me to finish up dat whitewashin'.*"

FIGURE 2. "Recruiting." Two recruiting agents enroll a black man. *Frank Leslie's Illustrated Newspaper,* February 13, 1864. (Courtesy of Special Collections, Hornbake Library, University of Maryland, College Park)

tween draft policies and the acceptance of black enlistment because most of these troops were black substitutes for whites. Following the national pattern, most New Hampshire colored soldiers were recruited in the last two years of the war, 1864 (45 percent) and 1865 (23 percent), when substitutions were authorized on a federal basis. If the Granite State provides an example of the importance of black substitutes to Northern war efforts, it nonetheless typifies a regional situation: by the end of 1863, the recruitment of Southern blacks had become functional, and therefore acceptable, to Northern states, and resistance to recruitment had been constrained to the Border States.[133]

The growing importance of bounty money for black enlistment does not mean that blacks volunteered only for the prospect of a financial reward. Choosing the most advantageous terms for enlistment was one of the few options available for men who could not choose their units and who suffered inferior treatment while in the ranks. Furthermore, differential payments as well as the absence of federal enlistment bounties until late in the war enhanced the role of local bounties in the minds of prospective recruits. Many of these black soldiers also had families to support and were reluctant to accept less than the best offer for their services.

## Fighting for Union and Freedom

The recruitment of African American soldiers illustrates some of the complex ramifications of racial issues during the Civil War. In 1861, ethnicity, class, status, and place of birth fragmented black people in America. Obvious contrasts distinguished Southern and Northern recruits from one another as well as from the free blacks and slaves within the Confederacy.

In the North, blacks came from the native free population and from Southern and foreign countries as immigrants. Some of these volunteers were educated and active members of the abolitionist movement, accustomed to working in a biracial organization. Although some Northern blacks had known slavery by experience, others had never seen a slave. Many blacks volunteered to fight for freedom, but others who served under Northern quotas were forced to fight by draft officers and Northern agents.[134] In the South, many recruits were ex-slaves, suddenly freed to enlist. Others were runways who were compelled to enlist by Northern agents operating in the "contraband camps." There were also free black communities who fought in order to maintain their relatively higher status after the war.

The motivations of the free black volunteer, his conduct during the war, and the associations that he formed with the white officers who led him into battle were different from those of the freedman enlistee. For many freedmen, the army was an escape from slavery, a ready source of employment, and a chance to take up arms against their former masters. The free black soldiers did not share these motivations. They viewed the army as an

121

opportunity to prove their worth as men and as an argument for gaining equal rights under the law as well as a means to destroy slavery. In spite of their differences, both groups had much to win and much to lose by enlisting.[135] Samuel Cobble, a Southern runaway who enlisted in the Fifty-fifth Massachusetts Infantry as a private, exemplifies some of these feelings. In a letter to his wife, still a slave in South Carolina, Cabble stated some of the reasons why he enlisted:

> I would like to [k]no[w] if you are still in slavery if you are it will not be long before we shall have crushed the system that now oppresses you for in the course of three months you shall have your liberty. Great is the outpouring of the colored people that is now rallying with the hearts of lions against that very curse that has separate[d] you and me. Yet we shall meet again and oh what happy time it will be when this ingodly rebellion shall be put down and the curses of our land is trampled under our feet. I am a soldier now and I shall use my utmost endeavor to strike at the rebellion and the heart of this system that so long has kept us in chains.[136]

For many black people, Northern and Southern, the decision to enlist was not an easy one. Enlistment meant, in practice, the surrender of their freedom to white authority and military discipline. It also meant a separation from family and friends, as well as a disruption of work and income. For some in the South, there was the additional risk of meeting slave pickets who patrolled the Confederate borders. A Northern commander observed that courage was an attribute of every Southern volunteer because "there were more than a hundred men in the ranks who had voluntarily met more dangers in their escape from slavery than any of my young captains had incurred in all their lives."[137] This insecurity was especially painful for those with relatives who remained behind in the hands of former masters and who might suffer some form of revenge. Testimony from a black soldier's widow gives an idea of the perils to which soldiers' families were exposed: "My husband . . . had only been about a month in service when he was killed. From that time [my master] treated me more cruelly than ever whipping me frequently without any cause and insulting me on every occasion. . . . When my husband was Killed my master whipped me severely saying my husband had gone into the army to fight against white folks and he my master would let me know that I was foolish to let my husband go he would 'take it out of my back,' he would 'Kill me by piecemeal" and he hoped 'that the last one of the nigger soldiers would be Killed.'"[138]

Unlike the situation faced by the majority of white troops, there were few avenues for advancement for blacks inside the military organization. The color bar was much stronger in the American army than in the Brazilian army, where hierarchies worked against most soldiers, not only the black ones. In the USCTs, blacks could not become officers, nor could they elect their commanders. Noncommissioned officers did not receive higher salaries. Many of them could not choose their regiments, as most whites had previously been able to do. With the exception of some chaplains and doctors, few blacks became officers, and even officers were subjected to extreme discrimination in their camps. African Americans had to serve in segregated regiments commanded by white officers, and they faced all kinds of prejudice. Their inferior camp conditions were evidenced in the greater rate of death by disease as well as the larger number of punishments inflicted and capital sentences recorded.[139]

African Americans who served in the Union army did so under more difficult conditions than their white compatriots. They were assigned more onerous duties, which exposed them to a greater risk of disease. When they became ill, they received substandard care. They were less likely, even as the war continued, to be assigned to combat. For blacks this was duty only when healthy, and often they were not. A black sergeant describing the troops in his regiment at Fort Redoubt, Florida, wrote, "At one time nearly all of our men were sick. My company could not muster but seventeen men fit for duty, and some of the other companies could not muster as many."[140]

## Hierarchical Relations in the Army

Joseph Glatthaar described "an alliance," that united black soldiers and white officers around a common ideology during the Civil War;[141] however there was much diversity among white officers who led black units. Many were educated, Christian, anti-slavery activists well known in abolitionist circles who revealed a strong paternalism in commanding their troops. However, later appointments were often noncommissioned officers who had served in white volunteer regiments.[142] Many of these officers showed strong prejudice when dealing with black soldiers and their families. Although some, like Colonel Isaac F. Shepard, defended his black soldiers when they were molested by whites,[143] others, like the infamous Lieutenant Augustus Benedict, exhibited such callous discrimination that it produced a mutiny among his troops.[144]

Concern about the quality of officers of USCT units led the federal government to create a board of examination.[145] The board effectively broke with the patronage system in its designation of white officers for black regiments. Candidates had to undergo special training and take a series of exams,[146] but merit alone did not eliminate racial prejudice. A private of the Forty-third USCI warned the readers of the *Christian Recorder,* a black newspaper, about the consequences of prejudice for military discipline: "Our officers must stop beating their men across the head and back with their swords, or I fear there will be trouble with some of us."[147] Yet, fourteen of the nineteen Union soldiers executed for mutiny were blacks.[148]

Another sensitive area involved soldiers' pay, of fundamental importance in military life and essential to the process of standardization. Although some governors had initially promised equal pay, federal legislation sanctioned economic discrimination, with blacks receiving less. The clauses of the Militia Act stated that blacks were entitled to $10 a month, less $3.50 for clothing expenses. By contrast, whites received $13 plus $3.50 for clothing.[149] Officers and politicians justified the difference in terms of different military risks: initially blacks were supposed to perform fatigue duties, not to fight. As the war progressed, these excuses became less and less tenable. Black troops fought in Virginia and other theaters, suffering a great number of casualties. James Henry Gooding, a corporal in the Fifty-fourth Massachusetts, expressed the situation well and simply in a letter addressed to the president: "Now if the United States exacts uniformity of treatment of her Soldiers, from the Insurgents, would it not be well, and consistent, to set the example herself, by paying all her Soldiers alike?"[150]

Early recruits felt betrayed by abrogated promises of equal pay made by governors and agents. They complained bitterly in Northern newspapers about camp conditions: "Do we not fill the same ranks? Do we not cover the same space of ground? Do we not take up the same length of ground in a grave-yard that other do?" wrote a soldier in the Fifty-fourth Massachusetts.[151] Protests led to repeated cases of insubordination, a famous example being that of Sergeant William Walker from Company A of the Third South Carolina Colored Infantry. Walker was charged with leading his company in a strike to protest the lower rate of pay for black troops. Although some officers sympathized with Walker's conduct, he was court-martialed on January 9, 1864, and shot on March 1 of the same year without a chance to appeal.[152]

Many at home refused to enlist until the problem was settled.[153] Yet the struggle for equal pay furnished an opportunity to enlarge the debate concerning equal rights. Although prejudice was strong, the army was an arena where many blacks, for the first time in their lives, could testify against whites and complain publicly against racial discrimination. By March 1864, the War Department agreed that those already free at the time of their enlistment were entitled to equal payments as well as to reimbursements dating from the period of their service. In June 1864, Congress enacted legislation equalizing the pay of black soldiers, making it retroactive to the first of the year to all soldiers and to the beginning of enlistment to those who were free when they enlisted. Prejudice was temporarily subordinated to administrative uniformity.[154]

## Immediate Consequences

Black enlistment in the Union army encouraged social reform in the defeated South. By the end of the conflict, many African Americans recognized the essential opportunities the war had offered them. It provided a valuable platform for combating decades of racial prejudice, raising new expectations, opportunities, and awareness. Thousands of black soldiers were politicized, creating a proud and determined black political leadership, and accelerating the quest for equality both during and after the war.[155]

Federal recruitment of African Americans played an important role in the destruction of slavery and initiated the reordering of American race relations. Enlistment, especially for those who fled slavery, provided opportunities to help defeat the Confederacy and promote changes for blacks, the most important of which was the Thirteenth Amendment granting freedom to all slaves, approved by Congress in January 1865.

Unfortunately, the army's degree of integration was relative at best. It presented a genuine step in the democratization of American society, but it was limited by cultural stereotypes still prevalent in Northern states. If the structure of society had been changed, racial attitudes and stereotypes survived and, in the long run, recovered part of their prewar strength. Still, the war equipped black people with the means to continue the struggle for social equality. This process was unparalleled in any other multiracial society and was perpetuated in national memory by the occupation of the Southern states by black soldiers, and later by the dependence of Civil War veterans on military pensions during the decades following Appomattox.[156]

In contrast to the American experience, the way freedmen were integrated into the Brazilian army did not allow black participation in the war to become the basis for a postwar movement aimed at black social improvement. Black interests were diluted, as freedmen were integrated into a military organization in which the roles of the soldier and the citizen were not connected. At the end of the War of the Triple Alliance, the quick demobilization of troops prevented army veterans from formulating new social demands under the shelter of the army. Those who served returned to civilian life as dispossessed individuals living in poverty in a country of abundance.

Another essential difference was the importance of black public opinion for black recruitment in America. Although many black men were drafted, public pressures from black communities in the North encouraged voluntary recruitment. African Americans were active participants in the political debate over recruitment. They kept pressure on the president and Congress to abolish slavery, enlist new USCTs, and provide for racial equality. They had their own black churches, secular leaders, and newspapers that kept many informed about the situation at the front. They formed freedmen's aid associations, which helped in recruiting in certain parts of the North. This kind of pressure was absent in Brazil despite the presence of influential blacks in the army, such as engineer André Rebouças. Free blacks enlisted of their own free will in Brazilian towns and villages, but these enlistments were propelled by civic and patriotic proclamations, not through the formation of blacks' self-help or abolitionist societies.

Perhaps the most similarities can be found in the relationship between officers and men. Many examples exist of sympathy and care across ethnic boundaries or between officers and their hierarchic subordinates, especially at times of crisis. This does not mean that ethnic differences disappeared in the course of the struggle. Alfredo D'Escragnole Taunay, who served in the Paraguayan War, produced one of the best reports on battle solidarity in his 1867 A Retirada da Laguna (Lagunas's Retreat). In this description of the Mato Grosso 1867 campaign, Taunay describes how Brazilian Iimperial officers could show the tenderest solicitude for their soldiers without bridging the social chasm that separated the classes and the races in the army. Taunay himself showed great compassion for his soldiers, but he never overcame his own entrenched prejudices. He never admitted that his troops had the capacity for personal initiative or intellectual command. Indeed, officers are supposed to take care of their men, and it is not clear that USCT was different from Brazilian regiments in this matter, although exceptions can always be found.[157]

Although slavery was not transformed by the war in Brazil as it was in America, it was clear to the Emperor that the institutions constituted a hindrance not only to military capacity but also the country´s image. To Pedro II, eliminating slavery had become part of a modernizing agenda; however, a careful, long-term strategy was necessary to avoid increasing tensions in the home front.

# FIVE

# Manumitting and Enlisting the Slaves in Brazil, December 1866–August 1868

On November 14, 1867, José Jobim, a respected doctor and imperial political councilor wrote to his friend, Thomas Gomes, describing the misadventures of a recently acquired domestic slave, a young man named Carlos. Jobim had gone to a traditional slave market to buy a replacement for a recently manumitted cook.[1] A particular black woman caught his eye; she came with good references from the coffee district of São Marcos in the Paraíba Valley. During the auction the prospective slave cook was able to negotiate the inclusion of her two children in the deal: first, her daughter and, later in the day, her teenage son, Carlos. Together the slaves cost around the equivalent of $830 U.S. dollars for the new cook and her daughter, and $460 for Carlos.[2] Slaves were expensive in the late 1860s, a consequence of the interruption of the African slave trade almost fifteen years earlier. The letter does not reveal the regional origins of the new slaves, so it is impossible to know whether the mother was Brazilian or African-born, or if she and her children had come from the northeast through interprovincial trafficking. The three slaves performed domestic functions: mother and daughter were cooks, and the son was an oxcart driver.

Shortly after arriving in the doctor's household, however, Carlos began to stir up trouble. Complaining to Gomes, Jobim declared that the young slave lied and stole. He also chased most of the slave women, causing great anger among the other male servants. Carlos constantly disappeared from work and encouraged other male slaves to follow him into the streets, where, armed with iron weapons, they joined disorderly mobs. Finally, after Carlos had intentionally destroyed the oxcart, Jobim decided to sell him to the army as a soldier for the Triple Alliance War.

Among Brazilian masters, splitting up families was a common form of punishment for disorderly slaves.[3] Drastic measures often lead to strong domestic resistance, however. Carlos's mother protested his sale, and finally attempted to poison Jobim's food. The plot was exposed by a loyal slave (or possibly one with a grudge against Carlos) before the cook could carry out her plan.

Surprisingly, when inspected for recruitment, Carlos told the military committee that he was a "broken slave," not healthy enough to serve in the army.[4] His statement may have contained some truth, because, after a brief examination, the committee refused to induct him.[5]

Now the unhappy Dr. Jobim realized that he had been deceived twice: first, in paying a high price for an unhealthy individual; secondly, in buying a troublesome slave. In desperation he decided to send Carlos back to the Paraíba Valley, probably hoping to sell him as a fieldworker to a coffee plantation.[6] But Carlos, who had no intention of working on farms, escaped on his way to the valley.[7] After a series of short escapades, Carlos returned to Rio de Janeiro, where the police caught him at last.

The fact that Jobim was notified of Carlos's final capture by the owner of the slave market where the young man had been purchased, not by the authorities, suggests some interconnection between the police and the slave catchers. The doctor probably had good connections with the military authorities as well. After some negotiation, the army accepted Carlos with no further medical objection. Carlos was sold to the nation for $640, the highest possible price for a slave in his condition. Dr. Jobim recovered his original investment, and the intermediaries received another $180 commission. With some satisfaction, the owner and agents could wrap themselves in patriotism. They had helped to defend the nation even as they disposed of an undesirable slave. Moreover, Jobim finally got his revenge. His letter proclaimed that Carlos was tricked into enlisting.[8]

This picaresque tale of Jobim and Carlos goes beyond a mere description of a doctor's slave troubles or his attempt to salvage his reputation within the "good society" of Rio de Janeiro. It provides a good example of how Brazilian slaves were recruited for the Paraguayan War. It also offers an opportunity to analyze relations between slave owners and the Imperial state. Intermediaries often facilitated such relations, and the great changes that occurred in the structure of Brazilian slave markets during the 1860s, as well as the relations between public and private agents in Brazil, are important factors in recruitment. Additionally, it portrays the key role of personal relations in all sectors of Imperial society. Finally, it offers impressive evidence of how the war effort, nationalism, and emancipation policies were linked together in Brazil during the 1860s.

Although many Northern merchants in the United States did business with Southern slave owners, slavery itself had become a sectional institution in the United States by the 1860s. In contrast, slavery was a national institution in Brazil. As a later politician wrote, slavery's influence was so pervasive that "nothing escaped, nothing was beyond or above or outside the slave institution."[9]

Most slaves resided in southeastern provinces, but slavery was present at different levels in all provinces, and slave ownership was widespread among different races and classes. This caused huge differences in how slavery affected the everyday lives of people in each country. In the Northern United States, slavery and African Americans could be ignored, whereas in Brazil, people of color, free and slave, were ever present. Thus, the absence of a strong color bar in Brazil made many mixed individuals fit to serve in the armed forces.

As Jobim's letter implied, military service was seen as a way to get rid of undesirable slaves. The state paid high prices for fighting men, even if they were troublesome or unhealthy. Owners recouped their initial investment, and intermediaries made substantial commissions. Enlisting slaves was a selective business controlled by the masters, some of whom profited from the enlargement of the army. The slaves themselves played no active role (except a precarious one for slaves, like Carlos, choosing between disobedience and escape). For most slave recruits, their final destinations were in the interests of their white masters, and Brazil paid the bill.[10] Of course, not all slave experiences were like that of Carlos. The relations between slaves, free men of color, and the armed forces were much more complex. But seigniorial behavior toward slaves and the state could often be more utilitarian than patriotic.

The Brazilian army did not officially accept slaves until they were "manumitted" by their owners. From the beginning of the war, individual or collective slave donations had taken place in many parts of the country. But these were limited initiatives, not large enough to solve the chronic problems related to recruitment. By mid-1866, slave enlistment had become a priority for Imperial leaders. The recruitment of freed slaves offered another acute challenge to the structure of civil authority in Brazil, as it implied an expansion of the state's capacity to extract more resources from its citizens in times of trouble. No issue disturbed the power balance between center and periphery as much as the emancipation of slaves for recruitment, and no other crisis so clearly indicated the urgent need for a broader cycle of reforms.

*Was that freedom?*

Slaves were not, as for the Union in the U.S. Civil War, an abundant, cheap, and readily available source of contraband labor. In Paraguay, all slaves had been quickly enrolled in the army. Captured Paraguayan slaves became prisoners of war, not contraband that could be repurposed for the war effort. This means there was no abundant source of soldiers available to Imperial troops. Slaves were important property assets, and the Brazilian government had to negotiate with slave owners and compensate them in exchange for freed slaves.

## Preliminaries

The relationship between slavery and military service in Brazilian society was paradoxical. Slavery prevented a large number of individuals from serving in the military, but it also made slaves a potential source for substitutes. Manumission for military service did not begin during the War of the Triple Alliance. It was part of a tradition that originated in Brazil's early colonial history, as the Luso-Brazilian military had occasionally armed its freed slaves in times of crisis. Slaves fought for and against Portugal in conflicts for the control of sugar producing regions before Brazilian independence. They served in distinct military organizations during the colonial period, comprising an important element of hierarchical relations and the apparatus of power.[11]

Describing the unpopularity of recruitment and the poor state of the militia in Portuguese America, C. R. Boxer acknowledged that recruiting black people was one of several extreme measures taken by the colonial authorities to improve Brazil's military capacity. Despite the occasional reluctance of local whites, freed and slave blacks, Indians, and whites served together in segregated infantry regiments. Such regiments were organized under a hierarchy of color, each armed group commanded by a white, but dark-hued officer.[12]

Slaves and freedmen were also organized into informal armed gangs that followed their masters or patrons in the intermittent struggles for frontier land. Individuals who enrolled in these personal militias hoped to advance in the social hierarchy through use of their military skills. Consequently, the military services they performed were not occasional, as in colonial British North America. Their service was part of the customary obligations that connected servants to their masters and clients to their patrons. Slaves saw these obligations as a way to rise within the seigniorial hierarchies that governed plantation relationships in the same way that certain slaves were rewarded by some farmers with the positions of drivers and overseers.[13]

The organization of segregated black militias and armed slaves was common in the northern and southern provinces of Brazil. In the northeast, during the seventeenth-century colonial war against the Dutch, battalions of black men fought under the command of Captain Henrique Dias, a freedman of color who supported the Portuguese.[14] In the southeast region, some provinces also admitted African descendants as soldiers. The French naturalist Auguste Saint-Hilaire observed that, in the province of Minas Gerais, regiments that should have been composed solely of whites would sometimes accept mulattos in their ranks. For the naturalist, such concessions were due "to favor," not to the military needs of the Portuguese colonial state. But the situation was probably more complex. An abundance of slaves and freed blacks, lack of financial resources, and the desire of the Portuguese crown to enlarge its base of support among all sectors of the free population helped to disseminate the creation of Henrique's battalions made up of men of color during the second half of the eighteenth century.[15] Francis Cotta found at least four kinds of institutionalized black militias operating in Minas Gerais at the end of the eighteenth century, a diversity that shows how deeply such militias were involved in the captaincy's social control.[16]

In these circumstances, the enlistment of African descendants in Brazil did not promote egalitarian racial attitudes, nor did militia service rendered by the former slaves result in full citizenship for them, although some individuals could improve their social standing.[17] Even when freedom was obtained, manumissions were linked to what the historiography of slavery classified as "onerous manumissions," that is, manumission exchanged for money or services.[18] No special programs existed to settle former soldiers in distant regions, nor were programs available to help them adapt to their newly acquired free status. As the historian Carl Degler points out, the "use of Negroes as soldiers in the colonial period in Brazil, in short, was not the result of the prior acceptance of the black man as an equal but of the need of him as a fighter."[19]

After independence, emerging Brazilian leaders adapted these practices to the new environment. The provisions of October 23, 1823, and September 10, 1824, permitted slave owners to be compensated when they gave slaves to fight in the Brazilian War of Independence.[20] Slaves served in the patriotic forces that engaged with Portuguese loyalist armies in Bahia. But these limited circumstances did not engender great emancipationist movements as had occurred with Bolivar's troops in Venezuela. Yet, the law of January 21, 1828, declared under the authority of Emperor Pedro I, foresaw the need to acquire slaves for an eventual war with the Argentine Confederation. Law No. 560 of November 3, 1837, provided the final step toward desegregation of the Imperial army. During the provincial revolts of the 1830s and 1840s, freed slaves and those still in bondage fought on both sides, for the empire as well as for its provincial opponents.[21]

Black or mixed-composition units predominated in Brazil's professional army, making apparent the high proportion of African descendants among the Imperial forces. Once recruiting from the lower social stratum of Brazilian society began, Brazilian soldiers increasingly came from social groups where dark-skinned men predominated.[22] Thus, enlistment was not related to broader conceptions of citizenship, and the structure of the army reflected prevailing social prejudices. Small in size and institutionally weak, the army maintained many beliefs dating to the ancien régime. It was not an "armée de citoyens," like those that marched across continental Europe from the 1790s to 1814 during the French Republican and Napoleonic eras. The Brazilian Imperial army was not a laboratory for citizenship and the expansion of individual rights; rather, it was a pre-bureaucratic agency with manifest incapacities.[23]

In spite of the widespread presence of blacks and mulattos in the ranks, Brazilian military service was not open to slaves. The Imperial Constitution of 1824 expressly guaranteed property rights, and, as private property, slaves could not officially be expropriated by the Imperial or provincial governments. Even if the government compensated them, owners would have to manumit their slaves before enrolling them in the army. Consequently, enlistment was open only to those who possessed civil liberties or slaves freed by their masters to defend the nation-state under exceptional conditions. But no consensus existed about what constituted an "extreme" situation or what compensation slave owners would receive. In Bahia during the War of Independence, slave recruitment led to the dismissal of General Pierre Labatut, a French-born military commander who had served in the Peninsular and Bolivarian campaigns. His timid emancipation measures faced rising opposition from planters and merchants, and he was finally replaced by a Brazilian-born officer.[24]

From the beginning of the campaign against Paraguay, ex-slaves reinforced the ranks of the Brazilian army. These men were impressed, donated by their masters, or substituted for men of higher social standing. Some slaves ran away and enlisted as if they were free. The state made no specific arrangements to acquire slaves because it was generally assumed that the war would be short and that the Paraguayans would give up after one or two battles. At the beginning of operations, most Brazilians agreed with Bartolomé Mitre, who called on all citizens to "run to the Barracks in twenty-four hours, to the battle-fields in sixty days, and to Asunción in six months."[25]

Despite initial expectations, many sectors of the free population refused to go to war. For these individuals, the easiest way to avoid enlistment was to present a qualified substitute. Such was the case in Vassouras, in the Paraíba Valley, where an informal bargain took place. Twenty-nine National Guardsmen had been designated for the war. In a reaction becoming increasingly common, the recruits took refuge in the forests on the outskirts of town, creating a focus of social tension in the middle of the important coffee-growing region. Rich political bosses solved the problem by donating thirty freed slaves for the war effort. As compensation, the Army released the original twenty-nine National Guardsmen from their military obligations. These men had neither left town, nor been punished for desertion. In this case, influential local bosses and quick replacement worked in favor of the original recruits.[26]

Substitution was widespread in practice. Using substitutes, proprietors could exempt protégés from military service or acquire new recruits for the army or navy. More importantly, substitution did not violate property rights, which appeased potential frictions between slave owners and the Imperial state.[27] Thus, substitution was an important escape valve in both the Paraguayan conflict and the Civil War. Figure 3 depicts a cartoon published in Rio de Janeiro on December 23, 1866. This image portrays the irony of an influential farmer presenting slaves to substitute for his sons. The caption reads, "Mr. Mathias Rôxo and his sons turn slaves into citi-

FIGURE 3. Mr. Matias Roxo presents slaves as substitutes. *A semana ilustrada,* December 23, 1866. (Courtesy of Biblioteca Nacional, Rio de Janeiro, Journals Division)

zens. The emperor's heart and the fatherland's voice show them as examples to be followed."

During the early part of the war, the market for substitutes flourished, with both free men and slaves providing the means of exchange. Either enlisted soldiers or their relatives could present substitutes. The Ministry of War recorded only 948 slave substitutions nationwide for the five years of war. The city of Rio de Janeiro provided the most substitutes, with 437, followed by Rio Grande do Sul, with 305.

Elias, a thirty-four-year-old Gaucho from the region of Pelotas, was a typical substitute. The son of "a mulatto of free condition" and a captive mother, Elias was still a slave when Luiz Xavier da Silva bought him for $550. Da Silva's letter of manumission clearly stated that Elias would be freed on the condition that Camilo Xavier da Silva, Luiz's son, be exempted from both recruitment in the army and service in the National Guard. Such a substitution would require Elias to serve between six and nine years in the ranks, if he survived the campaign.[28]

As the war progressed and the price of slaves increased, the quality of those sent to the army became increasingly questionable. The complaints of the Marquis of Caxias, who became commander in chief of the Brazilian forces in October 1867, reflected tensions that existed between the military command, the political bosses, and the recruiting agents. In April 1868, Caxias refused to accept seven freed slaves as substitutes and kept the originally designated National Guardsmen in the ranks. This dispute took place in the midst of a struggle between Caxias and provincial president of Rio Grande do Sul, as Caxias sought to concentrate military decision making and prerogatives in his own hands. But pragmatic factors also played a role. Most recruits had already received some training. Consequently, replacement meant an exchange of experienced soldiers for untrained, raw recruits. As the old marshal described it, "I cannot accept such substitution because these individuals do not have the qualities needed in a soldier in times of war. They will never be ready to replace the soldiers already in service."[29]

What was the fate of the returned slaves? That is a difficult question to answer. From to the available evidence, it seems that most of them, once refused, did not return to slavery. In some cases, the government maintained payments even when slaves were rejected during enlistment exams. Others, while free, had to fulfill obligations to their former masters before achieving legal autonomy. These individuals had to negotiate their freedom, working for their former owners for a certain number of years. One example is Thomas Furtado. A rejected substitute, Furtado signed a contract promising to work for his master for eleven years, until his debts were paid.[30]

Runaways were also common in many provinces, and conflicts arose between the army officers and the slave masters. In the face of the reduced number of individuals willing to march to war, and aided by both the precarious bureaucratic organization of the enlisting committees and the absence of a national system of personal identification, it was not difficult for slaves to adopt false names and present themselves to the army, especially in periods of massive mobilization.

Brazil had no free-soil region to which slaves could escape; thus the army provided a refuge for slaves who could blend into the corps. In this sense, the Brazilian situation differed remarkably from the American case. In the United States, especially after the War of 1812, a color bar was maintained to exclude blacks, both slave and free, from the army. Despite the courage demonstrated by persons of African descent, the U.S. Army progressively closed its doors to those individuals until events during the Civil War modified such attitudes.[31]

For many, life in the army was an improvement over conditions they had known in the fields. Such seems to be the case for a slave called Bernardo who enlisted in the Island of Marajó in the Amazon province of Pará. After enlistment, Bernardo was claimed by and returned to his master, José Joaquim Saraiva de Miranda. Sometime later, Bernardo, preferring the army to working for his master, misbehaved to the extent that his master returned him to the ranks "as a punishment for his bad behavior."[32]

With a multiracial army recruited from the free and freed sectors of the population, men who were often not visually distinguishable from captives, it was not possible for authorities to avoid the occasional recruitment of runaway slaves.[33] For successful runaways, the uniform worked to disguise their previous servitude, in addition to providing them with the sympathy of fellow soldiers.

Although runaways often blended in with other members of the corps, they could be returned to their masters if discovered. The Imperial government returned at least thirty-six runaways and took measures to avoid recruiting others.[34] In a circular letter to the president of Rio de Janeiro, the minister of war stressed that "We should avoid the repetition of cases where, voluntarily or through recruitment, the army accepts individuals who are later discovered to come from the slave condition. We need to be very careful and check cautiously the individuals that are presented."[35]

Sometimes the experiences of free individuals demonstrated that the status of freed slaves was not completely autonomous after manumission. In some cases, newly manumitted persons still owed cash payments to their former masters for a certain period of time. For them, freedom did not supersede personal subordination; slaves emerged to freedom still dependent on their previous owners. For example, the soldier Ricardo was freed before the war started. He lived in Rio Grande do Sul, where he enlisted in the army in 1866. After he left town, his former owner, a widow, petitioned the provincial president to recall her servant, lamenting her poor condition and declaring that "he could not enjoy liberty without paying me the amount of $534." The provincial president refused to release Ricardo, declaring that the letter of manumission left no doubt about his freedom, and that the contract between Ricardo and his previous owner could not be used to exempt him from military service. In this case, the urgent need to enlarge the army favored public freedom over private obligations.[36]

Impressments of slaves could happen in ways very similar to the impressments of free individuals. In many provinces the difference in color between slaves and free poor people was slight, and slaves could be impressed while walking in the streets or running errands for their masters. If the slave preferred army life, he could disappear into the ranks. Press gangs likely accepted lighter-skinned individuals thinking they were freed blacks, not slaves.[37]

Once recruited, many slaves changed their names to avoid being discovered. This was the case with a captive called Baltazar, impressed during the Uruguayan campaign (August 1864 to February 1865) and enlisted in the Third Battalion of Volunteers. In November 1866, his owner petitioned the provincial president demanding his return, but the quartermaster general declared it impossible to find his name on the list. Many times, the links of camaraderie that developed between slaves and their officers provided the best protection they could have. At other times, the precarious state of the military records contributed to hide fugitives when they escaped into the ranks.[38]

Although a large number of free people were eligible for military service, their recruitment was subject to obstacles imposed by patrons and protectors. This limited the ability of the state to obtain regular "tribute[s] of blood" from the Brazilian people, or adequate troops for the Imperial Army. Stymied by local patronage, military agents had to concentrate their recruiting efforts on the unprotected poor. Given the permanent scarcity of volunteer soldiers, slaves represented a natural source of substitutes, especially in areas where their concentration was considered a threat to the public order, that is, in the main cities and particularly at the Court. If cities provided ideal refuges for runaways, they were also places where a runaway was as likely to be recruited as any vagrant.[39]

Slave donations were less common and restricted to the first stages of the campaign, and the first wave of patriotic demonstrations. In one example of many, Manoel Antonio Ayrosa manumitted Pedro, a light mulatto, under the condition that he serve in the army for the duration of the campaign. Donations of slaves made in the early years were considered ample proof of patriotism, and donors were rewarded with titles of nobility.[40] However, this type of manumission became rarer as the war progressed, and virtually disappeared after 1866.

Unlike the situation in the United States, no popular demonstrations protested the mixing of free and freed troops. If there was internal discontent among soldiers, it is difficult to know. Popular racial prejudice was curbed by the racial composition of the Brazilian ranks. Evidence lies in the press coverage given to the eleven companies of Zouaves. Freedmen soldiers from Bahia, the 676 troops departed from Salvador during the first year of the campaign.[41] But segregated companies did not last long: as soon as they arrived in Paraguay they were mixed into nonsegregated battalions. No segregated battalions fought during the War of the Triple Alliance, in marked contrast to the United States, where blacks served either in state segregated battalions or in the federally raised United States Colored Troops (USCTs).

As in the United States, however, the war in Paraguay offered free blacks the opportunity to prove their value and bravery in combat and enhance their social position. In the province of Bahia, black veterans of the War of Independence organized eleven companies of Zuavos (Zouaves). Another company was raised in Pernambuco. Enlisted as "Volunteers of the Fatherland," these Zouaves fought in Uruguay and during the initial phases of the invasion of Paraguay. But between June and August of 1866, they were merged with regular army troops, ending the short experience of racially segregated battalions during the Paraguayan campaign.[42] Among the free black men who served was Cândido Fonseca Galvão, also known by his self-proclaimed title of Dom Obá II. The grandson of an African tribal king, Dom Obá volunteered to take part in the campaign along with thirty comrades from the town of Lençóis in the Bahian backlands. He was also one of the few public black veterans whose records were preserved. Mustered out in Montevideo, Cândido settled in Rio de Janeiro for the rest of his life. His postwar trajectory illustrates the importance of military service for Rio de Janeiro's black community. Cândido had personal access to the Emperor and demanded recognition of the rights of soldiers who had fought in Paraguay.[43] He became a model for the aspirations of veterans in general and African descendents in particular, although authorities granted few of his demands.

To summarize, the recruitment of slaves during the initial stages of the Paraguayan campaign was not numerically significant, but it offered an opportunity for some to escape exploitation and obtain a better life, despite the severe hardships of the military and the dangers of combat. If slave recruitment before 1866 was limited by the motivations of their owners, war conditions fundamentally changed the attitude of government agents, particularly as the draft of free men met violent resistance in several provinces. In the northeast, São Paulo, and Minas Gerais, mob attacks on enrollment officers forced provincial presidents to deploy troops to enforce the draft.[44] Thus, Brazil's military situation between 1866 and 1868 created a perception of national crisis that made slave recruitment the lesser evil, and reinforced the imperial state's appeal to slave owners for manpower.

## The Military Situation

The struggle against Paraguay resulted in only a fleeting burst of patriotism. After the enthusiasm of the first months had cooled, government efforts to recruit and train citizens met enormous resistance. Few free individuals were willing to risk combat and disease in a foreign war.[45] Powerful bosses and even imperial agents defended personal domains and conspired against impressments, making recruitment efforts pointless in some regions.

The primitive state of bureaucratic development in Brazil reinforced the huge obstacles that restricted the government´s attempts to build a powerful army. There was no national census and no civil registers to provide authorities with an accurate picture of population distribution. The lack of popular enthusiasm, endemic after 1866, undermined government efforts to send fresh troops and compounded the empire´s military deficiencies. Commenting on the different nature of the war, the Counselor Pimenta Bueno, a member of the emperor's inner circle, reminded his peers that "this is not a campaign that will be ended through one or two battles that will bring glory to the Prince. This is a war of resources, a series of attacks against trenches and fortifications, an ongoing guerrilla warfare, that will be very depressing."[46]

The prolonged campaign created a series of conflicts at the national level that reflected increasing social tensions in both city and the countryside. Little by little, the war effort exacerbated divisions within Imperial society, especially in relations between central and local powers. These circumstances were linked to a series of logistical problems at the front. By the end of 1866, it was not clear whether the Triple Alliance would prevail. The troops were bogged down in a swampy region on the right bank of the Paraguayan River, "a land in which no one does well," as a corporal described it.[47] The swamps offered poor footing for tactical maneuvers and dangerous conditions for cavalry.[48]

Brazil's economic situation was delicate, and no concrete prospects existed for an early, successful termination of the war. To make matters worse, the Paraguayan government gave no sign of surrender. Territorial protection is normally a powerful drive in defensive campaigns, but the Paraguayans' defense of their homeland turned to be one of the most determined and costly in the history of warfare.[49]

As long as Paraguayans kept control of the Humayta fortress, a well-fortified collection of trenches, they controlled the upper Paraguay River and blocked the main route to Asunción.[50] After a series of military disasters, however, the Paraguayan army retrenched as it struggled to prevent an invasion. Like the Confederacy during the Civil War, the Paraguay government's goal was defense against conquest. The small country placed its hopes in an honorable armistice that would preserve territorial and political autonomy. From June 1865 on, the Paraguayans could "win" the war only by not losing.[51] This view was expressed in the testimony of a Paraguayan soldier, collected by a young Brazilian officer, Benjamin Constant Botelho de Magalhães, captain of an engineering battalion. Writing to his wife, Constant described his contacts with the enemy:

> For three days the shooting stopped completely and the Paraguayans (soldiers and officers) came to our lines to talk to us. They brought us presents like bowls (cuias), and said that they had no intention to keep fighting us. They know everything that happens in our army, in our politics, and keep calling our men to talk [saying]: we are your friends and don't like to shoot you. The supreme government will take care of the peace negotiations.[52]

For the Brazilians, the war's most immediate threat came not from Paraguayan resistance but from the possibility of a rupture in the Triple Alliance. Few sectors in Brazilian society were comfortable in a diplomatic and military alliance with any Spanish-speaking republic. Memories of regional rivalries dating to the colonial period were still strong enough to generate mistrust of the Spanish republics among Brazilian regional leaders. Gaucho officers were especially sensitive due to a long history of border conflicts with the Argentineans. During the war, the leaders of Rio Grande do Sul pledged to maintain a special brigade on the provincial border because no one completely trusted the Uruguayan and Argentinean allies. Benjamin Constant defined the reluctant cooperation among allies: "This alliance, far from diminishing the racial hate that existed between Brazil and those miserable republics, has been serving to give them a stronger development. God willing, before we return to Brazil, we could rip apart [this Alliance] on the battlefield."[53]

According to treaty agreements, all Brazilian troops fighting for the Triple Alliance served under the command of the Argentinean president, General Bartolomé Mitre. For the first two years, this provision was respected, although Brazilian officers found it extremely difficult to serve under the command of a traditional rival. Consequently, relations were marked by deep mistrust on both sides. The commandant of Brazil's Second Army Corps, the Viscount of Porto Alegre, believed that Mitre's actions demoralized the Brazilian military.[54]

Many factors contributed to the designation of the Argentinean president as commander-in-chief of the Alliance's armies. Most significant was the chosen invasion route, which passed through Argentinean territory. Equally important, though less tangible, Buenos Aires elites saw the war as a tool for political centralization, which would strengthen the central government against provincial autonomy.

In the mid-1860s the Argentinean political situation was still very delicate. Many provincial chiefs openly criticized the Buenos Aires hegemony and its economic control of the rest of the country.[55] Having Mitre as supreme commander of the Triple Alliance armies was useful for pro-center forces in their long struggle for consolidation. For these Argentineans, the war provided the long-desired opportunity to defeat Federalist adversaries both in Uruguay and Paraguay. As they fought external enemies, Argentineans expected to undermine dissension in their own country.[56] Thus, for Argentina, the Paraguayan War was both an external conflict and a civil war, and as such it involved national loyalty much more intensely than in Brazil.[57]

Between 1866 and 1867, Brazil's participation in the war grew, with Brazilian troops increasing from 58 percent to 89 percent of the total army. But this increase in proportion was not accompanied by an expansion in the number of troops. Especially after the second half of 1867, the number of recruits decreased when compared to the first two years of the war.

In spite of internal turmoil, the imperial decision to soldier on prevailed. Resistance to recruitment in Brazil was intense, but no group within the country had enough political clout to change the course of events.[58] There were strong regional differences in the scale of provincial sacrifices. Disagreements were local in character, involving disputes among provincial factions over which would dominate the oligarchy.

National disputes also lacked an ideological motivation. Brazilian parties committed to the war effort as long as they were in power, but once in opposition, they criticized government conduct. Consequently, the unpopularity of the war was directed, not towards either of the two national parties through electoral changes, but toward Emperor Pedro II himself.

## The Argentinean War

If Brazilians were both divided and equivocal in their support of the war, enthusiasm in Argentina was limited to direct clients of the state, especially ranchers and merchants who could profit by provisioning the armies with horses and salt beef. According to David Rock, Mitre's supporters became known as the "Purveyors' Party."[59] Argentinean war efforts exacerbated political conflicts that had already erupted in bloody insurrections. These earlier rebellions linked provincial oppression to national tensions, sparking turmoil in many provinces. Federalist ideas in Argentina had stronger appeal than they had in Brazil and were supported by the Constitution of 1853. Consequently, the war generated even greater divisions in the country, which undermined national mobilization and forced the impressment of foreign immigrants. By 1868, foreigners, mainly Belgians and Italians, constituted an important percentage of the Argentinean troops.[60]

Argentinean Federalists disrupted efforts to organize a large army as much as they could. Even Justo José de Urquiza of Entre-Rios, who nominally supported the war, did not permit his province to send troops to the battlefields. Mobilization was the sole responsibility of Buenos Aires, and recruitment led to increasing regional opposition against the powerful centralist factions. Resistance to those groups took the form of armed confrontations as well as debates in the national press, the Congress, and in public opinion.

## The Black Image in the Rio de La Plata Mind

The War of the Triple Alliance was fought on many fronts. For the Paraguayans and their allies in the Argentinean provinces, propaganda and diplomacy became alternative battlefields in a desperate struggle for survival. The writer and diplomat Juan Bautista Alberdi (1810–84) was the intellectual mentor of the Argentinean Constitution (1853), and his book *Bases y Puntos de Partida* (Basis and Starting Points) had served as a blueprint for the Argentinean national state.[61] From Paris, where he lived during 1865 and 1866, Alberdi wrote a series of articles that became the most important public condemnation of Argentina's participation in the war. The articles had a clear objective: to undermine Bartolomé Mitre's position in Argentinean politics, thus opening the window for a Federalist-oriented regime.[62]

Alberdi attributed the war to Brazilian territorial rapacity. In his thinking, the social and cultural limitations imposed by the torrid weather in most of Brazil compelled the empire to turn to more temperate lands on the Platine estuary to satisfy territorial ambitions. The small republic of Paraguay stood in its path, protecting the "new world" against the slave-holding and expansionist Braganças of Brazil.[63] A Brazilian victory would lead to territorial expansion and the replacement of a white native population by black slaves. According to this perspective, Argentina had been mistaken in joining the Triple Alliance, because its people had historically opposed Brazilian expansionist aims. Alberdi predicted an eventual clash between the two powers over Paraguayan spoils. He blamed the empire in particular for circumventing its historical boundaries and seeking control of the natural resources and political destinies of the Rio de la Plata region.[64]

It does not matter whether or not Alberdi's vision corresponded to reality. Geopolitical nationalism was infected with racist attitudes and dogma that effectively promulgated a derogatory vision of Brazil's wartime intentions. Positivism and racial determinism were interconnected ideologies in the mid-1860s. Such pseudoscientific points of view made it easier to cast the Brazilian alliance as a nasty and backward return to colonialism.[65] Alberdi's writings underscored Paraguayan propaganda and the racist polemics appearing in the Platine press, especially in the provinces most deeply affected by the war.[66]

The racial composition of the Brazilian army was a major news theme. Paraguay's illustrated newspapers like *Cabichui* ("Wasp" in Guarany) and *El Centinela* (Sentinel) used allegory and caricature to denigrate the African background of Brazilians. Racist cartoons portrayed the Brazilian emperor and his military commanders as monkeys, and Brazilian soldiers were referred to as "cambas," the Guarany term for "monkeys." Many cartoons depicted the deplorable condition of the Brazilian army camped around the Paraguayan river, and suggested that the incompetence of Brazilian commanders was due to the African roots of Brazilian leadership. Others mocked Brazilian war efforts. Figure 4 depicts impressment in the streets of Rio de Janeiro as a conflict in which black recruiters attempted to sub-

FIGURE 4. "Reclutamiento en las calles de Rio de Janeiro." Paraguayan cartoon portraying impressment in the streets of Rio de Janeiro. *Cabichuí,* Jan. 23, 1868. (Courtesy of Centro de Artes Visuales, Museo del Barro, Asunción)

jugate white victims. The text emphasized that the Imperial government "violated all fundamental guarantees to citizen's rights, catching men to be thrown to the war's bonfire."[67] These cartoons became a serious concern for imperial authorities because they confounded the self-image the empire was trying to project in South America as a bulwark of European civilization.

The Argentinean province of Corrientes was the base of operation for the Triple Alliance armies; thousands of soldiers were camped around its capital. The provincial population of this upriver Argentine province resented its economic subordination to the port city of Buenos Aires, however. The situation deteriorated steadily with worsening sanitary conditions among the Brazilian forces. After October 1865, troop concentrations close to the city of Corrientes brought epidemics of cholera, which strained even more the delicate relationship between Correntinos and Brazilians. According to Benjamin Constant, half of the original population, or eight thousand persons, fled to the interior to escape both contamination and recruitment. Describing the situation, Constant emphasized the Correntinos' strong racist prejudices against Brazilians: "The Correntinos say that the Cholera is the worst of all evils we brought to them because it is devastating their population. They blame 'the monkeys' for the epidemics. You can't imagine how disgusted they are with us."[68]

A series of revolts erupted in the Argentinean northwest at the end of 1866, putting the Brazilian military campaign at risk. These revolts were led by the caudilhos Saá and Felipe Varela. From San Luis, San Juan, La Rioja, Catamarca, Salta, and Jujui, the insurgent wave threatened Cordoba, Santa Fé, Entre-Rios, and Corrientes, forcing the Argentinean government to recall six thousand soldiers from the Paraguayan front.

Chaos in the country ensued. The wave of revolts forced General Mitre to abdicate military command. His resignation in February 1867 gave Brazilian military officers complete control of the strategic decisions related to Corrientes as well as to the Paraguayan campaign. Four hundred Brazilian troops landed in the city, established peace, and secured provincial loyalty to the war effort. As the revolts were subdued, an important source of unrest in the Argentinean republic dissipated. With the assassination of Urquiza the next year, Federalists lost their principal figurehead with nationwide appeal. Provincial power declined during the next decade, although revolts continued sporadically throughout the 1870s.[69]

Ironically, wartime circumstances compelled the Brazilian Army to fortify central authority in Argentina's northeast by enforcing provincial subordination to Buenos Aires. Thus, Brazil had to insure the political stability of its historical adversary to stabilize its military base of operations.[70]

Even though the Federalist uprising was put down, the Argentinean crisis had dire consequences for the Triple Alliance. The Brazilian army had to fight virtually alone during the most severe phases of the campaign, and their need for human and material reinforcements became even greater. From September 1866 to July 1867, Brazilians prepared a new offensive against Paraguay while simultaneously enforcing peace in northern Argentina. Intensification of the war efforts occurred just as recruitment faced its most severe obstacles.

The Argentinean crises dispelled any illusion that Imperial authorities might have had that the war could be won without extreme measures on the home front.[71] The situation required immediate action. To prevail on the battlefield required enforcing emergency policies to obtain men and supplies, testing the internal limits of power. This view was expressed in a confidential letter from the minister of war to the president of Rio Grande do Sul, in which the links between the Argentinean situation and the need to conscript more slaves was made crystal clear:

> The outbreak of the revolution in [some provinces of] the Argentine Confederation is very intense and can turn into a national revolution, requiring the transference of Argentine forces to repress the rebellion. This measure will weaken the forces in operation against the government of Paraguay and can put us in the contingency of having to pursue the war without Allied support. . . . Your Excellency needs to free the slaves that should be designated to the service of war, be they offered for free or through an amount designated by the Ministry of Finances. The Imperial government considers the manumission of slaves to serve as a relevant service and recommends Imperial recognition through Imperial munificence to those who cooperate.[72]

Recruitment forced government officials and slaveholders into a delicate dialogue about the future of slavery in Brazil. A critical shortage of manpower at the front should have cleared the way for government support of wholesale slave emancipation. Pedro II emphasized the inevitability of abolition sometime in the near future. At least temporarily, the emperor became head of the limited emancipation efforts undertaken by the national state, a situation that slaveholders found especially threatening.

## The Decision to Enlist Slaves

In November 1866, the emperor announced a significant increase in the number of slaves who would be freed and armed to fight against Paraguay. It was not "one decision" but rather a series of maneuvers and negotiations always aimed at increasing the size of Brazilian military forces. Unlike in the United States, neither organized social movements nor the pressure of public opinion influenced the government's action. Slave recruitment was discussed behind closed doors as a matter of national security. Lengthy reflections and debates became a series of steps toward designing more encompassing and enforceable legislation concerning emancipation. In making his announcement, the emperor followed the advice of the Council of State. These advisors met periodically with the emperor to discuss important matters of politics and public administration.

The question was carefully analyzed in the November 6 meeting of the council of state. Most councilors were important members of the Imperial elite at the peak of their careers. Council membership was small. Its discussions covered the pivotal themes of governance, and opinions were freely expressed. As a tool for consultation, the council had great influence over Imperial decisions.[73]

During the Paraguayan War, the number of council meetings sharply increased due to the urgency and importance of the questions considered. Seventeen sessions occurred from January 21, 1865, to August 31, 1867: two in 1865, eight in 1866, and seven in 1867. Six sessions were largely devoted to war themes: financial problems, recruitment, the presence of the Prince Consort at the front, cancellation of provincial elections, and the transformation of slaves into soldiers.[74]

Records of the proceedings show that most councilors supported the continuation of the war. In their general opinion, any peace without a complete victory would reinforce the notion of the empire as weak, incapable of defeating even a small nation like Paraguay. One of the most active voices, Counselor Nabuco de Araújo, strongly asserted that "the government should avoid the contingencies of a kind of peace that would bring shame for present generations and indignation for future generations."[75]

Three questions were the focus of the November 6 meeting: (1) If the war were to continue, would it be good policy to manumit slaves to increase the army's size? (2) Which kind of slaves should be given preference for enlistment: those owned by the government, those from religious orders, or those coming from private owners? (3) What steps should be taken next?

Records of the proceedings show that opinion was divided about the need to enlist a large number of slaves. During the meeting, five of the ten councilors voted in favor, and five voted against. Councilors agreed, however, to prioritize enlisting slaves owned by the state, the Imperial house, or by religious orders over those owned as private property and employed on plantations.[76]

Pedro II's announcement was only a first step. It was a measured response to the army's urgent need for reinforcements, restricting slave recruitment to the Imperial household, convents and monasteries, state-related sectors on the fringe of the economy.[77] Soon, however, the freedom of state-owned slaves in support of the war efforts would become a precedent for other sectors.

## Slaves as Direct State Property

The slaves of the state were individuals owned by the government through national farms and state-owned industries, such as powder and iron factories. National farms also received custody of African contrabands, slaves illegally brought to Brazil after the international prohibition on slave trafficking.[78] These African-born individuals languished in Imperial custody for a number of years before being released.[79] Their semi-captive status permitted the state to dispose of them as it wished: a few were sent to public farms, and others were sent to Imperial iron and powder factories or to the arsenals. Antônio, a free African working in the war arsenals after 1849, is an example of a slave held by the state. In March 1862, Antônio petitioned the Ministry of War to be emancipated since he had fulfilled his probationary period. His petition clearly indicates that free workers at the arsenal encouraged him to pursue his rights.[80]

When discussing the subject, Nabuco de Araújo underlined a point that deserves attention in the historiography of slavery: the supposedly better treatment of state-owned slaves ("slaves of the nation" as they were called) and slaves in the Imperial Household, compared to conditions faced by "normal field workers."[81] In consequence, Nabuco reminded his peers that proposals for the freedom of such slaves could be problematic since the slaves might prefer bondage to a freedom that meant being sent off to war. Because "such slaves and those coming from the Nation have been living under very idle conditions it is possible they will refuse this benefit [freedom to serve] and will try to hide themselves. It is why their capture should be done in secret and with all possible caution. The best possible solution would be to send the police chief, the delegate, and the judge with the doctors and inspectors to catch, examine, and evaluate those slaves."[82]

When discussing the manumission of state-owned slaves, councilors recommended that their wives should also be freed.[83] Such concerns point to the growing importance of families among slaves. The process of family formation was advancing on state-owned properties, probably due to better living standards.[84] The report of the Ministry of Finances for 1866 shows a total population of 1,427 state-owned slaves. From a male population of 707, 339 were recruited. Officially, 287 of these men were sent to the front, as were 67 others owned by the Imperial house.[85]

## Slaves as Indirect State Property

Religious orders owned a number of slaves spread over many church properties across the nation, with an estimated 1,420 male slaves capable of military service.[86] In spite of religious principles and philanthropic works, Catholic institutions and most individual priests showed no special commitment to the emancipation of slaves. Unlike in the United States, where some Protestant denominations furnished ideological fuel and personnel for antislavery crusades, Brazilian society debated these questions strictly under the umbrella of the state. The church was completely absent in public discussions.[87] Councilor Torres Homem noted the great contradiction of slave ownership by the church: "It is also a strange anomaly that after eighteen centuries of Christianity, the convents still own a large number of slaves when the Catholic Church has always refuted, struggled and condemned slavery as an institution opposed to the spirit of the Gospel."[88]

As public servants, priests defended positions that were similar to, if not more conservative than, those of Brazilian bureaucrats. The fact that the Catholic Church and the nation-state were united in the Luso-Brazilian world was characteristic of that tradition. It is not surprising that no abolitionist sentiment developed among Brazilian priests as a whole. Priests were loyal to the church's institutional needs, and slaves performed a variety of duties on church properties, and in convents and monasteries. According to the future abolitionist leader, Joaquim Nabuco, the possession of men and women by convents and the clergy in general completely demoralized all religious feelings of masters and slaves.[89]

## Privately Owned Slaves

The third group, slaves owned by private individuals, was by far the largest, numbering around 1.5 million individuals, according to the 1872 census. Constituting 15 to 20 percent of the total Brazilian population by 1865, the slave population itself was fragmented by ethnicity, status, and personal loyalties. There were no accurate registers to give an account of the exact number of slaves in the country. Before 1872, there was no legal requirement to register slaves, and slave owners did not need certificates that proved ownership.[90] No regular demographic census existed, only estimates based on the counties and provinces where lists were produced. Widespread resistance entrenched in all classes confronted the expansion of the civil registers. This prevented the government from knowing precisely the number of slaves eligible for enlistment. It could not "see like a State."[91] Data from an 1849 census conducted in both the province and the city of Rio de Janeiro counted a population of 450,000 slaves, a larger number than Cuba had at that time. Some councilors optimistically believed that around 24,000 soldiers could be obtained from private owners, by recruiting just 10 percent of the estimated total.[92]

But these slaves were males between twelve and fifty years old, at the peak of their productive lives, and they were as essential to Brazilian planters as they were to the army. Worse, by the middle of the 1860s, the termination of the Atlantic slave trade, poor birthrates, and greater childhood mortality made healthy workers a scarce commodity on plantations. The institution of slavery faced its worst crisis in Brazilian history. Table 4 shows that more than half of the slave population was concentrated in the southeast region, home to the coffee plantations, and increasingly on larger properties. Consequently, resistance to slave recruitment grew among planters, particularly those with large holdings.

Debates focused on the question of how to release slaves pressed into the service. Many councilors condemned expropriation without compensation. The Marquis of Olinda feared any such measure could bring unintended consequences because "slavery is a misfortune that should not be touched." For others, the release of slaves was dangerously linked to the prospect of immediate emancipation. Finally, a third group, more concerned with public administration than with property rights, feared

TABLE 4. Brazil's slave population by region, 1872

| Region | Population (% of total slave population) |
|--------|----------------------------------------|
| North | 28,437 (1.88) |
| Northeast | 480,409 (31.8) |
| Southeast | 891,306 (59) |
| South | 93,335 (6.18) |
| West | 17,319 (1.14) |
| Total | 1,510,806 (100) |

Source: Directoria Geral de Estatística. Recenseamento da População do Império do Brasil de 1872. (Rio de Janeiro: Leuziger e Filhos, 1873–76)

that the country's poor finances could not support compensating slave owners.

Yet, proponents saw slave recruitment as essential to the nation's military needs. The Viscount of Abaeté went so far as to propose the expropriation of slaves, as needed, for national defense. Councilor Nabuco de Araújo anticipated that difficulties in mobilizing free sectors would increase due to the scattered distribution of the population, the absence of regular forces to apprehend runaways, political intrigues, and other circumstances. Consequently, basing Brazil's military power only on the free sectors would take too long. Prolonging the war would require more labor from industry and agriculture, aggravating the shortage of free workers because "Brazilians were characterized by enthusiasm, not by their steadiness." Nabuco defended the enlistment of slaves, especially those who were a threat to public order. He focused mainly on urban slaves, a group subject to less rigid rules of social control. Urban slaves would become the main target of his recruitment efforts. There would be no contradictions in this because "the slaves bought [by the state] are freed, consequently they will become citizens before they are turned into soldiers: they will become soldier-citizens. Thus, at the same time and through the same act it is possible to make a great service to emancipation, which is the cause of civilization and another service to the war, which is a national cause; thus [the army] will receive soldiers endowed with the values of freedom, disciplined by their habit of obeying."[93]

In the urgent need for mobilization, Nabuco saw an opportunity to resume debates on abolition, which had been frozen since 1850, when international traffic was abolished. He argued particularly for the recruitment of rebellious urban slaves, individuals like Carlos, the slave described at the beginning of this chapter, whom civilian authorities found difficult to control. By targeting urban slaves, the war effort would reduce one of Brazil's main security problems without undermining the agricultural activities so important for the national economy. Recruitment would thus complete the task that the ban on internal slave traffic had advanced: freeing cities of the turmoil and threat that resulted from concentrations of slaves living in permanent contact with freed and free members of urban society.

Councilor Pimenta Bueno also spoke in favor of enlisting slaves, this time from a much more racist perspective. Pimenta Bueno divided his answer into five points:

(1) Politically, instead of diminishing the free population, the state should shrink the number of slaves.

(2) The policy would be a kind of emancipation that provided both direction and occupation to those emancipated.

(3) Although this labor would be useful in agriculture, the sons, relatives, or clients of free workers are much more necessary. Many of them represented the nuclei of future working families, nuclei that the war would snuff out.

(4) Because Brazilian society is not homogeneous, it is preferable to spare the most civilized and virtuous class of society, and not the other, less civilized, less virtuous and possibly dangerous. Between evils it is better to choose the lesser. And finally,

(5) The recruitment of free men would become more and more difficult.

In Pimenta Bueno's Social Darwinist line of reasoning, of which he was the only proponent, the war would bring about a racial improvement of the Brazilian population by using slaves as cannon fodder. This line echoes some Yankee positions years earlier. Sending blacks to their deaths on the battlefields would diminish their proportion of the total Brazilian population. Consequently, war sacrifices would, in his opinion, "improve" Brazil's racial composition, while at the same time solving urgent military needs.[94]

Opponents of any official policy concerning slave recruitment appealed to both material and moral considerations. The Viscount of Jequitinhonha classified such action as "inconvenient, indecorous, ineffective and very onerous to the public coffers." Faced with the possible formation of freedmen battalions, Jequitinhonha went to the extreme of proposing a return to the use of foreign mercenaries, a practice long abandoned by the Brazilian army. Jequitinhonha was supported in advocating this "lesser evil" position by the Viscount of Itaboraí, for whom "foreign [mercenaries] are less dangerous than the slaves taken from the state of abjection in which they live to be armed on the next day, enhancing in their hearts the bad will, indisposition, and the anger they accumulated during their captivity because they understand that their freedom came not by feeling[s] of justice or generosity but just by the need to oppose them to their masters' enemies."[95]

## Comparing Slave Societies

During the meeting of November 6, councilors constantly appealed to comparative analysis. Most examples cited were of European countries and colonies. Councilors linked the elite national self-image with a Brazilian monarchy that mirrored the values and practices of European nations. But the recently ended American Civil War was also an important reference. Because American recruitment policies grew out of similar circumstances, they were the subject of inquiries and comparisons.

Both defenders and opponents of slave enlistment referred to the American situation. Pimenta Bueno employed the U.S. example to defend enlistment, connecting the Union situation to classical models from Greece and Rome, "which were not embarrassed to appeal for the help of their captives in times of trouble." Nabuco de Araújo emphasized Lincoln's Emancipation Proclamation (September 1862) and the final Emancipation Act (January 1863) as good precedents for Brazil. From his perspective, the American experience showed that recruiting freed slaves could be accomplished without social turmoil.

Refuting similarities between American and Brazilian experiences, Councilor Torres Homem pointed out that the Union's massive enlistment of blacks was related to emancipation in the South, a cardinal point of that struggle. Recruitment was not a threat to Northern society, which had a relatively small number of African descendants. The freedom granted to all Southern slaves didn't affect economic and social conditions in the North, where a free labor economy flourished even during the colonial period. Enlisted former slaves fought for their own freedom, which was reason enough to maintain strict discipline. Moreover, emancipation would (eventually) be universal. Slaves who did not participate in the fight would benefit from the victory. In Brazil, by contrast, freed slaves fought for a slave state. The lack of any prospects for immediate abolition would encourage revolt instead of social cooperation.

In their discussions about slave motivation, councilors always took it for granted that slaves would behave as a single "interest group." They did not consider that personal relations, patronage, ethnicity, and parental loyalties might fragment the social and racial orientation of the captives. In the councilors' minds, slave reactions were measured in terms of a monolithic "black behavior." Again, the shadows of Santo Domingo were present.

Curiously, the councilors did not discuss examples of other Latin American countries. In South America, many of the Spanish-speaking republics had used freed slaves as soldiers during the first half of the nineteenth century.[96] Simón Bolivar made extensive use of former slaves and freed blacks in his campaigns against royalists. Juan Manuel de Rosas also "appealed" to the black population of Buenos Aires when raising regiments to fight against rebel provinces. The British explorer Richard Burton noted in his "Letters" that both Argentina and Uruguay thinned the ranks of their local black populations by utilizing them as cannon folder.[97] During the War of the Triple Alliance, Paraguay used its small black population, freeing slaves for the army.[98] The only reference to neighboring republics was made by Councilor Torres Homem, who feared the impression this special kind of recruitment would produce in "the neighbor republics and in the civilized world." Torres Homem feared that the empire would be criticized for recruiting slaves to fight against one of the smallest nations in the Americas.

Councilors also feared that recruitment could foment rebellions among slaves who remained on the farms, disturbing economic activities to the rear. To ensure monarchical stability, councilors insisted that slaves must be prevented from confounding recruitment with immediate abolition. Torres Homem emphasized that it made no difference whether slaves were freed by the state in the name of civilization, or to produce soldiers for the war; the moral effects on the remaining slaves would be the same. He also remarked on the resentment of free soldiers, who would suddenly find themselves in the ranks on equal footing with former slaves.[99]

After reflecting on the councilors' opinions, and considering the precarious state of the army, the emperor reached a decision regarding the enlistment of slaves. Two steps were taken to make it clear that enlistment did not mean emancipation. Concurrent with the next council meeting, the emperor manumitted all slaves held by the state and religious orders through Decree 3725. The Decree emphasized that slaves would be freed on the condition that they immediately enter the Army and serve for a period of nine years. Soldiers' wives were automatically freed by the same decree. This serious step had now been taken, and the emperor would have to face its consequences. In spite of transforming freed institutional slaves into a tool to reinforce the army, the decree was soft on private owners.

## Extracting Manpower from Slave Owners

Although the number of individuals freed during the first wave was small, there was still resistance to the government's plan, particularly from the church. The Carmelite Order illustrates the lack of cooperation that Imperial authorities found even in sectors deeply connected to the monarchy. In an official letter from December 1865, the archbishop of Bahia informed the minister of war that "due to the deplorable state of the Carmelites' properties it would not be possible to furnish a significant number of individuals." He declared that, of the 106 slaves living on the best Carmelite farm, only 8 were in condition to march. Although the Benedictine Order had given 10 slaves at the same time, the Archbishop emphasized that "giving eight individuals, poor as the Carmelites were, represented much more than those given by the richer order of Benedictines."

An anonymous letter of November 1866 from a "loyal servant of his majesty" cast doubt on the Carmelite's argument:

> The Carmelite order possesses around one thousand slaves of both sexes of different ages in the provinces of Rio de Janeiro, São Paulo, Espírito Santo, and Pará. From those it is possible to take a lot of people. But the current Superior Priest rented many of their farms, with good slaves, to speculators. From these farms it would be possible to extract a large contingent for the army. I should advise the government not to accept any excuses that could frustrate the government's intentions. The government should rescind all contracts and nominate an honorable person to choose the better slaves for the service of the army. This will bring profits for the country and for civilization.[100]

It seems that the writer was correct in his criticism. In April 1867, a superior from the Carmelite convent announced that the order could free forty-five individuals, distributed among many properties, some of them rented,[101] and increasing sixfold its initial offer.[102] Also noteworthy, Carmelite monasteries in the Court and the northern province of Pará gave more individuals than those in the provinces of São Paulo and Rio de Janeiro.[103] In another letter, the Carmelites reminded the Imperial government of the "necessary compensation." Ecclesiastical authorities objected to the expropriation of property and demanded money in exchange for their servants. Final reports list a total of ninety-five recruits coming from convents and monasteries.[104]

If the government faced problems in extracting slave-soldiers from the church, how would private citizens respond? Clearly the council was unwilling to pressure slave owners. At no time during the war were slaves recruited against their masters' wishes. Instead, government officers made a "series of appeals" expressly aimed at convincing masters to voluntarily donate slaves to the nation. Some answered these appeals, but others opposed them, including José de Souza Breves, one of the richest planters in the province of Rio de Janeiro. His response to an official letter from the provincial president expresses a common argument against the government requests: "During the past year . . . I released six slaves [to serve] but these showed bad will and sought protection with some of my friends, refusing the benefits of freedom. . . . At the same time, eleven of my slaves, 'mixed and Creoles,' after committing smaller offenses also left my farms, and it seems they entered the ranks as Volunteers offering to march to the theater of war. Given this situation, I offered freedom to all of those that enlisted as well as to the others that followed the same fate. I believe my patriotic intentions are justified."[105]

For rural bosses who voluntarily donated some slaves, other questions arose. Who would transport the slaves to the Court in Rio de Janeiro? Expressing concern about this problem, the president of São Paulo declared that, if "the slave owners have to pay, none would send their slaves to the court and risk receiving them back when refused."[106]

In spite of the good intentions of some planters, the number of slaves freed was small, only one or two per planter. A total of 799 slaves were freely donated, together with 948 designated as substitutes. This was about half the number of 1,807 individuals who were freed by public funds. The Imperial government realized that, if the military situation did not improve, serious difficulties would arise during the next year, as planters and their associates in major cities became less willing to cooperate with efforts to free and enlist slaves. The contrast was nowhere more evident than in the northwestern province of Ceará: Imperial and provincial governments together freed 350 slaves, but just one was freed by a private owner.[107]

The tide of war, however, turned in favor of the empire. Beginning in December 1867, a series of victories led to the crucial capture of Humayta fortress in August 1868. After that, Paraguayans could no longer muster enough resistance to alter the outcome of events. The war, for all practical purposes, had been won, and conquering the remaining Paraguayan posts was only a question of time and weather conditions.

## Numbers and Losses in the Enlistment of Slaves

The problems in determining the number of freed soldiers who served during the Paraguayan War are the same as those in determining the number of free recruits. The figures generated by the Ministry of War do not match. In the Report of 1872, officials tried to give some uniformity to this ocean of data, summarizing totals for the five years of combat.

Most emancipation efforts were concentrated on state-related institutions. Fifty-six percent of all emancipated individuals came via Imperial donation, from the Imperial Household or farms, or from indirectly related institutions such as the church. Half of the private contributions were filled through substitutions. Private donations represented only about 2 percent of all recruitment efforts. The unwillingness of planters to contribute slaves can be attributed to the permanent slave labor crisis. But even considering difficulties within the plantation economy, the cooperation of this sector fell far below the councilors' most skeptical projections. No expropriation took place, although some slaves may have been mistakenly taken from their owners. Overall, the state bore the heaviest burden of recruitment, and yet it, too, failed to extract a significant number of individuals. Information from the territorial division of recruitment supports these conclusions.

These data show the great contribution of the city of Rio de Janeiro to the war efforts. On the surface, they appear to confirm councilor Nabuco de Araújo's supposition that slave recruitment should focus on urban slaves, especially those in the capital. But a more careful analysis indicates that proximity to the Court and to the machineries of state aided in the recruitment effort. As the capital of the empire, the Court at Rio was much more sensitive to political pressures and its slaves more susceptible to Imperial manumissions. Of the 2,196 slaves freed for recruitment in the city of Rio de Janeiro, 60.5 percent came from state-related activities, most of them bought or released by the government (see table 5).

The distribution of regional recruitment followed the same patterns presented by internal slave traffic. The northeast and the south contributed proportionally much more than the southeast, which held half of the country's slave population. This evidence supports the hypothesis that coffee planters did not cooperate as expected but retained their slaves despite Imperial government demands. To the 4,003 slaves officially freed for the army, 2,257 more who enlisted in the navy must be added, making a total

TABLE 5. Recruitment of slaves by region, 1865–1869

| Region | Number (% of total recruitment) |
|---|---|
| North | 66 (1.6) |
| Northeast | 985 (24.5) |
| Southeast (including the Court[a] in the City of Rio de Janeiro) | 2,555 (64) |
| South | 396 (9.9) |
| Total | 4,002 (100) |

Source: "Mappa da Força . . ." Report from the Ministry of War, 1872.
[a] The Court alone recruited 2,196 slaves or 55 percent of the slaves.

of 6,260 individuals. This number corresponds to 4.4 percent of the 91,298 soldiers who fought in the war, according to the Report of 1872. But true figures are probably larger, although proportions between free and freed individuals may be the same.[108]

This small proportion becomes more significant, however, when compared to the declining number of troops sent to the front from November 1866 to August 1868, the final years of the war when manumissions for the army were officially suspended. Alternative lists provided by the reports of the Ministry of War show that during 1867 and 1868 just 15,000 troops were sent to the front, 3,897 of whom were freed slaves (26 percent). In 1868, an estimated 1,873 slaves were recruited. They made up 23 percent of the 8,241 soldiers sent to Paraguay that year. Thus, the recruitment of freed slaves maintained the supply of new troops at acceptable levels, and was fundamental for Brazilian victory. If freed slaves made up a relatively small proportion of the total army contingent, they were nonetheless essential during the last three years of the campaign, when sources of free soldiers were drying up. It is very probable that freed slaves played a crucial role in the occupation of Paraguay after the end of the war. What started as a volunteer and patriotic campaign turned into a fight of freed slaves and impressed recruits.[109]

## Immediate Political Repercussions of Enlistment

During the empire's last foreign war, issues surfaced around recruitment and the ways slaves could eventually be freed to support the armies being raised. Slave enlistment became an important element in the debate over the future of slavery in Brazil. Emancipation in British, French, and Danish colonies and the victory of the Union in the American Civil War made powerful Brazilian groups realize that conditions had decisively turned against slavery. Any explicit defense of the institution would be fruitless. The coffee industry, heavily dependent on slave labor, realized the need to negotiate favorable conditions for termination, but discussions of these terms led to tensions between coffee growers, the Conservative Party, and the emperor that reflected longstanding frustrations.

The conduct of the Paraguayan War reflected the Imperial attitude toward slavery. During the war, slavery was viewed as detrimental to military efforts because it undermined mobilization and incited fears on the home front. Such concerns were added to long-term international criticism of Brazil's unwillingness to end an institution widely condemned in Europe and now in the victorious United States.

Not coincidentally, the future of slavery was discussed along with the war efforts. The war seemed to show that the nation could not be strong as long as there were slaves at home, ready to rebel. Under these circumstances, Brazilian politicians reflected on the experience of the United States and discussed the similarities and differences between the two countries. In general, slaveholder representatives defended a path appropriate to their different understanding of Brazilian society and history.

This attitude deeply embittered the emperor, shook his confidence in the monarchy's supporters, and led him to challenge the representative practices of the Brazilian Parliament.[110] Since 1864, Dom Pedro II had been very concerned about the outcome of the American Civil War. In a private conversation with his newly appointed liberal prime minister, Zacharias de Góis e Vasconcelos, the emperor declared that events in America compelled the Brazilian government to consider the future of slavery.[111]

By 1867, the third year of the Paraguayan War, the enlistment of slaves had become a fundamental strategy for the defense of the Imperial state. This led to a new series of discussions centered on the Crown's initiative, introduced by the Emperor Pedro II. In his Speech from the Throne of May 1867, Dom Pedro II clearly signaled his position in support of emancipation. The Brazilian government informed the world in the name of the emperor that measures would be taken toward emancipation as soon as the war was over: "The captive element in the Empire will deserve your consideration in such a way that the higher interest linked to emancipation will be considered, respecting current property and without causing great instability to our industry and agriculture."[112] Writing sixteen years later, the abolitionist leader Joaquim Nabuco declared that the Imperial Speech from the Throne was to emancipation, "like a bolt of lightning in a cloudless sky."[113] Such an initiative, coming from the highest Brazilian authority four months after the manumission of most state-owned slaves, alarmed planters and supporters of slavery around the country. These barons feared the government was moving too quickly in the direction of abolition. Fears of immediate interference in the slave market were not realized, but they had a profound impact on the mood of the powerful planter class that felt threatened by what it perceived as an excessively autonomous and authoritarian national state. If the planters' immediate interests were not entirely homogeneous, the defense of slavery unified them around convergent long-term policies.[114]

One of the stronger critics of the emperor's position was the writer and politician from Ceará, José Martiniano de Alencar. Referring to the high expenditures related to the Paraguayan conflict, Alencar called Dom Pedro II "the soul of the war," blaming him for the persistence of the campaign and the sacrifices it had imposed on the Brazilian people. Alencar was especially critical of the "Speech from the Throne," which he described as a surrender of national interests to the "fanaticism of progress." His argument was useful not only in support of constitutional principles, but also in support of private property.[115]

Alencar defended the slaveholders with arguments that resembled those used by Thomas Dew and George Fitzhugh in the antebellum U.S. South.[116] He accused the emperor of being more sympathetic to "foreign passions" than to the interests of Brazilian planters: "You did nothing to liberate the country from the infection of immorality. Your lack of interest about everything not connected to the War and your obstinacy about it leads you to tolerate things that are terrible for those who admire your character."[117]

The situation faced by the Brazilian Empire exhibits similarities and differences compared to that of the Union during the American Civil War. Black soldiers served the Union in segregated battalions raised mostly during the conflict's last two years. In contrast, African-descendants in the Brazilian army were numerous from the start, with free and freed elements serving alongside white, indigenous individuals and those of mixed race. Freed slaves became the center of Imperial policy when public slaves were freed and appeals for manumission were directed to private slave owners at the end of the war's second year. But the monarchy's determination to wage war to the bitter end slowly alienated the planters.

Participation in the U.S. Civil War helped to consolidate emancipation in the Southern states. Freed slaves serving in Brazil's Imperial army, however, returned to a depressed and unchanged society, where the values and practices of slavery still mattered. They were free, of course, and the central government was compelled to protect them against their former masters. But changes came too slowly to touch these veterans. The poor state of Imperial finances did not help. Enlistment promises made to volunteers were difficult to fulfill, especially pensions and other monetary support.

If the long-term social and racial benefits differed in the two countries, the deployment of troops taken from slavery was essential to both victorious armies. The enrollment of African Americans helped to maintain the Union's military superiority against a weakened but unbowed South. Of the 198,000 African Americans enlisted, an estimated 140,000 came from the Confederate states. After the end of the war, around 80,000 black troops were kept in the South as an army of occupation.

Although raw numbers in the United States were impressive, Brazil's armies likewise relied on the poorest sectors of society, enlisting thousands of individuals related somehow to slavery. The Union army faced strategic dilemmas similar to those of the Imperial army, and in the empire as well as in the Union North, the recruitment of black soldiers turned out to be fundamental to maintaining the work of an army of invasion.

# Conclusion

## Processes, Effects, Distortions

I claim not to have controlled events but confess plainly that events
have controlled me. Now, at the end of three years [of] struggle
the nation's condition is not what either party, or any man devised
or expected. God alone can claim it.

—Abraham Lincoln

It is lamentable that partisan politics . . . led to the understanding
that National revenge is a monopoly of some political faction.

—Marquis of Caxias

As the preceding chapters have demonstrated, both Brazil and the United
States found themselves in unprecedented but similar situations in response to the wars of the 1860s. The critical need for troops and materials
forced each nation-state to centralize to enforce military recruitment. The
uneasy triumph of centralization over tenacious forms of localism affected
both societies despite differences in demography, in the scope of racial
prejudice, and in the amount of popular political participation.

The move toward a more centralized governing structure was impeded
in both countries by lack of bureaucratic expertise and poor military organization. Efforts to consolidate political authority and extract resources
from individuals led to internal conflicts, popular criticism, and rebellion
that illustrated the central states' limited capacity to acquire the materials
they needed. The autonomy of national recruiting agents proved especially
problematic by igniting resentment among local authorities and their constituents. Attempts to increase recruitment undermined social cohesion
and national unity in both cases. Whereas the Union possessed more sophisticated political tools to circumvent popular resistance, the empire's

inadequate resources limited the monarchy's ability to make demands on its periphery.[1]

The similarities between the years 1863 in the United States and 1867 in Brazil justify careful comparison. In those years, government officials confronted unexpected crises resulting from the expansion of state action. Both governments chose to pursue complete military victory despite severe obstacles and high human costs. Relentless enemy resistance forced both the Union and Imperial governments to push beyond original victory objectives, and simultaneously shaped the path for further internal compromises.

Impressments and emancipation were central issues in the debates about mobilization. Armed mobs in the far interior of Brazil, as well as anti-draft riots in America, were perceived as dangerous menaces to progress and social stability. The threats posed by local resistance were more symbolic than real, however, reflecting desperate attitudes in the face of changing conditions, and rarely became a real risk to the social order. Still, they threatened each state's ability to conduct war, and, as such, affected public policy formation in subsequent decades. In Brazil, they led to new proposals on the organization of the army and the gradual abolition of the National Guard. In the United States, they led to the expansion of federal power in the South, as well as the birth of a national citizenship, with the extension of the franchise to former slaves and freed blacks.[2]

The social conflicts that emerged in each case help us understand the limits of state action during periods of national emergency, especially when centripetal, nationalistic demands confronted local interests. Most of these conflicts centered on the extension of recruitment and its consequences for social stability. Great debates involving the war effort and its consequences shaped each victorious postwar society.

## Differences between the United States and Brazil

The Civil War and the War of the Triple Alliance arose from very different longstanding contentions. The American Civil War culminated decades of internal political and regional tensions caused by different visions of social organization, political power, and racial hierarchies. It resolved many inconsistencies and inefficiencies in the founding documents of American government (although not racism or inequality), which had been aggravated by territorial expansion during the first half of the nineteenth century. Wartime Congress imposed tariffs, centralized economic decisions, circulated greenbacks, and expanded access to western lands, an agenda favored by the North since the 1820s. Thus, the Civil War began to resolve many of the practical problems that had contributed its outbreak.

The War of the Triple Alliance was an international conflict connected to the process of state formation in the Rio de la Plata region. It united the Brazilian Empire, the Argentine Confederation, and the Oriental Republic of Uruguay in opposition to the Paraguayan Republic. Most of the action took place outside Brazil, far from centers of plantation agriculture. With the exception of the Provinces of Mato Grosso and Rio Grande do Sul, Brazilian territory was spared invasion, plunder, and pillage. The Brazilian population was not spared the hardships and privations brought by war efforts, however. Designation not only disrupted the lives of the national guards, it also disorganized families, social life within communities, and society in general.

The war had no direct influence on the agricultural changes that had been taking place since the 1850s. The interruption of international slave traffic expanded internal trade, concentrating slaves in coffee-growing areas and stimulating the employment of free poor in the northeast region. Agriculture was most affected in these northeastern provinces through wartime demands on landowners' human and financial resources.

## Similarities between Brazil and the United States

For both Republican and Imperial leadership, territorial integrity was paramount. For Brazilians, protecting territorial integrity meant an articulation with the colonial past as well as the preservation of its chief Imperial achievement: Brazil was the only Latin American country to retain its colonial boundaries. With the exception of the Cisplatine (current Uruguay), all other provinces remained under the empire's umbrella. During the 1830s and 1840s the monarchy and its local allies defeated each provincial secessionist revolt. By 1860, national unity was beyond dispute. Despite internal divisions, few issues united the Brazilian population with their Emperor as readily as territorial integrity. An editorial published in a northeastern newspaper a few months after mobilization began shows the appeal of territorial integrity even among provinces located far from the battlefields: "Nations as well as individuals have their days of sacrifice, of peril, of distress; as [well as] their days of safety, of satisfaction, and of glory. The life of states depends on their unity and honor; consisting of their territorial integrity and power autonomy."[3]

For Union men, territorial integrity implied the survival of principles viewed as essential to the American polity. Many of these principles were associated with notions of American exceptionalism, President Lincoln's "mystic nationalism."[4] In his annual message to the Congress in December 1862, Lincoln emphasized the symbolic and practical meanings of territorial preservation in terms that would have sounded familiar to a Brazilian Imperial bureaucrat: "The territory is the only part [of a nation] which is of certain durability. . . . It is of the first importance to duly consider, and estimate, this ever-enduring part."[5]

## Mobilization and Resistance

The wars against the Confederacy and Paraguay forced the Union and the Imperial governments to expand their regular armies, recruiting men from all regions. Army expansion pushed command hierarchy and national bureaucracy to the edge of capacity. Both successes and failures became vital to strengthening the response of the Union and Imperial armies. As a result of large mobilizations, centralization became a necessity of circumstance, reinforcing the role of national governments in coordinating recruiting, arming, transporting, and supplying troops on the frontlines.

Rapidly raising professional troops increased tensions between military and national interests on one hand and local prerogatives on the other. A crucial step in army expansion was centralized military recruitment, in which individuals independent of local and agrarian influences worked to enlist soldiers. Recruitment became crucial when traditional militias failed to maintain troop strength in the field. Subsequent conscription efforts were related less to a fundamental struggle over the future of national military organization than to the temporary needs of tough campaigns. Nonetheless, these efforts imposed unprecedented levels of extraction on civilians, and those most affected by these changes thought their world had been turned upside down by powerful external forces.

No central interference was more unpopular in Brazil than the transfer of National Guard units to the front. The National Guard had been an essential institution for the repression of slave revolts and the maintenance of internal peace in Brazil. Local political bosses commanded Guard militias and supplied their clients with arms. These bosses possessed the weaponry and the authority to use it. Such rights were seen as a civic privilege. The transfer of National Guards to the Paraguayan front temporarily undermined the efficiency of the system of social control, generating a problem that was potentially more serious than arming freed slaves would have been.

State interference in an area fully connected to local, private interests was seen as a threat to local management of recruiting. It created many conflicts concerning Guard command and troop deployment. In 1866, many slaveholders still believed that slave rebellion threatened the empire, and viewed the National Guard as essential for maintaining internal peace. These fears were exaggerated, but perceptions counted.

In the same way, the Enrollment Act threatened local control of recruitment in the United States. Democratic practices related to military discipline and hierarchies, practices that connected officers to their men, seemed vulnerable in the face of national demands. A wave of revolts pushed recruiting escorts out of villages and towns. The suspension of the writ of habeas corpus and other emergency measures disturbed the war support the government received from these communities. The Enrollment Act worked as both a carrot and stick for communities struggling to fill quotas through substitution or commutation, practices that prevented impressments, but simultaneously changed the composition of volunteer armies raised by the Union.

The temporary growth of military institutions affected the operations of client networks that had been so important for military organization. Above all, local bosses in Brazil opposed the enrollment of their clients and protégés. These men feared a permanent extension of central powers and viewed even small changes with suspicion. Likewise, individuals and communities in the American Union noticed changes in their relations with the federal government. A minority supported the need for stronger government, but this agenda was difficult to sustain, even among Republican Party supporters. In Brazil, after the second year of war, even small groups of supporters were hard to find. A newspaper article published in 1869 revealed the despondency present in parts of the country: "There is no longer an army here, what exist are an angry and discontented people, without hope, without trust. In the barracks as well as in the streets soldiers themselves . . . complain bitterly about the war's direction and procrastination."[6]

Some groups reacted according to their capacity to prevent their own removal to the front. They appealed to party bosses and to community leaders, they looked for legal exemptions, and they raised funds for paying substitutes or simply rebelled when any of these options proved futile. In the United States, anti-draft riots were common in the northwest as well as in some eastern cities, such as New York and Philadelphia. In Brazil, collective unrest was basically a rural phenomenon. Some rural rebellions brought together deserters and fugitive slaves, threatening social hierarchies and political stability.

## Recruitment and Socialization of Freedmen

A remarkable difference can be found in the impact the recruitment of freedmen had on each society. This difference was especially evident in American struggles for emancipation. The Civil War created the environment necessary for emancipation in the Confederate states, and no group was more affected by the changes wrought by the war than Southern African Americans. Conflicts involving the nationalization of citizenship marked the postbellum United States. These conflicts were inflamed by the emergence of African American citizens and voters who took advantage of growing federal intervention to obtain civil and political rights both in the postbellum South and in the victorious North, where they were a real minority.

During the war, an expanded national polity emerged in the United States. Unlike its antebellum predecessor, this state exhibited a strong commitment to creating citizenship based on equal rights, at least for some time after the end of the Civil War. Although this organization reflected the contradictions of the coalition of interests that supported the Union, it compensated for this deficiency through the exercise of a victorious authority, a bloody mandate to enforce social and racial transformations in the defeated Confederacy.

Nothing comparable occurred in Brazil after its victory over the Paraguayan Republic. The army had recruited free blacks since Brazilian independence. Including slaves in the army during periods of emergency had long been practiced and was continued during the Paraguayan War. Slaves conditionally freed to serve were subject to controls that prevented their recruitment from becoming a key to emancipation. Because of these differences in experience, we find stronger distinctions between state power and racial transformations in the United States and Brazil during the final war years and the immediate postwar period.

Brazilian slave owners had a peculiar vision of their social reality. For them, private economic interests should set limits on state actions. The state should defend slaveholders from international interference. State intervention would not be seen as a transgression against prevalent laissez-faire economics if it protected the social and economic status quo. Slave owners as a group did not deny the importance of the war; rather, they saw it as a secondary issue and tried to impede Imperial action.[7] Like Southern slaveholders in the antebellum period, Brazilian farmers wanted the national state to protect their interests. They were upset with the growing lack of fieldworkers and feared their voice was not being heard by the decision makers in Rio de Janeiro.

But the world had changed too much by 1867. Slavery in the Southern states has been utterly demolished by the Civil War. The demise of the Confederacy left Cuba, still a Spanish colony, as the only other remaining slave economy in the Western Hemisphere. International conditions made it impossible to restore Brazilian slavery to what it had been at its height. The war affected the confidence of rich land bosses in the Imperial state at a moment when the interests of slave owners had been weakened by enormous changes in slave markets and in the products produced by slaves. The war effort gave planters the impression that expropriation—a phantom that had haunted the Brazilian oligarchy ever since independence—could be the next step. The emperor's pronunciations and his policies supporting the free-womb law freeing all the children born from slaves, approved in September 1871, that is, after the war's end, soon created resentment in the country's major agricultural regions. Suspicion arose that the Imperial state had become detached from the interests of the reactionary groups that dominated local politics and would increasingly interfere with private and representative interests. The replacement of a Liberal-Progressive cabinet by a purely Conservative one in July 1868 placated suspicions but did not solve the problem.

## A Chronology of Changes

The long-term results of slavery—immediate emancipation and citizenship in the United States; delayed emancipation with few political rights in Brazil—can be followed chronologically: Lincoln presented his Emancipation Proclamation in September 1862, decreeing that all slaves under Rebel authority would be free by January 1, 1863. In February 1865 the Thirteenth Amendment freed all remaining slaves, including those still belonging to loyal masters in the Border States. The Brazilian Imperial government enacted a Free Womb law in 1871, despite severe criticism from slave owners, Conservative party leaders, and abolitionists, who saw the measure as dilatory. Seventeen more years would pass before they enacted the Golden Law, freeing more than one and a half million slaves.

In the United States, Lincoln's action had the support of a Republican majority. It was carefully balanced against Northern public opinion. Racial prejudice was strong in the North, but the war effort and the needs of the army helped to circumvent public sentiment and push Lincoln to reelection in November 1864. In the end, military victories prevailed over strong pockets of Northern resistance to the Emancipation Proclamation.

In Brazil, however, the intervention of Emperor Pedro II undermined the political system. Increasingly, political and personal differences interfered with the performance of the army in the field. Imperial patriotic appeals conflicted with the more utilitarian needs of slaveholders and other powerful local groups. The barons' lack of cooperation and the government's timid retaliation upset professional military officers who risked their lives in Paraguay. When the emperor replaced Liberal-Progressives with Conservatives and proposed legal changes promoting gradual abolition, both parties and the monarchy were damaged in fundamental ways.

A possible explanation for these differences may be found in the ways that war efforts confronted elite interests in each country. In Brazil, emancipation and recruitment of freed slaves came to be seen as an attack on the regime's main supporters. These landowners had been affected by changes in the nature of slaveholding, especially by the lack of replacement slaves following the end of international slave traffic. Consequently, these landowners were haunted by slave recruitment, especially in the most important plantation areas.

By 1863, Northern Republicans saw themselves as attacking the Confederacy by emancipating slaves and putting them into the army. As the war progressed, many Republicans were convinced that the South could not return to its prewar status and sought to use military victory as a way to revolutionize conquered states. For the next ten years, the national government was the strongest defender of civil rights, in a clear inversion of the

Jeffersonian republican doctrines that had prevailed in antebellum America. Two main institutions operated by the federal government extended government initiative for change: the army and the Freedmen's Bureau.

If we take the enormous transformations propelled by warfare in the whole of the United States, and compare them to lack of structural changes in Brazil, it puts the Civil War in a different perspective. Some historians have analyzed the war in terms of government difficulty extracting recruits. If instead we take social and political transformations into account and compare the extent and nature of these transformations, the American Civil War must now be considered a Total War, more than Brazil, where changes were more gradual and not as substantial.

## Slaves, Freedmen, and the Army

During the Civil War, slaves who escaped to enlist found an institution regulated by values different from those of the plantation. The Union army expressed the ambivalences of Northern racial construction. Until the Civil War, military service was linked to whiteness; it was a privilege of race. During the first eighteenth months of the war, Northern blacks were not officially accepted as soldiers. Many Southern "contrabands" were returned to their masters before their contribution was seen as a relevant tool against the Confederacy. Black troops increased after 1862 but were segregated in camps. This unfair treatment pushed many soldiers to use the opportunities created by the war to advance their struggle for citizenship. Such were the cases arising from the conflicts over equal pay and promotion. Literate members of the United States Colored Troops (USCTs) wrote letters to newspapers and congressmen, a testimony of their will to change arbitrary conditions. The army provided them with a valuable opportunity to contest decades of racial prejudice. The political system magnified their chances to acquire social and political rights and to bring about a social transformation.

The effects of sectional difference were clearer for the former slaves in the South than for the free African American population. Blacks in the South achieved gains that could not be taken back. Prominent among them were the reorganization of black families, the establishment of black churches, and freedom of movement. To some extent African Americans were able to extract democratic advantages from the racist assumptions of American civic culture.[8]

Nothing similar happened in Brazil. There was no nation to be reconstructed, no political alliance with dispossessed groups, and no assimilation of alternative political leaders to the mainstream of national debates.[9] Free or freedmen, Brazilian blacks who had served in the Imperial army found themselves returning to a country that remained unchanged, one that did not provide most of them with the means to overcome hierarchical barriers prevalent in society. Although some individuals joined with former comrades in making specific demands for Imperial recognition, these constituted a few, exceptional cases. By war's end, the Imperial political system was severely damaged by factional and personal conflicts. Its finances were exhausted by repayment of loans to foreign investors, and there were no funds for providing help to the exhausted veterans. Initiatives for reforms were restricted to the Imperial inner circle, and debates took place in the same closed coteries that had existed during the war. The Council of State and the Parliament were the arenas in which representative political forces responded to state-centered initiatives. No expansion of the electoral franchise took place, nor did reform result in increased popular participation. As has traditionally been the case, the initiative for reforms came from the government, not from public opinion. Consequently, the debates over the nature of the nation in Brazil were much smaller and much less purposeful than Union pamphlets of the Civil War. Writers as distinct as José de Alencar, Menenio Agrippa, and Saldanha Marinho published harsh criticism of the emperor and what they considered to be the Crown's despotism in the name of war. They criticized things they considered to be unjust, but they were not able to use the war to propose long-term changes. In many ways these critics restricted their reflections to the limits presented by the Imperial debates. Thus, it was not possible to take from the war any lessons concerning the future of the nation or including a larger number of its citizens in the political system. Nor was it possible to improve and extend national infrastructure through material improvements that could add dynamism to the country's economy.

The postwar decade in Brazil saw the institution of the first census, as well as the introduction of the metric system, a free womb law, and an extension of the railroad system. But the Triple Alliance War did not shape Brazil in the same ways that the Civil War changed America. In the United States, industrialization and expanded political participation had been achieved during the antebellum period and were effective tools in canvassing social support for Union reforms. Brazilians, meanwhile, remained connected to an agrarian economy less hospitable to structural changes. The Brazilian railway system was not significant and did not work as a tool for national integration.[10] Troops had to be transported to Argentina by boat and, after landing, marched along a devastated territory. An American traveler observed the paradox of a campaign that did not fund critical infrastructure, asserting, "If Brazil had invested one-half the treasure she squandered to enrich these mercenary allies, in constructing a railroad to Matto Grosso from her capital, she would have saved for herself her money and the lives of a hundred thousand of their people, which, like the cash, she could not well afford to lose."[11]

In comparison, American political organization provided the Federal government with more alternatives. The virtue of the Northern party system lay in the strong links between local and national organizations and in the vitality of the Republican Party. The party became a fundamental instrument for maximizing the war effort. The combination of the Republican political structure and material progress made it possible to mix war support with economic modernization, speeding and concentrating economic decisions in ways imperfectly understood by contemporaries. In Brazil, on the other hand, military initiative was an apparatus of the central state with no ideological agenda. Those in power would recruit their adversaries, and vice versa. No essential moral or political rationale united state and national efforts. This scenario helps us understand why patriotic appeals led to political strife, which in turn impaired recruiting efforts. In addition, no political faction was capable of shouldering the burden of unpopular war measures. Political and social discontent was directed toward the emperor and the monarchy, exemplified by the protest that accompanied the enlistment of slaves.[12] Although the American government overstepped its formal constitutional powers during the Civil War, its actions remained consistent with the liberal traditions of the country. Furthermore, the political costs of the war could be more evenly divided between the government and the party. War efforts helped centralize business operations. The management of railroads, textile mills, and coalmines became much more standardized than before. According to Phillipe Paludan, this was not a state-led process but it led to similar results. Business answered government demands for efficiency, centralizing schedules and procedures in ways that subverted independent management of industrial activities. In political terms, management centralization also reinforced the Republican national command. The party acted as a strong motivational force both at the local and national levels, maintaining the allegiance of a substantial part of the population in towns and states. This role was exercised during the debates over commutation and substitution. With commutation viewed as a triumph of the idea of "a rich man's war but a poor man's fight," other sources of troops had to be identified. Black recruitment worked as an escape valve to keep local Republican support alive while alleviating the burden on poor white males. These features were bolstered by economic development and the extensive use of the industrial and transportation networks in support of the war efforts. This reinforced what General William T. Sherman viewed as part "of the process by which Americans attached themselves to their nation. This crucial union; of citizens, not just of states."[13]

## Immediate Political Repercussions of Recruitment

What were the main changes to relations between state and society in Brazil and the United States as a result of troop mobilization? Most comparative literature on state building discusses the effects of European wars on countries like France and Germany, confirming the correlation between military mobilization and an increase of state power in these specific national landscapes. In the American and Brazilian cases, however, such connections were weak. Neither country subscribed to western European patterns of military organization; nor did they adopt the extraction-coercion cycle that was the underlining feature of European state-building processes. Americans despised European military centralization, with its connections to despotism and civic corruption, and Brazilian elites lacked a national state strong enough to impose these patterns upon its population. Centralization was either tortuous or unwanted; consequently, the capacity of elites to create impersonal bureaucracies and impose a "tribute of blood" on underprivileged populations was limited. Government efforts achieved little in terms of bureaucratic development, circumventing accepted practices only to get larger numbers of recruits. In the United States, the threat of a draft mobilized communities to fill their quotas to avoid the risks associated with impressments. In Brazil, regional imbalances spared the more quarrelsome areas, concentrating recruitment in the northeast provinces. There, weaker elites showed themselves less able to protect free workers than those of the Paraiba Valley and Minas Gerais in the southeast. War efforts demonstrated the limits of political parties, courts, and civic organizations when it came to the enormous responsibilities associated with raising large armies. National governments retreated from the main stage, with the exception of occupation forces that remained in Paraguay and in the former Confederate states. Overall, economies remained unregulated.

One of the few constructive consequences of the wars was the development of a different structure of authority, and a specialized bureaucracy that could implement more rational ongoing strategies to tax citizens and recruit soldiers. Had such a structure been in place, the wartime experiences of Brazil and the United States would have been much different. As observed by Charles Tilly, European national states went through this trajectory, developing bureaucratic structures from the equation "war plus war preparation." The needs of war reformulated governments, including the collection of tributes that could fund and sustain a regular army.[14] European wars helped form modern states because they demanded an efficiency that could be provided only by more sophisticated political structures. In the United States, such a role was performed by the political parties and the courts, as well as by regular army bureaucratic elements such as the Quartermaster's Department. Although the Union government lacked such specialized organization, it relied on an institutional apparatus that allowed authorities to see their society "like a State," to borrow a famous phrase from the historical sociologist James Scott.[15] A decennial census had been taken since the 1790s, and political parties and civic organizations helped connect islands of communities through the mail and transportation systems.

Nothing could be more different from Tilly's perspective than the Brazilian situation. After the initial enthusiasm vanished, recruiting efforts faced permanent obstacles, and populations in the far interior reacted as if the true invader was the Imperial government, not the Paraguayans. The war did not help develop state capacity. Only through renewed and repeated efforts could Imperial agents obtain the needed resources. Even then, some resources, for example, the liberation of slaves for the army, were not extracted, but bought with public funds or emancipated by the Imperial House. The demands of the war against Paraguay created the opportunity for innovation. But war efforts did not weaken local loyalties, nor did they strengthen the liaisons between the population and the nation-state. As shown by Miguel Centeno, state capacity is not an absolute but a relational phenomenon. It is not a question of force, based solely on the direct relationship between coercion and extraction; it also depends on the ability of society to accept and collaborate with state interference, thus creating the bases for an enlarged citizenship.

The American Civil War created an environment conducive to expanding the productive organizational structures that existed in the North before the war. The demands of war also centralized the command of economic interests, including railroads and coalmines. In contrast, economic activities in Brazil were not driven by the state action or by business development. This failure likely occurred because many members of the Imperial political elite were not in favor of continuing the war after the Paraguayans were expelled from Brazilian territory. Another factor at play was the negative image of military service among the population, an image that strengthened in light of a long war fought far from the nation's heartland. The Brazilian case showed the failure of a central government and its provincial agents to infiltrate rural society, whereas the Union insinuated its influences throughout society. The best the empire could do was to fight a limited war. Extractive capacities remained limited, and the national state provided most of the needed resources, adding to a national debt that impoverished the country.[16]

The two wars in the Americas led to very different outcomes. The U.S. Civil War signaled the beginning of an expanded capitalist experience. Furthermore, preserving the Union and ending slavery became engraved on the pantheon of noble American achievements and helped unite the country (except for the South) around shared sacrifice and triumph. In contrast, the War of the Triple Alliance had no effect on the disastrous balance among various powers and social interests that haunted Brazilian politics. Things remained unchanged; imperial efforts were not capable of transforming society. Indeed, they failed to convince the population to support massive mobilization for the duration of the war. Brazilian war efforts generated debts, resentments, and few practical benefits or ideological principles that might have given meaning to the bloody military victory.

# Notes

## Abbreviations

| | |
|---|---|
| AHEX | Arquivo Histórico do Exército (Rio de Janeiro) |
| AHMI | Arquivo Histórico do Museu Imperial (Petrópolis) |
| | DPP, Arquivo Pedro Paranaguá |
| | POB, Arquivo Pedro Orléans e Bragança |
| AHRS | Arquivo Histórico do Rio Grande do Sul (Porto Alegre) |
| ANRJ | Arquivo Nacional (Rio de Janeiro) |
| | SPE, Sessão Provincial e Estadual |
| | IG, Série Guerra |
| APRJ | Arquivo Público do Estado do Rio de Janeiro (Rio de Janeiro) |
| APRS | Arquivo Público do Estado do Rio Grande do Sul (Porto Alegre) |
| *Atas* | *Atas do Conselho de Estado* |
| CBC | Museu Casa de Benjamin Constant (Rio de Janeiro) |
| *C.G.* | *Congressional Globe* |
| GCLO | Gilder Lehrman Institute of American History (New York City) |
| IBGE | Instituto Brasileiro de Geografia e Estatística (Rio de Janeiro) |
| IHGB | Instituto Histórico e Geográfico Brasileiro (Rio de Janeiro) |
| MHN | Museu Histórico Nacional (Rio de Janeiro) |
| NARA | National Archives and Records Administration (United States) |
| *O.R.* | *War of the Rebellion: A Compilation of the Official Records of the Union and Confederate Armies* |
| RMJ, 1866 | *Relatório do Ministério da Justiça apresentado à Assembléia Geral Legislativa na Quarta-Sessão da Décima-Segunda Legislatura pelo Respectivo Ministro e Secretário de Estado José Thomas Nabuco de Araújo* (Report from the Ministry of Justice) |

RMJ, 1867    *Relatório Apresentado à Assembléa Geral Legislativa na Primeira Sessão da Décima Terceira Legislatura pelo Respectivo Ministro e Secretário de Estado Martin Francisco Ribeiro de Andrada*

RMJ, 1868    *Relatório do Ministério da Justiça Apresentado à Assembléa Geral Legislativa na Segunda Sessão da Décima Terceira Legislatura pelo Respectivo Ministro e Secretário de Estado Martim Francisco Ribeiro de Andrada*

RMT    *Proposta e Relatório do Ministério da Fazenda Apresentados à Assembléa Geral Legislativa na Quarta Sessão da Décima Segunda Legislatura pelo Ministro e Secretário de Estado dos Negócios da Fazenda, João da Silva Carrão* (Report from the Ministry of the Treasury)

RMW, 1865    *Relatório Apresentado á Assembléa Geral Legislativa na Terceira Sessão da Décima-Segunda Legislatura pelo Ministro e Secretario de Estado dos Negocios da Guerra Visconde de Camamú* (Report from the Ministry of War)

RMW, 1866    *Relatório Apresentado à Assembléa Geral Legislativa na Quarta Sessão da Décima Segunda Legislatura pelo Ministro e Secretário de Estado dos Negócios da Guerra Angelo Moniz da Silva Ferraz*

RMW, 1867    *Relatório Apresentado à Assembleia Geral na Primeira Sessão da Décima Terceira Legislatura, pelo Ministro e Secretário d'Estado dos Negócios da Guerra, João Lustosa da Cunha Paranaguá*

RMW, 1872    *Relatório apresentado Á Assembléa Geral Legislativa na Quarta Sessão da Décima-Quarta Legislatura pelo Ministro e Secretario de Estado Interino dos Negócios da Guerra Visconde do Rio Branco*

RFO, 1865    *Relatório da Repartição dos Negócios Estrangeiros apresentado Á Assemblea Geral Legislativa na Terceira Sessão da Décima-Segunda Legislatura pelo respectivo ministro e secretário de estado João Pedro Dias Vieira* (Report from the Ministry of Foreign Affairs)

RPA, 1865    *Fala Dirigida á Assembléa Legislativa Provincial das Alagoas no dia 05 DE MAIO DE 1865 pelo Ex. Sr. Desembargador João Baptista Gonçalves Campos Presidente da Província* (Report from the president of Alagoas)

RPA, 1866    *Relatório com que o Dr. Esperidião Eloy de Barros Pimentel, Presidente da Província das Alagoas Entregou a Administração da Mesma Província no dia 10 de Abril de 1866, ao 10. Vice-Presidente Dr. Galdino Augusto da Natividade e Silva*

RPB, 1866    *Relatório Apresentado á Assembléa Legislativa Provincial da Bahia pelo Excelentíssimo Presidente o Comendador Manuel Pinto de Souza Dantas no dia 10 de Março de 1866* (Report from the president of Bahia)

RPMG, 1865    *Relatório que à Assembléia Legislativa Provincial de Minas Gerais Apresentou no Ato da Abertura da Sessão Ordinária de 1865 o Desembargador Pedro de Alcântara Cerqueira Leite, Presidente da mesma Província* (Report from the president of Minas Gerais)

RPMG, 1867    *Relatório que Apresentou ao Ex. Sr. Vice-Presidente da Província de*

| | *Minas Gerais Dr. Elias Pinto de Carvalho por Ocasião de Passar a Administração em 3 de Julho de 1867* |
| RPRJ, 1865 | *Relatório com que o Sr. Conselheiro de Estado Bernardo de Souza Franco passou a Administração da Província do Rio de Janeiro ao Ex. Desembargador José Tavares Bastos* (Report from the president of Rio de Janeiro) |
| RPRJ, 1868 | *Relatório apresentado à Assembléa Legislativa Provincial do Rio de Janeiro na primeira sessão da décima-oitava legislatura no dia 15 de outubro de 1868 pelo presidente da mesma Província, o conselheiro Benevenuto Augusto de Magalhães Taques* |
| Statutes | *Statutes at Large, Treaties, and Proclamations of the United States of America* |

## Introduction

1. A comparison with the Confederacy also could be relevant, but two factors prevented me from choosing the Confederate States of America as the focus of my comparison: the Confederacy did not recruit slaves until the very end of the war, and it did not survive as a nation-state. Since the book is about the role of slave recruitment during wartime, and state building in its aftermath, a comparison with the Confederacy would confuse the argument. A valid comparison would be between the Confederate and the Paraguayan situation during the Triple Alliance War. For discussions concerning the recruitment of slaves by the Confederate army, see Levine, *Confederate Emancipation.*

2. Förster and Nagler, *On the Road to Total War.*

3. Berlinger et al., *Why the South Lost the Civil War,* 440–42; McPherson, *Battle Cry of Freedom,* 856.

4. For recent scholarship that interprets American history within a transnational perspective, see Doyle, *Nations Divided;* Bender, *A Nation among Nations;* Timothy M. Roberts, *Distant Revolutions.*

5. For more recent contributions, see Whigham, *The Paraguayan War;* Kraay and Whigham, *I Die with My Country;* Doratioto, *Maldita guerra;* Salles, *Guerra do Paraguai;* Leuchars, *To the Bitter End;* Izecksohn, *O cerne da discórdia;* Capdevila, *Una guerra total;* and Costa, *A espada de Dâmocles.*

6. Although Brazilian shipyards and arsenals did put a few high-tech weapons in the field.

### ONE. Military Traditions Confront Mass Mobilization in the United States and Brazil

1. Tilly, *Coercion, Capital, and European States,* 76.

2. For the colonial experiences of New England, see Anderson, *A People's Army,* 63–164.

3. Parker, *The Military Revolution,* 6–44.

4. Of course, there are exceptions in America. In Virginia's racially divided society during the Revolutionary War, recruits were subjected to low esteem. According to McDonnel, Virginia's leadership believed that only the "lower Class of People" should join the regular army. Service in the Continental army was analogous to slavery. See *The Politics of War*, 403–4.

5. Needell, "Party Formation and State-Making," 259–308; Barman, *Brazil*, 189–216.

6. For recent debate on the war's causes and course, see Menezes, *A Guerra é nossa*, 133–66.

7. Williams, *The Rise and Fall of the Paraguayan Republic*, 211–28; Leuchars, *To the Bitter End*, 211–32; Saeger, *Francisco Solano López*, 159–62.

8. Once enrolled, soldiers also performed compulsory public works. Capdevila, *Guerra total*, 26.

9. López-Alves, *State Formation and Democracy in Latin America*, 193–211.

10. Yerba mate is a hot herbal drink similar to tea. Blinn Reber, "Commerce and Industry in Nineteenth Century Paraguay," 29–53.

11. Saeger, *Francisco Solano López*, 94.

12. In the Paraguayan case, another factor impelling the decision to go to war could be what Thucydides called "honor," that is a sense of being valued, a sense of being respected, a sense of prestige. See Thucydides, *History of the Peloponnesian War*, Book I, 35–123. The theme of "honor" as the main motive for going to war has been recently recovered by Kagan, *On the Origin of War*, 15–80. According to Kagan, honor has been a more common reason for the outbreak of conflicts than many economic and political designs.

13. On the ambivalence of the application of the concept of "balance of power" for the Platine scenario, see Abente, "The War of The Triple Alliance," 47–67; and Izecksohn, *O cerne da discórdia*, 10–27. On the concept itself, see Haas, "The Balance of Power," 318–29.

14. For the history of Paraguayan diplomacy during the Argentinean Civil War see O'Leary, *El Paraguay en la unificación Argentina*.

15. For an appreciation of the role of Argentina in the outbreak of the Triple Alliance War, see McLynn, "The Causes of the Triple Alliance," 21–44.

16. Farinatti, "Cabedais militares," 81–100.

17. Goldman and Salvatore, *Caudilhismos rioplatenses*, 7–30.

18. Thus, in opposition to the 1851 agreement between Brazil and Uruguay.

19. A summary of the Uruguayan events can be found at Report from the Minister of Foreign Affairs, (1865), 1–28. The "friendly note" from the Brazilian plenipotentiary is on p. 8.

20. According to Murphy, "Latin American State Formation in Regional Context," 9, until 1855 the Brazilian Empire kept 5,000 military troops based in Uruguay; 15 percent of the Uruguayan population by then were Brazilian gauchos, who occupied 30 percent of Uruguayan territory.

21. That situation is defined by Abente as "Power Transition," that is, a condition in which the main country players cannot understand correctly the shifts

that a system of states is undergoing. Abente, "The War of the Triple Alliance," 47–60.

22. For an accurate description of the Paraguayan mistakes during this first phase of the operations, see Doratioto, *Maldita guerra*, 21–81.

23. According to George Thompson, a British engineer who participated in López's inner-circle and who was one of the few foreigners commissioned as lieutenant colonel, from a total of 12,400 men who marched in the Paraguayan expeditionary force to Uruguay, 1,900 died or got sick. Of the remaining 10,500, 2,500 were killed in the battle of Yatay, and 8,000 surrendered at the town of Uruguayana (Brazil). Thompson remarked that most rifles were so old they could not repeat a shot. Thompson, *A Guerra do Paraguai*, 83–92.

24. The Paraguayan troops in Mato Grosso lacked any regular supply system. One of the reasons why the Imperial army regained the city of Corumbá through a surprise attack was that the remaining Paraguayan garrisons were fishing while the Brazilians approached. This episode was well described in the memoirs of one Paraguayan general. Resquin, *Datos históricos de la Guerra del Paraguay contra la Triple Alianza*, 74.

25. Blinn Reber, "The Demographics of Paraguay," 283–319; Whigham and Pottash, "The Paraguayan Rosetta Stone," 174–86; Santos, "A Guerra do Paraguai;" 102–3.

26. The nature of this treaty was a subject of great controversy. It was to have been kept secret until the end of the war. Its revelation by the English ambassador in Argentina resulted in bitter criticism by many governments, such as the Bolivian and Peruvian, of its draconian clauses undermining Paraguayan autonomy.

27. On the internal uprisings in Argentina see, De la Fuente, *Children of Facundo*, 17–32.

28. IBGE, *Estatísticas históricas do Brasil*, 32–33.

## TWO. The Crisis of the American Recruitment System

1. *Miscellaneous Documents of the U.S. Senate, 38th Cong., 1st Sess.*, Doc. No. 71.

2. On the role of military bureaucrats in the workings of a national supply system, see Wilson, *The Business of Civil War*, 34–71.

3. The expression was used during a conversation with Charles Sumner in January 1863. Quotation from McPherson, *Battle Cry of Freedom*, 591.

4. Although conscription has always been discussed in studies of the Civil War, focus on the political and social repercussions of recruitment dates from Robert Sterling's 1974 doctoral dissertation, "Civil War Resistance in the Middle West." During the early 1990s further contributions focusing on draft resistance emerged from such authors as Grace Palladino, Iver Bernstein, and David Osher. These studies helped to establish a connection between the impact of federal legislation and specific local long-term issues. See Palladino, *Another Civil War*; Bernstein, *The New York City Draft Riots*; Osher, "Soldier Citizens for a Disciplined Nation."

5. The Confederate conscription law was passed in the spring of 1862; see Bensel, *Yankee Leviathan*, 130–86.

6. Cameron, *Report of the Secretary of War*, December 1861, 10. Quoted in *Message of the President of the United States, December, 3 1861*.

7. Hattaway and Jones, *How the North Won*, 274.

8. Bensel, *Yankee Leviathan*, 292–95. Bensel compares Republican state building to the Bolsheviks' actions in revolutionary Russia.

9. "The Draft, or Conscription Reviewed by the People," in Freidel, *Union Pamphlets of the Civil War*, 791.

10. It would be impossible to measure the impact of the war effort on all aspects of Northern society; the Union's enormous geographic and social diversity precludes such consideration in the context of this chapter. For a summary of the impact on the most affected regions, see Paludan, *A People's Contest*, 316–38.

11. Stampp, *And the War Came*, 179–203; Potter, *Lincoln and His Party in the Secession Crisis*, 134–55; Crofts, *Reluctant Confederates*, 66–129; Freehling, *South vs. The South*, 3–47.

12. Potter, *The Impending Crisis, 1848–1861*, 90–120; Ashworth, *Slavery, Capitalism, and Politics in the Antebellum Republic*, 1:366–492; Grimsley, "Conciliation and Its Failure, 1861–1862," 317–35.

13. Crofts, *Reluctant Confederates*, xvii.

14. For accounts of the force of Unionists in Georgia, see Freehling and Simpson, *Secession Debated*, 51–114; Johnson, *Toward a Patriarchal Republic*, 79–107.

15. Even in those states that opted for secession, differences were very narrow. According to David M. Potter, in Louisiana, the pro-secession difference was 1,763 votes out of a total of 38,665. In Alabama, the so-called "Cooperationists," who opposed immediate secession, had between 36 and 43 percent of the votes: the difference was 7,500 out of a total of 28,100. In Texas, Governor Sam Houston opposed secession and refused to convene the legislature. Outside of South Carolina, margins for secession were not strong enough to make anybody certain that secession was inevitable. Potter, *The Impending Crisis, 1848–1861*, 496–97.

16. Degler, *Neither Black nor White*, 47–51; Stampp, *The Peculiar Institution*, 132–40; Jordan, *Tumult and Silence at Second Creek*, 1–19; Channing, *Crisis of Fear*, 252–98; Dew, *Apostles of Disunion*, 4–21; Ashworth, *Slavery, Capitalism, and Politics*, 2:471–650.

17. Potter, *Impending Crisis*, 477.

18. *Charleston Mercury*, 11 October 1860, quoted in Stampp, *The Causes of the Civil War*, 151.

19. Thomas R. R. Cobb Secessionist Speech, Monday Evening, November 12, 1860, in Freehling and Simpson, *Secession Debated*, 25. The extent of Southern panic was well expressed at an incident in November 1860. In Georgetown, South Carolina, slaves were whipped for celebrating Lincoln's election by singing a hymn with the verse, "We'll soon be free Till the Lord shall call us home." The Southerners accused the slaves of meaning "The Yankee" when singing "the lord." Taylor, *Reminiscences of My Life*, 32.

20. Lincoln, "The Cooper Institute Address," February 27, 1860, in Fehrenbacher, *Abraham Lincoln*, 137.

21. Wiebe, *The Search for Order, 1877–1920*, 44–75; Ferraro, "Lives of Quiet Desperation," 333–50.

22. The populations of such regions not only opposed secession but rendered substantial numbers of recruits to the Union armies. Hahn, *The Roots of Southern Populism*, 129. Numbers are presented in Hattaway and Jones, *How the North Won*, 17–18.

23. McPherson, *For Cause and Comrades*, 16.

24. Donald, *Gone for a Soldier*, 3.

25. "That whenever the laws of the United States shall be opposed, or the execution thereof be obstructed, by combinations too powerful to be suppressed by the ordinary course of judicial proceedings, or by the powers vested by law in the marshals, it shall be the duty of the President to call forth such portion of the militia as may, in his opinion, be necessary to suppress such combinations, and to cause the laws to be duly executed." Henry Knox to George Washington, Communicated to the Senate on Jan. 21, 1790, 1st Cong., 2nd Sess., No. 2, "Organization of the Militia," *American State Papers: Military Affairs*, Volume 1.

26. "Address of his Excellency John A. Andrew, to the Two Branches of the Legislature of Massachusetts," January 5, 1861, 8.

27. *Madison Wisconsin Daily State Journal*, April 19, 1861, quoted in Perkins, *Northern Editorials on Secession*, 810.

28. McPherson, *For Cause and Comrades*, 16. In this sense, many young volunteers were experiencing some of the same feelings from late colonial America campaigns of the Seven Years' War, as described by Fred Anderson in, *A People's Army*, 26–62.

29. *Springfield Daily Republican* (Mass.), April 20, 1861, quoted in Perkins, *Northern Editorials on Secession*, 1064.

30. Palladino, *Another Civil War*, 85. Erasing partisan competition was a spontaneous process in certain regions and the result of political craft in other areas. According to Robert Sterling, the Democratic leaders in Illinois used their influence to remove the war issue from the realm of partisan politics. Sterling, "Civil War Draft Resistance in the Middle West," 32–35.

31. Osher, "Soldier Citizens for a Disciplined Nation," 95.

32. Hesseltine, *Lincoln and the War Governors*, 115–80; Bogue, *The Earnest Men*, 125–50, and *The Congressman's Civil War*, 29–59.

33. Costa and Kahn, *Heroes and Cowards*, 52.

34. "Oneida County Proceeding of the Republican Party Convention" held at Rome, N.Y., September 26, 1862, published in the *Utica Morning Herald*, quoted in Skowronek, *Building a New American State*, 30.

35. Ledman, "A Town Responds," 38.

36. McPherson, *Battle Cry of Freedom*, 327.

37. On the role of personal courage among volunteers' early motivations, see Linderman, *Embattled Courage*, 43–60.

38. McPherson, *For Cause and Comrades*, 54, 77–89. According to James Geary, the majority of men, 1,342,110, joined Union forces prior to the Conscription Act, when patriotism was still a significant motivation. Geary, *We Need Men*, 82.

39. Caleb J. Allen to Matilda T. Allen, September 4, 1861, in the Samuel T. Allen Papers, Center for American History, University of Texas, Austin. Quoted in Herrera "Guarantors of Liberty and Republic," 35.

40. *O.R.*, 3rd ser., 2:298–300.

41. P. Fessenden to Simon Cameron, May 9, 1861, *O.R.*, 3rd ser., 1:181–82; Osher, "Soldier Citizens for a Disciplined Nation," 113.

42. McPherson, *Battle Cry of Freedom*, 332.

43. Ibid.

44. A number of prominent Democrats were given military commissions to improve the party's commitment to the Union cause. Some, for example George B. McClellan, had previous experience in the army. Others were not military professionals, before receiving their commissions. Political connections mattered. Even among professional soldiers who attended West Point and were sympathetic to the administration, political commitments helped advance careers. Important future military commanders such as Ulysses S. Grant and William T. Sherman were appointed in part because of their political connections with Republican state political bosses. Their understanding of the connections between war and political needs was key to their success as commanders during wartime.

45. *The Life and Writings of Frederick Douglass*, 3:94.

46. These fears were not new. Leon F. Litwack has analyzed how Northern blacks had been systematically excluded from the best opportunities provided by the urban marketplace during the antebellum period. The war intensified such tensions due to fear of a mass migration of runways. Litwack, *North of Slavery*, 153–86; Voegeli, *Free But Not Equal*, 1–9, 98–99. This study furnishes a detailed description of the socio-political environment of the North during the Civil War.

47. Corporal James Henry Gooding to Abraham Lincoln, Sept. 28, 1863, quoted in Adams, *On the Altar of Freedom*, 118–20.

48. McClellan to Lincoln, August 4, 1861, quoted in Glatthaar, *Partners in Command*, 59.

49. McClellan to the Union Men of Western Virginia, Cincinnati, May 26, 1861, quoted in *Civil War Papers of George B. McClellan*, 26.

50. *Diary of Orville Hickman Browning*, 1:55, 558–60.

51. McPherson, *For Cause and Comrades*, 19.

52. Wiley, *The Life of Billy Yank*, 40.

53. Costa and Kahn, *Heroes and Cowards*, 62.

54. *The Collected Works of Abraham Lincoln*, 4:263.

55. *New York Times*, May 10, 1861, quoted in Perkins, *Northern Editorials on Secession*, 2:830.

56. In this sense, they probably reasoned as German strategist Carl Von Clausewitz, who declared three decades before that "fighting is to war . . . what cash payment is to trade, for however rarely it may be necessary for it actually to

occur, everything is directed to towards it, and eventually it must take place all the same and must be decisive." Quoted in Keegan, *The Face of Battle,* 28. According to Keegan, this economic analogy so delighted the Marxist philosopher Friedrich Engels that he included Clausewitz in the Marxist Temple du Génie.

57. A curious example of federal caution is in recruitment. While most Border States did not fill their recruitment quotas in 1862 and 1863, no draft was ordered in those areas.

58. James A. Bayard to T. F. Bayard, Dec. 14, 1860, Bayard Papers, Library of Congress. Quoted in Hancock, *Delaware during the Civil War,* 38.

59. In his analysis of the hinterlands of Augusta, Georgia, J. William Harris pointed out that, although poor men could go "shoulder to shoulder" with slaveholders, such cooperation was not free from hierarchical and social tension. As the war progressed and conscription expanded, rich men managed to avoid Confederate service more often than did the poor. Consequently, the Southern "façade" of social unity was progressively shaken in that region as war sacrifices mounted. See Harris, *Plain Folk and Gentry in a Slave Society,* 140–66. For a different vision of similar problems, see Bearman, "Desertion as Localism," 321–41.

60. George B. McClellan to Secretary of War Edwin M. Stanton, April 7, 1862, quoted in *The Civil War Papers of George B. McClellan,* 232.

61. On Confederate nationalism, see Faust, *The Creation of Confederate Nationalism;* Potter, *The South and the Sectional Conflict;* and Gallagher, *The Confederate War.* According to Faust, "Scholars have continued to fear that accepting the reality of Confederate nationalism would somehow imply its legitimacy," 3. For an analytical comparison between challenges posed by the American Revolution and the Civil War, see John M. Murrin, "War, Revolution, and Nation Making"; Bensel, *Yankee Leviathan,* 135–39.

62. Moore, *Conscription and Conflict in the Confederacy.* J. William Harris analyzed how opposition to conscription affected Georgia's devotion to republican liberties in *Plain Folk and Gentry in a Slave Society,* 147–53. For the significance of conscription to the Southern war effort, see Geary, *We Need Men,* 3–5, which made the point that the South could not rely on high bounties to raise troops because of the scarcity of financial resources. Hattaway and Jones, *How the North Won,* 721, estimates that around 87 percent of Southern white males of arms-bearing age served in the Confederate army.

63. Osher, "Soldier Citizens for a Disciplined Nation," 101; Wilson, *The Business of Civil War,* 191–226.

64. Sterling, "Civil War Draft Resistance in the Middle West," 39. All these hazards were described in detail in the letters soldiers wrote home. In these uncensored documents, recruits described the worst aspects of camp life. They complained about poor food, sickness, fatigue, boredom, and delayed payments. To add to the confusion, the contents of such letters were often read to a broad public, a circumstance that made the work of recruiting officers still more difficult. Disturbed by the poor living conditions, one of these soldiers described problems faced while in route to front: "We were huddled together more like a lot of pigs

than human beings. . . . I was compelled to sleep on the floor. . . . Our rations we could hardly force down. In fact most of it was rotten or nearly so. The water was very dirty. Yet we were glad to get enough of it." Niven, *Connecticut for the Union*, 95.

65. Andrew Knox to his wife, January 6, 1862, GLCO 3523.20

66. Rufus Kinsley, Jan. 10, 1863, in Kinsley, *Diary of a Christian Soldier*, 119.

67. According to Bolster and Anderson, the connection of photography and war during the American Civil War proved "another step in the modernization of combat," becoming "as much a part of the Civil War as the rifle." *Soldiers, Sailors, Slaves, and Ships*, 10.

68. In December 1861, Stanton's predecessor, Secretary Cameron, issued instructions that governors were not to send any more regiments forward unless they were requested to do so. If this decision was intended to save money, or to give better direction to army procurement, its reckless effects were heavily felt during the winter. This decision probably stemmed from the lack of administrative organization during Cameron's term.

69. Such was the enthusiasm of the Northern ranks that about June 1, 1862, slaves on St. Simon's Island were told there would soon be a settlement of the war. See Taylor, *Reminiscences of My Life*, 38.

70. On McClellan's administrative capacities and his relations with the Democratic Party and the Lincoln administration, see Glatthaar, *Partners in Command*, 51–94.

71. Barnes, *Memoir of Thurlow Weed by His Grandson Thurlow Weed Barnes*, 420–21.

72. The Battle of Shiloh (April 1862) cost General Grant 13,000 casualties. Resources were progressively wasted, and good news became scarce as the season came to an end. Macdonald, *Great Battles of the Civil War*, 31.

73. Lincoln to August Belmont, July 1, 1862, in *The Collected Works of Abraham Lincoln*, 5:810.

74. Barnes, *Memoir of Thurlow Weed by His Grandson Thurlow Weed Barnes*, 422.

75. The most important transformations would be connected to the emancipation of slaves and the recruitment of black soldiers by the Union army, subjects that will be treated separately in chapter 4.

76. Burt, *My Memoirs of the Military History of the State of New York during the War for the Union, 1861–1865*, 85. Quoted in Osher, "Soldier Citizens," 233.

77. Fessenden quoted in McPherson, *Battle Cry of Freedom*, 500.

78. According to Osher, "Soldier Citizens," 151–55, 300,000 was clearly an insufficient number in view of the growing challenges faced in the South. But these numbers have been contested by Costa and Kahn, *Heroes and Cowards*, 80–119.

79. Nonetheless, this prescription was never enacted because sheriffs, selectmen, and the state militia executed the 1862 drafts.

80. In clear contrast to the three-year term of duty of the July 2nd call.

81. One of most important consequences of the Militia Act was its repeal of the 1792 federal law barring blacks from participation in both state militias and the

regular United States Army. The Militia Act provided for the employment of free blacks and freedmen as soldiers, a point discussed in chapter 4. McPherson, *The Struggle for Equality*, 196.

82. Berry, *Military Necessity and Civil Rights Policy*, 43.

83. For a summary of active and passive resistance to the draft, see O'Sullivan and Mecler, *The Draft and Its Enemies*, 61–107.

84. *Hartford Courant* (Conn.), Aug. 22, 1862, quoted in Niven, *Connecticut for the Union*, 82.

85. Conscientious objection, an important issue for pacifist religious groups, was legitimate for Quakers and some other religious dissenters. For an interesting analysis of Quaker behavior during the Civil War, see Nelson, *Indiana Quakers Confront the Civil War*, 29–44, which contests general assumptions concerning the Friends' nonadherence to the war effort. Utilizing church records and manuscript collections, Nelson's work indicated that more Quakers from Indiana took up arms in the Civil War than is generally assumed.

86. According to Robert Sterling, by the war's end, various public and private agencies had expended almost three-quarters of a billion dollars in bounty money as inducements to reluctant volunteers. "Civil War Draft Resistance in the Middle West," 656. For Cape Elizabeth, see Ledman, "A Town Responds," 109–13.

87. For the significance of bounties as a selective incentive for enlistment, see Murdock, *One Million Men*, 154–69.

88. In spite of that, draft evasion was significant; estimates suggest that forty to fifty thousand men evaded the draft prior to 1864. See Hallock, "The Role of Community in Civil War Desertion," 123–34; Geary, *We Need Men*, 87–102.

89. Joseph E. Paine to Charles Sumner, July 7, 1862, quoted in Osher, "Soldier Citizens," 188.

90. Sterling, "Civil War Draft Resistance in the Middle West," 68.

91. The Peace, or Copperhead, faction of the Democratic Party believed that the increased, and increasingly centralized power of the Republican wartime government had brought hard times and political tyranny to the North. They emphasized the growing sacrifices faced by poor white men and requested a negotiated settlement to the war as the best way to restore normalcy. Curry, "The Union as It Was," 34–39.

92. *C.G.*, 37th Cong., 3rd sess., 1232.

93. Curry, "The Union as It Was," 208.

94. McClellan to Lincoln, July 7, 1862, in *O.R.*, 1st ser., 11:1, 73–74.

95. For a discussion of the events that culminated in the 1862 fall elections, see Hesseltine, *Lincoln and the War Governors*, 249–72.

96. Northern Democrats had been severely shaken by the crisis spawned by secession (a crisis in the Democratic Party, after all), but maintained regular organizations everywhere in the North and retained popular allegiance in many areas. With its electoral victories of November 1862, the party regained part of its prewar strength, taking thirty-five Republican seats and governorships, including those of New York and New Jersey. Silbey, *A Respectable Minority*, 30–61.

97. This is one instance where the Civil War records are inaccurate. A man could be paid to substitute for someone else before the latter person (the principal) was drafted, but he would be called a volunteer. If his principal had already been drafted, then he should have been called a substitute. In practice, however, recruiting officers generally called all substitutes volunteers.

98. Ella Lonn estimated from information recorded by regimental commanders that 113,697 men deserted between the beginning of the war and April 1863. *Desertion in the Civil War*, 153–54.

99. Levine, "Draft Evasion in the North during the Civil War, 1863–1865," 830. According to Levine, "Republicans' insistence on the lack of conflict between social classes and their basically middle-class perspective failed to obscure an obvious disdain for a permanent underclass incessantly toiling for wages and incapable of economic independence because of an inability to conform to the values and virtues necessary for success in a modernizing society." Ibid.

100. *C.G.*, 37th Cong., 3rd sess., 976.

101. Ibid., 1264.

102. Basset, *A Warning for the Crises Or Popular Errors Involved In the Present War*, 13.

103. *Statutes*, 13:731–37. For interpretations of the Congressional debates, see Geary, "The Enrollment Act in the Thirty-seventh Congress," 562–82; Sterling, "Civil War Draft Resistance in the Middle West," 132–65.

104. Lieber, *No Party Now but All for Our Country*, 2.

105. Bernstein, *The New York City Draft Riots*, 8.

106. H. D. Gordon to unknown, Sept. 11, 1864. GCLO 8214.

107. *C.G.*, 38th Cong., 1st sess., 227.

108. On the impact of the first national draft on Cape Elizabeth, Maine, see Ledman, "A Town Responds," 71–103, 121. Although the town had voted a recruitment bounty, it was primarily funded by citizens seeking to obtain their own substitutes.

109. Quoted in Lee, *Discontent in New York City, 1861–1865*, 90. See also Sales de Bohigas, "Some Opinions on Exemption from Military Service in Nineteenth-Century Europe," 268; McPherson, *Battle Cry of Freedom*, 602.

110. Sterling, "Civil War Draft Resistance in the Middle West," 166–250.

111. Ibid.

112. Stephen, *Jailed for Peace*, 15–22.

113. Final Report made to the Secretary of War, by the Provost Marshal General, H.R. Ex. Doc. No. 1, 39th Cong., 1st sess., 4th, ser., 1251–52 (1866). *C.G.*, 37th Cong., 3rd sess., 1863, vol. 41, pt. 2, 1214.

114. Murdock, *Patriotism Limited, 1862–1865*; Shanon, *The Organization and Administration of the Union Army, 1861–1865*.

115. Rudé, *The Crowd in History*; Hobsbawm, *Primitive Rebels*; Thompson, *Customs in Common*.

116. Sterling noted in "Civil War Draft Resistance in the Middle West," 3, that the complicity of local civil authorities in blocking the work of provost marshals.

Bernstein found draft-related conflict in New York City to be a "spontaneous eruption, volcanic and short-lived." *The New York Draft Riots,* 11. Palladino also underlined the role of women in early resistance in Pennsylvania carbon counties. In these areas, the most common sign of contempt was male evasion, with few violent demonstrations. *Another Civil War,* 99.

117. For cooperation between provost marshals and the coal companies in Pennsylvania, see Palladino, *Another Civil War,* 140–62. According to Palladino, the "Provost Marshals Charlemagne Tower, Samuel Yohe, and Stephen N. Bradford moved well beyond their mandate to enforce the draft . . . enforc[ing] managerial prerogatives in the mines," 140–41.

118. Hattaway and Jones, *How the North Won,* 440.

119. Quoted in Foner and Lewis, *The Black Worker,* 298.

120. John Hay, Aug. 14, 1863, in Hay, *Lincoln and the Civil War in the Diaries and Letters of John Hay,* 80.

121. Bernstein, *The New York City Draft Riots,* 8.

122. Edward Tatum to Charles Albert Tatum, July 23, 1863. GLCO 8967.

123. The draft in New York was resumed on August 19, 1863.

124. Peter Levine, in a statistical analysis of Civil War records, found illegal evasion in districts that tended to vote non-Republican and contain Catholics and foreign-born residents, while "legal" evasion was more likely to occur in areas containing native-born, non-Catholic populations. Overall, both groups (native Protestant and foreign Catholic) avoided the draft, but used different strategies. Levine, "Draft Evasion in the North during the Civil War, 1863–1865," 816–34.

125. In 1860, the population of the seceded states was 9,103,332. Of these, 3,521,110 were slaves. Approximately 520,000 slaves fled across Union lines during the war. Long and Long, *The Civil War Day by Day,* 702.

### THREE. From Inertia to Insurgence

1. The whole account can be found at ANRJ/SPE/IG56 (PB), doc. 231. Feliciano Toscano Brito to José Antonio Saraíva, Sept. 11, 1865.

2. For the judicial attributions of the sub delegate (deputy), see Holloway, *Policing Rio de Janeiro,* 107–65.

3. ANRJ/SPE/IG56 (PB), doc 231. Henrique Felinto de Almeida to Feliciano Toscano de Brito, Sept. 2, 1865.

4. These numbers correspond to official estimates. They are presented in Schulz, *O exército na política,* 216.

5. Social stratification was very strong among poor whites. Those involved in permanent work counted on planter protection, while vagrants and other unassimilated poor inhabitants were clearer targets of recruiter agents. I am using the term "baron" to characterize big local bosses with a certain amount of power over land and people. For an analysis of differences in status among the poor, see Beattie, *The Tribute of Blood,* 17–37.

6. For an analysis of previous conflicts over registration and rationalization, see Palacios, *A Guerra dos Marimbondos*.

7. The impact of recruitment on poor sections of Brazilian society can be found in Meznar, "The Ranks of the Poor," 335–51. On the relationship between honor and recruitment, see Beattie, *The Tribute of Blood*, 75.

8. According to Santos, to win the war, the ratio of Paraguayan casualties to Allied casualties would have to have been one to three. *A Guerra do Paraguai*, 315.

9. At the time, Brazilians did not use the term "conscription" to describe their recruitment procedures. They generally used the term "recruitment" (recrutamento) to describe men coercively recruited for military service.

10. ANRJ, RPA, 1865, 23–24.

11. ANRJ/SPE/IG125/AL, fl. 186, Augusto César Reis to Visconde de Camamú, April 25, 1865.

12. Arquivo Público Mineiro, SP PP1/15 Cx 78. Also quoted in Duarte, *Os voluntários da pátria na Guerra do Paraguai*, 13–16. The same episode is quoted in Salles, *Guerra do Paraguai*, 98. See also Mendes, "O tributo de sangue," 226.

13. ANRJ, RPB, 1866, 21.

14. ANRJ, RPRJ, Niteroi, 10 May 1865, 4.

15. However, according to Beattie, *The Tribute of Blood*, 39, "By creating a separate corps with special privileges and status the government recognized and confirmed popular disdain for regular service."

16. ANRJ/SPE/IG140/doc. 59. Correspondences from the President of Ceará with the Ministry of War. Francisco Marcondes Homem de Mello to Ângelo Muniz da Silva, March 18, 1865.

17. The President of the Council of Ministers was an office similar to that of prime minister in the English system of government, although in Brazil the emperor's confidence was much more important. For technicalities of the Brazilian system, see Needell, *The Party of Order*, 73–162.

18. MHN—GP4.10.11. Marquês de Olinda to João Maria Pires Camargo, Aug. 14, 1865. The word "fazendeiro" was many times used in the official reports to designate planters.

19. ANRJ/SPE/ IG1 159, Cx. 587, fl. 552, Correspondence from the Provincial President of São Paulo with diverse authorities. From João Crispinaro Soares to Conselheiro Henrique Bauepaire Rohan, Jan. 29, 1865.

20. ANRJ/SPE/IG1 159, Cx 587, fl.582. João Soares to Visconde de Camamú, Feb. 21, 1865.

21. Ibid. João Crispiniano Soares to Conselheiro Henrique de Bauepaire Rohan, Jan. 29, 1865.

22. ANRJ/SPE/IGI 159—cx. 587, fl. 741. Joaquim Floriano de Toledo to Ângelo Muniz da Silva Ferraz, May 25, 1866.

23. In 1973, the Brazilian Senate began publishing the minutes from the meetings of the Council of State, henceforth cited as *Atas*. For more information, see Carvalho, *Teatro de Sombras*, 107–38; Martins, *A velha arte de governar*, 255–328. *Atas*, 6:81.

24. Stein and Russet, "Evaluating War," 413.

25. According to Kraay, the practice of recruitment "was a system into which the State, the ruling class of land- and slave-owning planters, and a large segment of the free poor all contributed, and from which each participant derived considerable benefit." Kraay, "Reconsidering Recruitment in Imperial Brazil," 2–3.

26. ANRJ, RPRJ, Nicterói, October 1868, 2.

27. Ibid., 3–4.

28. Tuyuti is still the biggest battle in Latin American history. Of a total of around 17,000 causalities, 13,000 were Paraguayan. After that battle, the Paraguayans completely lost their strategic initiative. See Williams, "A Swamp of Blood," 58–64; Leuchars, *To the Bitter End*, 117–28.

29. According to Santos, in Curupayty, the Allies lost 4,061 soldiers: 2,011 Brazilians, and 2,050 Argentineans. This battle signaled the end of a significant presence of Argentine troops at the front. "A Guerra do Paraguai," 322.

30. A detailed description of battles and campaigns in Paraguayan territory can be found in O'Leary, *El Paraguay en la unificación Argentina;* Schneider, *Guerra da Tríplice Aliança.*

31. Pedro II to the Countess of Barral, Nov. 7, 1866, in Magalhães Jr., *D. Pedro II e a Condessa de Barral*, 89.

32. George B. Mathew to the Earl of Clarendon, April 9, 1870, in Barman, *Citizen Emperor*, 230.

33. Santos, "A Guerra do Paraguai," 313. In her analysis of Confederate nationalism, Faust shows similar concerns. Late nineteenth-century experiences can enlighten the discussion of such problems in a less militaristic approach. See *The Creation of Confederate Nationalism*, 3.

34. Izecksohn and Beattie, "The Brazilian Home Front during the War of the Triple Alliance, 1864–1870," 123–46.

35. ANRJ/SPE/IG40 (CE), n. 34. Angelo Moniz da Silva Ferraz to Francisco Ignácio Marcondes Homem de Mello, August 28, 1866.

36. AHMI, I-DPP–22.1.867—met.c. From Vicente Pires da Mota to Marquis de Paranaguá, May 24, 1867.

37. Ibid.

38. Ibid.

39. James Watson Webb to Secretary of State William H. Seward, Aug. 21, 1868. NARA, Microcopy 121, reel 35.

40. ANRJ/SEP/IG125—Cx. 530, fl. 76. Tenente Coronel José Caetano Vaz Júnior to Conselheiro José Antônio Saraiva, Aug. 14, 1865.

41. The city of Rio de Janeiro was the Brazilian capital from 1763 to 1960. From 1961 to 1964, it was the capital of the Guanabara state. It has been Rio de Janeiro's state capital since 1975. See Izecksohn, "Recrutamento military no Rio de Janeiro durante a Guerra do Paraguai," 179–208.

42. The political alignment between the Fluminense elite and the Imperial government was proposed as a hypothesis by Mattos, *O tempo saquarema*, 129–92, and Salles, *E o vale era escravo*, 41–55. For a different view, see Needell, *The Party of Order*, 73–163.

43. The small size of the initial contingents shows that the Imperial government also underestimated the dimensions of the war, probably expecting a quick surrender from the Paraguayan government.

44. The estimate of 10 million inhabitants for the entire Brazilian population would be better applied to the first census, made in 1872. IBGE, Census, 1872.

45. ANRJ, RPMG, 1865, 22.

46. MHN, GP.412, "Uma Proclamação de Dom Viçoso aos seus Diocesanos." Mariana (MG), Nov. 6, 1866. Later in his life, Saldanha Marinho became one of the most prominent leaders in the Republican movement. How much his experiences as a provincial president convinced him to change his political opinions is difficult to state.

47. AHMI, I-DPP-22.1.867—met.c. Vicente Pires da Mota to Marquis de Paranaguá, May 24, 1867.

48. ANRJ, RPMG, 1867, 21.

49. ANRJ, RPRJ, 1866, 18–19.

50. Substitutions were widely used as the surest way to leave service. In spite of the criticism associated with this practice, law sanctioned it. Fábio Faria Mendes, *Recrutamento militar e construção do estado no Brasil imperial*, 33–56.

51. APRJ, Documentos da Presidência da Província, 1862–1867. Coleção 215/216, caixas 175/176. João José Marinha to Eduardo Pendayba de Mattos, Nicterói, 1867.

52. Substitution was an international practice in societies where universal military recruitment was not instituted. See Sales de Bohigas, "Some Opinions on Exemption from Military Service in Nineteenth-Century Europe," 261–89.

53. In the provincial reports, the term "recruits" was often used as a synonym for either imprisoned men or conscripts, that is, those who were not recruited on a voluntary basis.

54. ANRJ/SPE/IG125—Cx.530—fl. 76, Tenente Coronel José Caetano Vaz Júnior to Conselheiro José Antônio Saraiva, Aug. 14, 1865.

55. ANRJ/SPE/IGI 159.Cx. 587, fl. 741. Joaquim Floriano de Toledo to Conselheiro Ângelo Muniz da Silva Ferraz, May 25, 1866.

56. ANRJ, RPMG, 1867, July 3, 1867, 21.

57. RMJ, 1867, 5. Similar exemptions for postal employees existed in the United States. Section 2 of the Enrollment Act, March 1863, provided exemptions for public officials. See *Statutes*, 13:731–37.

58. IHGB, Lata 312—Pasta 31—Coleção Marques de Paranaguá, General Osório to Visconde de Paranaguá, Dec. 15, 1866. General Venancio Flores was president of Uruguay between 1865 and 1868. Until the 1930s, General Osório was the patron saint of the Brazilian national army. On Osorio's life and myth, see Castro, "Entre Caxias e Osório," 103–18; Doratioto, *General Osorio*.

59. IHGB, Lata 312, Pasta 31, Manuel Luís Osório to Marquis de Paranaguá, Dec. 15, 1866.

60. IHGB, Lata 372, Pasta 17. Manuel Luís Osório to Marquis de Paranaguá, March 31, 1867.

61. ANRJ, IG125—Cx. 530, fl. 76. Lieutenant Coronel José Caetano Vaz Júnior to Conselheiro José Antônio Saraiva, Aug. 14, 1865.

62. ANRJ, RPMG, 1865, 22.

63. ANRJ—IGI 159, cx. 587, fl. 741. Joaquim Floriano de Toledo to Ângelo Muniz da Silva Ferraz, May 25, 1866.

64. IHGB, cx. 276, pasta 19. Joaquim Manoel de Macedo to Count of Eu, Sept. 5, 1867, Also quoted in Dudley, "Reform and Radicalism in the Brazilian Army, 1870–1889," 68.

65. RMJ, 1867, 7.

66. The political effects of Caxias's nomination will be shown below.

67. IHGB, Lata 312—Pasta 31—Coleção Marquês de Paranaguá. Severino Ribeiro D'Almeida to João Lustosa da Cunha Paranaguá, Dec. 31, 1866.

68. Elections normally took place inside churches.

69. *Atas,* Meeting held on August 23, 1866, 6:49–59. A broader explanation concerning the Council meetings appears in chapter 6.

70. AHMI—93—I—ZGVMel.c 1–6. Francisco Ignácio Homem de Melo to Zacharias de Góes e Vasconcelos, Feb. 19, 1867.

71. ANRJ/SPE/IG147, (RN). Olyntho Jose Meira to José Antonio Saraiva, Aug. 28, 1865.

72. ANRJ/SPE IG1587, fl. 741. President of São Paulo to the Minister of War, May 25, 1866.

73. Ibid. Report of the Ministry of Justice, 1867, 3. By Brazilian law, magistrates had the right to divide their districts into blocks of less than twenty-five families and to name a deputy for each block. These "inspetores de quarteirão" (block inspectors) were exempt from service in the National Guard. According to Flory, these exemptions "generated the keenest resentments." *Judge and Jury in Imperial Brazil,* 93–94.

74. ANRJ, RMJ, 1866, 4.

75. Ibid.

76. At the root of some provincial rebellions during the 1830s were assaults against jails resulting from local controversies over impressment. One of the greatest provincial revolts, the Balaiada, began with the forced release of nine conspirators from a Maranhense cell in 1838. For a contemporary description of the Balaiada, see Magalhães, "Memória Histórica e Documentada da Revolução da Província do Maranhão," 14–66; and Alencastro, "Memórias da Balaiada," 7–13. The rebellion began when a man called "Cara Preta" (Black Face), attacked a town jail to release some relatives.

77. RMJ, 1866, 4.

78. RMJ, 1868, 7.

79. RPJ, 1866, 3.

80. RPM, 1867, 3.

81. RPJ, 1866, 3.

82. RMJ, 1868, 12.

83. ANRJ/SPE/ IG1 159—Cx. 587, fl. 741. Joaquim Floriano de Toledo to Conselheiro Ângelo Muniz da Silva Ferraz, May 25, 1866.

84. RMW, 1867, 1.

85. On these fears, see Reis and Silva, *Negociação e conflito;* Azevedo, *Onda negra, medo branco.* On the Haitian Revolution see Dubois, *Avengers of the New World,* and *A Colony of Citizens.*

86. Schwartz, *Sugar Plantations in the Formation of Brazilian Society,* 488.

87. ANRJ—IG1 146, cx. 582, fl. 636. Antônio José Lino da Costa to Eduardo Pindahyba de Matos, Sept. 10, 1867.

88. In *Roll, Jordan, Roll,* Eugene Genovese described similar processes of negotiation over slaves' living and working in the U.S. South. See especially Book 1, "God is not Mocked," 1–158.

89. RMJ, 1866, 8.

90. The Balaiada (see n. 76, above) occurred in Maranhão during the late 1830s and early 1840s.This huge popular revolt united slaves with poor whites; its memory was sufficiently alive three decades later to raise fears among all parts of the elites.

91. ANRJ/SPE/IG125, cx. 530, fl. 44. Francisco Américo Menezes Dória to Visconde de Paranaguá, July 23, 1867.

92. AHRS—Secretaria de Polícia, maço 8. J. William Harris found similar conflicts in Georgia, during the final years of the U.S. Civil War. In 1863 and 1864, petitions requesting exemptions poured into the office of Governor Joseph Brown. See Harris, *Plain Folk and Gentry in a Slave Society,* 178.

93. AHRS—Delegacia de Polícia (Police station), maço 7.

94. Many Brazilian city streets, squares, and neighborhoods were named in honor of episodes and heroes from the War of the Triple Alliance. Izecksohn, *O cerne da discórdia,* 1–27. For general accounts of war, memory, and symbols, see Baldwin and Grimaud, "How New Naming Systems Emerge," 153–66; Agulhon, "La 'statuomanie' et la Histoire," 145–72; Mayo, "War Memorials as Political Memory," 62–75; Zikmund, "National Anthems as Political Symbols," 73–80; and Centeno, "Symbols of State Nationalism in Latin America," 74–106.

95. Centeno, "The Centre Did Not Hold," 54–76.

96. Centeno, *Blood and Debt,* 20–26.

97. On the impact of the war on the creation and raising of taxes and the sharp limits imposed on that kind of extraction, see Pena, "O surgimento do imposto de renda," 337–70.

FOUR. Forged in Inequality

1. Browning, *The Diary of Orville Hickman Browning. Volume I, 1850–1864,* 659.

2. Although it was only presented in September, Lincoln shared a draft of the Emancipation Proclamation with his Cabinet in a meeting held in Washington on July 21, 1862. Following the advice of Secretary of State Seward, he delayed the Proclamation until a military victory demonstrated that its release was not an act of desperation. Although the battle of Antietam was not a clear-cut victory, it served the purpose. See Vandiver, *The Long Loom of Lincoln,* 10–15; Schwartz,

"Salmon P. Chase Critiques First Reading of the Emancipation Proclamation of President Lincoln," 84–87; Franklin, *The Emancipation Proclamation*, 31–57.

3. This modified the racial exclusion presented by the 1792 Federal Militia Act. See *Statutes*, 11:592, 599, for details on black recruitment.

4. For the adaptability of the Republican leadership, see McKitrick, "Party Politics and the Union and Confederate War Efforts," 117–51.

5. On public debates in the American press, see Andrews, *The North Reports the Civil War*; and Stanchak, *Leslie's Illustrated Civil War*. On the Paraguayan War and the Brazilian press, see Silveira, *A batalha de papel*, 139–204; Toral, *Imagens em desordem*, 57–76

6. While affirming their role in promoting centralization, I do not assume that this process was a result of planning. Rather, it was the unintended consequence of a kind of war that challenged many American beliefs. Lincoln's attitudes have been the subject of vigorous historiographic debates. Authors diverge about the meaning of changes in presidential attitudes; some recognize those changes as part of a real political advance, and others underline the conservative aspects of Lincoln's war policies. Westwood, "Lincoln's Position on Black Enlistments," 101–12; Hubbel, "Abraham Lincoln and the Recruitment of Black Soldiers," 6–21; Fredrickson, "A Man But Not a Brother," 30–58; Vorenberg, "Abraham Lincoln and the Politics of Black Colonization," 23–45.

7. Wilson, *The Black Phalanx*.

8. Despite contributions made by Joseph T. Wilson and W. E. B. Dubois, the prevalent view before the Second World War portrayed black participation as insignificant. This notion was established in 1928 by the historian W. E. Woodward in his biography *Meet General Grant*, 7: "The American Negroes [were] the only people in the history of the world that ever became free without any effort of their part."

9. This position is better expressed in Cornish, *The Sable Army*, and Glatthaar, *Forged in Battle*, which, however, do not establish connections between black recruitment and the Enrollment Act. Benjamin Quarles's *The Negro in the Civil War*, is still highly informative. A few works—the bulk of which are postwar memoirs—described experiences at a regimental level.

10. This perspective was established by Sterling, "Civil War Draft Resistance in the Middle West," and developed in Geary, *We Need Men*, and Osher, "Soldier Citizens for a Disciplined Nation."

11. "In every instance [in Brazil,] the [free] Negro participated with the whites in their wars on equal terms, and some of them achieved the prestige of a national hero . . . [while in the United States,] they could not hold office in the black militia." Tannenbaun, *Slave and Citizen*, 90–91, 94–95.

12. Degler, *Neither Black nor White*. In this sense, Degler rejects the Tannenbaum-Elkins model concerning a more benevolent Brazilian attitude toward African descendants. The path opened by Degler led the way for inquiries into the role of political and institutional processes.

13. Ibid., 80–81. For an appreciation of the participation of blacks in previous conflicts, see Wilson, *The Black Phalanx*.

14. According to Robert A. Gross, in the town of Concord in colonial Massachusetts, only two groups were exempt from service in the militia: Harvard graduates and a dozen black slaves. The *Minutemen and Their World*, 70. On the limited size of the American army, see chapter 2, 30–41.

15. As shown in chapter 3, Brazilian recruitment during the nineteenth century also operated as a mechanism of social control, singling out socially dangerous individuals. Beattie, "Conscription versus Penal Servitude," 847–73; Costa, "Os Problemas do Recrutamento Militar no Final do Século XVIII e as Questões da Construção do Estado e da Nação," 121–55.

16. Winthrop Jordan, in *White Over Black*, develops this thesis. The discussion about white fears of a black revolt is in 562n. About different images attributed to blacks in literature and society, see Fredrickson, *The Black Image in the White Mind*, 97–129.

17. Frey, *Water from the Rock*, 77.

18. Voelz, *Slave and Soldier*, 29. Complete lists concerning examples of military use of blacks during emergencies can be found in charts 1–4, on pp. 24–28, 34–35, 46–47, 66–67.

19. Berlin, *Slaves Without Masters*, 15–24; Quarles, *The Negro in the American Revolution*, 68–93.

20. In Brazil, five provinces reacted against independence: Bahia, Maranhão, Piauí, Cisplatina, and Grão-Pará. The Brazilian Imperial government needed only a small number of loyal regular troops, supported by foreign mercenaries, to subordinate these provinces to the new order. Kraay, "Em outra coisa não falavam os pardos, cabras e crioulos," 202.

21. Maslowski, "National Policy toward the Use of Black Troops in the Revolution," 2–6; Duncan, *Slavery, Race, and the American Revolution*, 109–47; Neimeyer, *America Goes to War*, 65–88, incorporates an excellent discussion of African American participation in the Continental Army.

22. Davis, *The Problem of Slavery in the Age of Revolution*, 73–83. Davis defines the American Revolution as a movement of "conservative criollos."

23. For a case study, see White, *Connecticut's Black Soldiers, 1775–1783*, 17–39.

24. Jackson, *Correspondence of Andrew Jackson*, 2:51–54.

25. Appendix to the *Annals of Congress*, 1st Cong., 1st sess., 1392.

26. On the lost opportunity for African Americans at the end of the revolutionary period, two interesting case studies are Nash, *Freedom by Degrees*, and White, *Somewhat More Independent*. Both authors blame pervasive racism in the North for the lack of a vigorous abolitionist policy in the period following independence.

27. Rankin, "The Impact of the Civil War on the Free Colored Community of New Orleans," 379–416. The state of Louisiana paid free colored soldiers pensions, and the federal government granted them bounties. On the black presence in West India regiments see Geggus, "Slavery, War, and Revolution in the Greater Caribbean, 1789–1815," 1–50; Buckley, *Slaves in Red Coats*, 63–81.

28. Joshi and Reidy, "To Come Forward and Aid in Putting Down This Unholy Rebellion," 330. See also Ira Berlin et al., *Slaves No More*, 195.

29. Benjamin C. Howard, compiler, *Report of the Decision of the Supreme Court of the Unites States, and the Opinions of the Judges thereon in the Case of Dred Scot versus John F. A. Sandford* (Washington, D.C.: C. Wendell, 1857), quoted in Osher, "Soldier Citizens for a Disciplined Nation," 371.

30. *Douglass' Monthly* 3 (May 1861): 451.

31. On the constitutional impasses involving emancipation, see Nieman, *Promises to Keep,* 50–57.

32. Abraham Lincoln, "Annual Message to Congress, December 3, 1861," quoted in Fehrenbacher, *Abraham Lincoln,* 176.

33. Thomas Wentworth Higginson, "The First Black Regiment," *The Outlook,* July 1898, 521–31, quoted in Trudeau, *Like Men of War,* 66.

34. For a good account of black mobilization at the beginning of the war, see McPherson, *The Negro's Civil War,* 19–36.

35. Quoted in Degler, *Neither Black Nor White,* 78. A similar point of view about black soldiers was also formulated by some officers who told the Union Brigadier General Daniel Ulman, "We must not discipline them (blacks), for if we do, we will have to fight them some day ourselves," quoted in Glatthaar, *Forged in Battle,* 168. On the Southern debate over the enlistment of slaves in the last months of war, see Durden, *The Gray and the Black;* Rollins, *Black Southerners in Gray;* Preisser, "The Virginia Decision to Use Negro Soldiers in the Civil War, 1864–1865," 98–113; and Levine, *Confederate Emancipation,* 110–28.

36. For a description of the varieties of jobs performed by blacks in the Army of Virginia, see Jordan Jr., *Black Confederates and Afro-Yankees in Civil War Virginia,* especially, 185–200. See also McPherson, *The Negro's Civil War,* 245–48.

37. L. H. Minor to the Confederate Secretary of War, May 2, 1862, in "The Destruction of Slavery," in Berlin, *The Destruction of Slavery,* Doc. 264, p. 698.

38. James S. Slight to his wife, Jan. 17, 1862, quoted in Jimerson, *The Private Civil War,* 133.

39. Wiley, *The Life of Billy Yank,* 44; McPherson, *For Cause and Comrades,* 117–30; Silber, *Yankee Correspondence;* Jimerson, *The Private Civil War,* 86–123; Mitchell, *Civil War Soldiers,* 117–26; Hess, *Liberty, Virtue, and Progress,* 81–102. The extreme case seems to be Michael Barton's, *Goodmen,* which argues that Southerners and Northerners shared the same core value system.

40. According to Litwack, *North of Slavery,* the extent of antislavery and anti-Southern sentiment in 1860 cannot be taken as an index of the success of abolitionism, since many Republicans, probably a large majority, were explicitly opposed to the doctrine of immediate abolition. Blacks did not share in the expansion of political democracy during the first half of the nineteenth century. Only after many years and hundreds of thousands of victims did the radical wing of the Republican Party achieve the strength needed to organize its demands on a consistent political project. Only at the war's end would such a project be able to claim a deep transformation in the country's racial structures. On the Republican Party's free labor ideology before the Civil War, see Foner, *Free Soil, Free Labor, Free Men,* and *Politics and Ideology in the Age of the Civil War,* especially 23–24, 261–62.

Despite limitations of the Republican attitude, Foner claims it was qualitatively more progressive than the average Northern position.

41. Major E. Boney to Mr. Lincoln, 18 Feb. 1861, in Berlin, *The Black Military Experience*, 1, Doc. 162, p. 411.

42. Fredrickson, *The Black Image in the White Mind*, xii–xiii.

43. Dix to Colonel August Morse, 14 Oct 1861, quoted in Berlin, *The Destruction of Slavery*, 1, Doc. 129, p. 351. Dix also proposed to send "contrabands" north to alleviate the demographic pressure in the military camps. See Jordan Jr., *Black Confederates and Afro-Yankees in Civil War Virginia*, 265.

44. *C.G.*, 37th Cong., 1st sess., 32. Owen Lovejoy was a brother of the martyred abolitionist Elijah Lovejoy.

45. Taylor, *Reminiscences of My Life*, 32.

46. Testimony given by the former Virginia slave Harry Jarvis in Blassingame, *Slave Testimony*, 608.

47. This incident took place in May 22, 1861. See Gerteis, *From Contraband to Freedmen*, 11–13. According to Gerteis, 23, the population of blacks under federal control in Virginia rose from approximately 1,500 early in 1862 to nearly 5,000 by the end of the year. See also McPherson, *The Negro's Civil War*, 28. For the official correspondence of the whole affair, see *O.R.*, 1st ser., 2:52–54, 648–51; 8:370; 3rd ser., 1:243.

48. Women and children significantly surpassed the male population in many camps. A Dec. 12, 1863, report from a refugee camp in Natchez, Mississippi, recorded 495 men, 1,612 women, and 875 children, for a total of 2,982 refugees. *Liberator*, Jan. 15, 1864, quoted in Frost, "Blacks and Emancipation," 103–4.

49. *Statutes*, 12:319.

50. *Frank Leslie's Illustrated Newspaper*, Nov. 2, 1861. Open prejudices were part of what Michael Barton defined as the "Victorian Panorama." According to Barton, *Goodmen*, 50, "Victorians believed that the economy was a test of morals, and that the poor could not control their impulses. Rescuing the poor, therefore, meant teaching them willpower and new morals. Many of the poor believed this too."

51. On the Port Royal conflicts, see Rose, *Rehearsal for Reconstruction*, 199–216; Berlin, *The Destruction of Slavery*, 101–14; Foner, *Reconstruction*, 51–55.

52. May, "Continuity and Change in the Labor Program of the Union Army and the Freedman's Bureau," 245–54.

53. Louis Gerteis argues that the experience of blacks in Civil War Louisiana, where General Nathaniel P. Banks established a labor system that critics charged resembled slavery, shaped Reconstruction far more than events on the Sea Islands. *From Contraband to Freedmen*, 65–82.

54. *Frank Leslie's Illustrated Newspaper*, May 21, 1864.

55. According to Mays, of a prewar population of 4,000,000, approximately 520,000 African Americans in the Confederacy crossed the Union lines during the war. "Black Americans and Their Contribution toward Union Victory in the American Civil War, 1861–1865," 53.

56. Entry from September 21, 1862, Kinsley, *Diary of a Christian Soldier*, 109.

57. Donald, *Inside Lincoln's Cabinet*, 96, 99–100.

58. In late summer of 1862, Confederates reversed the initial progress of Union troops and recaptured Baton Rouge, the state capital. Complete control of the state was achieved only after the fall of Vicksburg and Port Hudson in July 1863.

59. In 1860, 18,647 free blacks lived in Louisiana, 10,689 of them in New Orleans. In 1830, some 750 free men of color owned 2,351 slaves. Rural Louisiana developed a significant class of slaveholding free blacks. See Tunnel, "Free Negroes and the Freedmen," 5–28.

60. For Congressional debates concerning Butler's recruitment efforts in Louisiana, see *C.G.*, 37th Cong., 2nd sess., 2620–21.

61. Higginson, *Army Life in a Black Regiment*, 1. According to Joshi and Reidy, "'To Come Forward and Aid in Putting Down this Unholy Rebellion,'" 326, on the eve of the Civil War, New Orleans freemen owned two million dollars worth of property, and fully 85 percent worked as artisans, professionals, and proprietors. The most prosperous owned large plantations and dozens of slaves.

62. Berlin, *The Black Military Experience*, 41–44.

63. In sequence, Hunter proclaimed the emancipation of all slaves in South Carolina, Georgia, and Florida, whether or not within Union lines.

64. The violence of the draft system was symbolically connected with the previous insinuations from masters that the Yankees would sell former slaves to the Caribbean plantations.

65. Higginson, *Army Life in a Black Regiment*, 15–16.

66. On James [Big] Lane recruitment procedures, see Cornish, *The Sable Arm*, 69–76.

67. The Thirty-Seventh Congress was one of the most influential in American legislative history, with fundamental contributions in land grants, colleges, confiscation, banks, and expropriation of property. See Curry, *Blueprint for Modern America*, 10–35. For Republican behavior in the Congress, see Herman Belz, *Emancipation and Equal Rights*, 23–46.

68. Henry W. Halleck to Ulysses S. Grant, March 31, 1863, quoted in Berlin, *The Black Military Experience*, Doc. 50, p. 144.

69. *New York Times*, November 21, 1862.

70. "Emancipation Proclamation," in Fehrenbacher, *Abraham Lincoln*, 212. See also Franklin, *The Emancipation Proclamation*.

71. Eric Foner, *Reconstruction*, 11–18. The phrase "inner civil war" was originally coined by George Fredrickson in 1965 when discussing Northern intellectuals.

72. Although Democrats could not prevent the victory of emancipation, they could filibuster to retard passage of emancipation legislation. See Curry, "Congressional Democrats, 1861–1863," 213–19.

73. Quarles, *The Negro in the Civil War*, 166–67.

74. Seymour, *Public Record*, 54, quoted in Seraile, "The Struggle to Raise Black Regiments in New York State, 1861–1864," 224.

75. Bellows, *Historical Sketch of the Union League Club of New York*.

76. On the problems presented by conscription in America, refer to chapter 2.

77. Senator John Sherman to General William Tecumseh Sherman, Aug. 24, 1862, quoted in Quarles, *The Negro in the Civil War*, 158.

78. According to Geary, 116,125 soldiers deserted during the last two years of the war. *We Need Men*, 14. See also Costa and Kahn, *Heroes and Cowards*, 80–119.

79. Welles, *Diary of Gideon Welles*, 1:324.

80. This sharply contrasts with the situation in the Empire. In Brazil, the force of a small public opinion was restrained by the structure of the Imperial Constitution that empowered the Emperor to change cabinets during political crisis. In addition to the executive, legislative, and judiciary powers, the Emperor counted on a fourth power called the moderative, which weakened congressional independence. Under the moderative power, the Emperor could call new elections to forge a majority when he needed it. Nabuco, *Um estadista do império*, 38–54. For a liberal critique of the operation of this power, see Góes e Vasconcellos, *Da natureza e limites do poder moderador*. During the war, provincial elections were suspended in the province of Rio Grande do Sul.

81. Amos A. Lawrence et al. to Honorable E. M. Stanton, Dec. 10, 1863, enclosed in S. Hooper to Honble. E. M. Stanton, Dec. 19, 1863, H-1807 1863m Letters Received, RG 107, NARA, L-159. Quoted in Ira Berlin, *The Black Military Experience*, Doc. 39A, p. 108–9.

82. *C.G.*, 38th Cong., 1st sess., 80.

83. A famous case was the First South Carolina Volunteers subsequently renamed the Thirty-third U.S. Colored Infantry. See Rose, *Rehearsal for Reconstruction*, 193.

84. Cornish, *The Sable Arm*, 94–111.

85. According to Quarles, of a total of 980 recruits enlisted in the Massachusetts Fifty-fourth; 287, or 29.2 percent, had been slaves. Quarles, *The Negro in the Civil War*, 187.

86. *Frank Leslie's Illustrated Newspaper*, Dec. 20, 1862.

87. David Givler to a friend, Feb. 14, 1863, in "Intimate Glimpses of Army Life During the Civil War; Autobiography, Diaries, Letters, of David B. Givler, Company C, 7th Illinois Infantry . . ." typewritten MS, Illinois State Historical Library, 101. Quoted in Hicken, "The Record of Illinois' Negro Soldiers in the Civil War," 538–39.

88. Samuel J. Kirkwood to General Henry W. Halleck, Aug. 5, 1862, quoted in Berlin, *The Black Military Experience*, Doc. 25, p. 87–88.

89. Geary estimates that between two and three thousand slaves enlisted in these experimental regiments. *We Need Men*, 30.

90. Higginson's diary, *Army Life in a Black Regiment*, is one the best sources for the story of this regiment. See also Emilio, *A Brave Black Regiment*.

91. Prevalent racist attitudes in certain parts of the North drove many free blacks to the Massachusetts regiments. See Seraile, "Struggle to Raise Black Regiments in New York State, 1861–1864," 215–33; Smith, "Raising a Black Regiment in Michigan," 22–41. In the Fifty-fifth Massachusetts Regiment, 106 (11 percent)

of its 961 soldiers were from Virginia. Jordan Jr., *Black Confederates and Afro-Yankees in Civil War Virginia*, 268.

92. Five regiments were initially raised in the North: the Fifty-fourth and Fifty-fifth Massachusetts Volunteer Infantry, the Fifth Massachusetts Colored Cavalry, the Twenty-ninth Connecticut Volunteer Infantry, and Fourteenth Rhode Island Heavy Artillery. Ira Berlin, *The Black Military Experience*, 407.

93. On the action and the role of the regiment's first commander, see Duncan, *Blue-Eyed Child of Fortune*; Emilio, *A Brave Black Regiment.*

94. Nevins, *The War for the Union*, provides a good account of the transformations in the Union army's organization.

95. Wilson, *The Business of Civil War*, 34–71.

96. Nearly 60 percent of eligible Kentucky blacks served in the army. Foner, *Reconstruction*, 8.

97. William H. Johnson, Eighth Connecticut Infantry, Roanoke Island, North Carolina, Feb. 10, 1862, *Pine and Palm*, Feb. 27, 1862, quoted in Redkey, *A Grand Army of Black Men*, Letter 7, 18.

98. *C.G.*, 38th Cong., 1st sess., Part 1, February 10, 11, 16, 26, 1863, 598–602. For a detailed account of the conflicts in Kentucky, see Smith, "The Recruitment of Negro Soldiers in Kentucky, 1863–1865," 364–90.

99. Local opposition in Kentucky delayed the enrollment of all blacks until March 1, 1864. See Blassingame, "The Recruitment of Colored Troops in Kentucky, Maryland, and Missouri," 533–45; Howard, "The Civil War in Kentucky," 245–56.

100. John W. Bowen et al. to Hon. Secretary of War, Sept. 26, 1863, quoted in Berlin, *The Black Military Experience*, Doc. 65, p. 174.

101. Costa and Kahn estimate that roughly three-quarters of the black soldiers serving in the Union forces were former slaves. *Heroes and Cowards*, 63.

102. After Union victories at Gettysburg and Vicksburg, the power of loyal slaveholders steadily decreased. McPherson, *Battle Cry of Freedom*, 689–716.

103. Adjutant General Lorenzo Thomas to Hon. Edwin M. Stanton, Feb. 1, 1864 in Berlin, *The Black Military Experience*, Doc. 98, pp. 253–54.

104. Address of His Excellency John A. Andrew to the two branches of the Legislature of Massachusetts. January 9, 1863, 73

105. *O.R.*, 3rd ser., 4:233–34, April 18, 1864. Of course, the last blow against slave owners' rights was the Thirteenth Amendment in January 1865. Vorenberg, *Final Freedom*, 211–50.

106. The first African American to receive the Congressional Medal of Honor, Sergeant William H. Carney of the Fifty-fourth Massachusetts, furnishes a good example of migration for enlistment. Born in Norfolk, Virginia, Carney fled to Massachusetts and enlisted at New Bedford. Jordan Jr., *Black Confederates and Afro-Yankees*, 272; Quarles, *The Negro in the Civil War*, 183–202.

107. *New York Tribune*, June 10, 1865, quoted in Genovese, *Roll, Jordan, Roll*, 112.

108. Some authors disagree with these numbers. Cooper, "Records of Civil War African American Troops Inspire Major Archival Project," 9–11, estimates 185,000

as the total number of African Americans who served in the USTCs. Metzer, "The Records of the U.S. Colored Troops as a Historical Source," 23–132, estimates the number at 186,017 or 17.7 percent of colored men ages 15 to 49. For methodological convenience, I am working from data from *O.R.*, the same source used by Ira Berlin, Joseph Glatthaar, and most authors on the subject.

109. Geary, *We Need Men,* 31.

110. Westwood, "Captive Black Union Soldiers in Charleston—What to Do?," 29–44; Cimprich and Mainfort Jr., "The Fort Pillow Massacre," 830–39; Huch, "Fort Pillow Massacre," 62–70; Urwin, "'We Cannot Treat Negroes . . . as Prisoners of War,'" 193–210.

111. Black soldiers comprised 21 percent of all executed federal soldiers. See Glatthaar, *Forged in Battle,* 118.

112. On March 9, 1863, the War Department issued a manual titled *United States Tactics for the Use of Colored Troops.*

113. For the changing nature of the Civil War, see Royster, *The Destructive War,* 321–404.

114. Quoted in Quarles, *The Negro in the Civil War,* xiv.

115. Andrew K. Black gives different numbers: 33,294 black soldiers died during the Civil War. From these, 3,331 died in combat, and 29,963 were victims of diseases. "In the Service of the United States," 317–33.

116. Although blacks participated effectively only during the last three years of the war, seventeen black soldiers and four black sailors won Congressional Medals of Honor. Mays, "Black Americans and Their Contribution toward Union Victory in the American Civil War, 1861–1865," 125–27. For descriptions of their acts of bravery, see Stark, "Forgotten Heroes," 70–80.

117. An order from the adjutant general's office dated March 11, 1864, stated, "Thenceforth all black regiments should be designated by numbers and include the word 'colored.'" See Quarles, *The Negro in the Civil War,* 200.

118. The Fifty-fourth Massachusetts Infantry is perhaps the most famous of these state-organized regiments. It was kept under state jurisdiction throughout its service. *O.R.,* 3rd ser., 5:661.

119. Of the 7,000 men who officered USCT troops, fewer than 100 were blacks, and those were heavily concentrated in the Louisiana Native Guards, an auxiliary institution whose existence preceded the formation of the USCTs. The regimental division by branch was: 145 of Infantry; 7 of cavalry; 13 of artillery; and 1 of engineers. Quarles, *The Negro in the Civil War,* 199.

120. Berlin, *The Black Military Experience,* Doc. 407, p. 33; Metzer, "The Records of the U.S. Colored Troops as a Historical Source," 123–32.

121. Letter from Jane Wallis, Dec. 10, 1863, in Berlin, *The Black Military Experience,* Document 47A, p. 138.

122. Statement of John Banks, Jan. 2, 1864, in Berlin, *The Black Military Experience,* Document 47C, 139–40.

123. The threat of a black draft was not restricted to the South. Eugene Murdock pointed out that in some cities police officers intimidated black men, accus-

ing them of invented crimes if they did not enlist. Through this expedient, they aimed to sell them as substitutes for whites. *One Million Men*, 289n.

124. Jordan Jr., *Black Confederates and Afro-Yankees in Civil War Virginia*, 270.

125. Andrew Pratt to Salomon, Nov. 22, 1863, Salomon Papers, quoted in Sterling, "Civil War Draft Resistance in the Middle West," 605.

126. Murdock, *One Million Men*, 178–80. On the debates concerning commutation, see *C.G.*, 38th Cong., 1st sess., 64–65, 80, 142, 143. Commutation issues generated an enormous debate inside the Republican Party. While Senator Jim Lane attacked it, many other Republicans, led by Senator Henry Wilson, defended maintaining it by arguing that it would furnish a positive benefit to the poor. For more information, see chapter 2.

127. It should be noted that, previously, various states cities, towns, and even individuals had been offering enlistment inducements (formally and informally) to blacks.

128. *O.R.*, 3rd ser., 4: 473; Berlin, *The Black Military Experience*, 77.

129. Cornish, *The Sable Arm*, 235. Nicolay's substitute was an African American from North Carolina, Hiram Child, who later died in battle.

130. Geary, *We Need Men*, 113. On Jan. 8, 1864, U.S. Senator Daniel Clark of New Hampshire referred to the permissiveness of this practice in his state. See *C.G.*, 38th Cong., 1st sess., 1:140. See also Marvel, "New Hampshire and the Draft, 1863" 58–72.

131. In Michigan, Michael O. Smith found that black substitutions accounted for 50.7 percent of the draft during the last two drafts of the war. See "Raising a Black Regiment in Michigan," 38.

132. This figure is impressive when compared with the percentage of blacks in New England's population before the war. According to the U.S. Census of 1860, 0.8 percent of New England's population was black. The proportion by state was: Maine, 0.2 percent; New Hampshire, 0.2 percent; Massachusetts, 0.8 percent; Vermont, 0.2 percent; Connecticut, 1.9 percent; and Rhode Island, 2.3 percent. Katz, *U.S. Department of Commerce, Bureau of the Census, Negro Population in the United States, 1790–1915*, 51.

133. Data collected and processed from Evans, *Revised Register of the Soldiers and Sailors in the War of the Rebellion, 1861–1866*, 1016–26.

134. Some regiments reflected the preponderance of specific groups. The Thirty-sixth United States Colored Infantry was organized among former slaves seeking refuge within the Union lines in eastern North Carolina and southeastern Virginia. The Fifth Regiment of Infantry USCT was raised among the free black community of Ohio. Recent regimental studies have explored such differences. See Bryant, "A Model Regiment"; Paradis, "Strike the Blow."

135. It should also be mentioned that a minority came from other countries, especially Canada and the Caribbean.

136. Samuel Cabble to his wife, 1863, NARA, Record Group 94, Records of the Adjutant General's Office. Quoted in Cooper, "Records of Civil War African American Troops Inspire Major Archive Project," 10.

137. Higginson, *Army Life in a Black Regiment,* 248.

138. Berlin, *The Black Military Experience,* Doc. 106, pp. 268–69. This woman ran away with her baby, leaving five of her children behind.

139. Black noncommissioned officers received the same salaries as private soldiers. For African American rates of mortality in the military service, see Black, "In the Service of the United States," 317–33. According to Black, white troops were twice as likely to die from disease as to die in battle, while black troops were almost ten times as likely to do so.

140. Sergeant Milton Harris, Co. F., 25th USCI, *Christian Recorder,* Dec. 17, 1864, quoted in Redkey, *A Grand Army of Black Men,* 151.

141. Glatthaar, Forged in Battle, 35–60.

142. Even among those deeply committed to abolition, promotion could be quick. Robert Gould Shaw, the famous commander of the Fifty-fourth Massachusetts, was promoted from captain (in the Second Massachusetts Infantry) to major and finally to lieutenant colonel in less than two months. Quarles, *The Negro in the Civil War,* 9.

143. Berlin, *The Black Military Experience,* Doc. 164, pp. 414–15.

144. On Benedict, see Rutherford, "Revolt in the Corps D'Afrique," 20–23.

145. The Free Military School for Applicants for Command of Colored Troops, which provided training for those who sought these positions, was established in December 1863.

146. The army produced special manuals, such as *U.S. Infantry Tactics, for the Instruction, Exercise, and Maneuvers of the Soldier, a Company, Line of Skirmishes, and Battalion, for the Use of Colored Troops of the United States Infantry, Prepared under the Direction of the War Department* (Washington D.C.: GPO, 1863). See Glatthaar, *Forged in Battle,* 103–4.

147. "Private," 43rd USCI, Bermuda Hundred, Virginia, quoted in the *Christian Recorder,* Jan. 26, 1864.

148. Westwood, "The Cause and Consequence of a Union Black Soldier's Mutiny and Execution," 222–36; Berlin, *The Black Military Experience,* 365–66, 388–95.

149. *Statutes,* 12:599.

150. Corporal James Henry Gooding to Abraham Lincoln, Sept. 28, 1863, quoted in Berlin, *The Black Military Experience,* Doc. 157A, p. 386. Only those who were free as of April 19, 1861, received equal and back pay, and they had to swear an oath to provide testimony from another source before receiving back pay retroactively from April 19, 1861, to Jan. 31, 1864. Not until March 1865 were all black soldiers guaranteed the same pay as white soldiers.

151. Private E. D. W., *Christian Recorder,* April 2, 1864, quoted in Redkey, *A Grand Army of Black Men,* 48.

152. For a summary of the events involving Walker's protest and execution, see Westwood, "The Cause and Consequence of a Union Black Soldier's Mutiny and Execution," 222–35.

153. Some 14,870 black soldiers deserted the Union army, approximately 8.2

percent of all black soldiers enlisted. See Sterling, "Civil War Draft Resistance in the Middle West," 605.

154. Higginson, *Army Life in a Black Regiment*, appendix D, "The Struggle for Pay," 280–85; Belz, "Law, Politics, and Race in the Struggle for Equal Pay during the Civil War," 197–222; Friedrich, "We Will Not Do Duty Any Longer for Seven Dollars per Month," 64–73.

155. The African American community in the North was informed of many aspects of black military life through the letters published in some newspapers that appealed directly to the black population: the *Christian Recorder* of Philadelphia, the *Weekly Anglo-African*, and *Douglass' Monthly* were published by black editors. Other newspapers, such as the *Liberator*, occasionally published letters from black soldiers. On blacks and the war press, see Redkey's preface in *A Grand Army of Black Men*, ix–xv.

156. For reviews on the USTC experiences, see Kynoch, "Terrible Dilemmas," 104–27; Geary, "Blacks in the American Military," 59–68; Cheek and Cheek, "White Over Black in the Union Blue," 104–27.

157. Taunay, *A retirada da laguna*. See also his *Cartas da campanha de Mato Grosso*; and *Memórias*.

### FIVE. Manumitting and Enlisting the Slaves in Brazil, December 1866–August 1868

1. It was impossible to discover the fate of the cook after she had obtained her freedom, if she was kept on at her master's house or if she was sent way.

2. The whole case is in José M. da C. Jobim to Thomas Gomes, Engenho Novo, 14 November 1867, AHMI, POB, 101—maço 141, doc. 6925). One dollar was equal to 2$174 (two thousand, one hundred and seventy-four mil-réis). Consequently, the three slaves cost 2:800$000 mil-réis. The mother and daughter together cost 1:800$000 mil-réis, while Carlos cost 1:000$000. For the exchange value between Brazilian mil-réis and U.S. dollars, see Duncan, *Public and Private Operations of Railways in Brazil*, 183.

3. On the subject, see Florentino and Goés, *A paz nas senzalas*, 113–28.

4. According to the narrative, Carlos informed the recruitment inspectors about his health condition.

5. Medical examinations of recruits were often superficial. In his war memoirs, General Dionísio Cerqueira described his own inspection as a young soldier. After presenting himself as a volunteer at the general headquarters, Cerqueira was examined by a careless physician who merely observed him, never touching his body. No medical exams, in the true meaning of the term, were performed. See Dionísio Cerqueira, *Reminiscências da campanha do Paraguai*, 48.

6. On the strategic importance of the Paríba Valley, see Stein, *Vassouras*, 29–116; Salles, *E o vale era escravo*, 17–40.

7. Carlos's evasion occurred at Barra do Piraí, then the last station on the railway that would link the city of Rio de Janeiro to the city of São Paulo through the Paraíba Valley.

8. It is possible that some urban slaves might well have judged their semi-free status as preferable to confinement in the army barracks. This hypothesis has been presented by Kraay, "The Shelter of the Uniform," 637–57, and Karash, *Slave Life in Rio de Janeiro, 1808–1850*, 338. Kraay concludes that most evidence contradicts the hypothesis, although the above case is clearly an exception.

9. Tannenbaum, *Slave and Citizen*, 117.

10. It was impossible to follow Carlos's fate after his enlistment.

11. During the sixteenth and seventeenth centuries, French and Dutch explorers repeatedly invaded many regions of Portuguese-America. For additional information on this subject, see Capistrano de Abreu, *Chapters of Brazil's Colonial History, 1500–1800*, 52–90; Cabral de Mello, *Olinda restaurada*, 257–316.

12. Charles R. Boxer, *The Golden Age of Brazil, 1865–1750*, 142.

13. Fragoso, "A nobreza vive em bandos," 14; Lima. "Escravos de Peleja," 131–52.

14. Thus, the origin of the expression "Henriques" for those battalions that were organized in the northeast to repel the Dutch forces. On Henrique Dias and the struggle against the Dutch in Brazil, see Boxer, *The Portuguese Seaborne Empire, 1415–1825*, 119, 162. For an analysis of the symbolic appropriation of the myths of Henrique Dias and his black warriors, see Cabral de Mello, *Rubro veio*. For a description of the rewards received by Dias and his family, see Mattos, "Henrique Dias," 29–45.

15. Saint-Hilaire, *Viagem pelas Províncias do Rio de Janeiro e Minas Gerais*, 321.

16. Cotta, "No rastro dos Dragões." "Dragões" (dragons) is a denomination of old calvary regiments.

17. For a comprehensive treatment of black soldiers in the colonial Americas, see Voelz, *Slave and Soldier*.

18. On the concept of "onerous manumission," see Slenes, "The Demography and Economics of Brazilian Slavery, 1850–1880," 516; Lara, *Campos da violência*, 219; Almada, *Escravismo e transição*, 148–9. For a summary of the discussions, see Einsenberg, "Ficando Livre," 175–226.

19. Degler, *Neither Black nor White*, 79. Such a perspective does not exclude the hypothesis that military life could bring positive changes for blacks directly involved, that is, former recruits coming from Brazil's poorest social groups.

20. As soon as independence was secured, such measures were canceled. They were probably never effective.

21. Except for the Malê Revolt (1835), no other riot directly questioned the existence of slavery.

22. This hypothesis was presented by Berrance de Castro, "O Negro na Guarda Nacional," 149–72.

23. On the levée en masse, see Forest, *Soldiers of the French Revolution*, 73–81.

24. Kraay, "Em outra coisa não falavam os pardos, cabras e crioulos," 109–26.

25. Quoted in *Oliveira, Diário do Coronel Manuel Lucas de Oliveira*, 54.

26. APRJ, PP 2.2–4, Cx. 16, Coleção 8. Ofícios, Oct. 18–23, 1867, quoted in Souza, *Escravidão ou morte*, 63.

27. As the price of an exemption 600$000 (US$276) was generally inferior to the average price of a slave, it could be good business just to buy an exemption instead of an individual for recruitment. But the poor were hardly able to pay such a high price.

28. APRS, J-69, Codice J-60, fl 1v.

29. Marquis of Caxias to Francisco Inácio Marcondes Homem de Mello, April 12, 1868. APRS, B1.071—Avisos do Ministério da Guerra—1868/1869.

30. Thomas Furtado to José Silveira Filho, Feb. 13, 1867. AHRS, fl. 55, livro 19. Quoted in Moreira, *Faces da liberdade, máscaras do cativeiro,* 67.

31. For the enlistment of African Americans previous to the Civil War, Rollins, *Black Southerners in Gray,* 1–35.

32. *Jornal do Pará,* May 16, 1868, 1, quoted in Bezerra Neto, "Nos bastidores da guerra," 100.

33. This was the source of great misunderstandings about the status of Brazilian soldiers. Some authors took for granted that the large number of people of black descent meant that they were slaves.

34. Carneiro da Cunha, "Silences of the Law," 427–43.

35. João Lustosa da Cunha Paranaguá to Esperidião Elóy de Barros Pimentel, Aug. 20, 1866. APRJ, Coleção 8, Pasta 10, maço 12 (1866).

36. APRS, Correspondência dos Governantes, maço 109—Ofícios do Presidente da Província ao Chefe da Polícia em 14. Feb. 1867.

37. Dean, *Rio Claro,* 72. Terms such as "pardo," "mulato," "crioulo," and "cabra" were some of the designations for both freedmen and slaves. These terms assumed different meanings as the century advanced.

38. From the Quartermaster General to Barão of Boa Vista, Nov. 7, 1865. AHRS, Lata 198, maço 1.

39. According to the data in Fábio F. Mendes, "O tributo de sangue," 217–19, voluntary enlistment decreased from 41.4 percent in 1864 (first year) to 8.16 percent during 1867–68.

40. "Relação dos Offerecimentos feitos ao Governo para as Urgencias da Guerra" in RMW, 1865, also quoted in Salles, *Guerra do Paraguai,* 101.

41. The name Zouave was copied from the French African armies in Algeria, where black soldiers fought on behalf of the French Empire during the colonial wars.

42. Kraay, "Os companheiros de Dom Obá," 121–61.

43. For a historical analysis of Dom Obá's life and times, see Silva, *Prince of the People.*

44. Many such cases were described in chapter 3.

45. According to Salles the Cholera epidemics killed 10 percent of the nominal contingent of the Brazilian army in 1867. *Guerra do Paraguai: memórias e imagens,* 158.

46. *Atas,* 6:65.

47. Francisco Borges Ribeiro to Agostinha Maria de Jesuz, April 16, 1869. AHEX requerimentos, JJ-259-6322. Quoted in Kraay, "Soldiers, Officers, and Society," 500.

48. Until the Paraguayan War, the Gaucho cavalry had been the basis of the Brazilian military's actions in the River Plate. See Ribeiro, "'Tudo isto é indiada coronilha ( . . . ) não é como essa cuscada lá da corte,'" 117–37.

49. Cooney, "Economy and Manpower," 23–43.

50. Some historians considered Humayta to be the South American Sebasto-pol, the Russian stronghold during the Crimean War. It seems that Alliance leaders overestimated the strategic importance of the trenches, which contributed signifi-cantly to the army's paralysis. During this period, many proposals for negotiation came from Bolivia, Peru, and Chile, as well as from the United States. The fact that they did not prevail does not diminish their importance.

51. This was the Paraguayan message at the meeting that reunited Solano López, Bartolomé Mitre, and Venancio Flores at a place called Yatayti-Corá on Sept. 12, 1866, when Solano López presented his proposal to end the war. For the meeting, see Baez, *Yatayty-Corá*.

52. Benjamin Constant to Cláudio Luís da Costa, Nov. 29, 1866, quoted in Mendes, *Benjamin Constant*, 118–19. See also Izecksohn, *O cerne da discórdia*, 105; Lemos, *Cartas da Guerra do Paraguai*, 63–64.

53. Benjamin Constant Botelho de Magalhães to Cláudio Luis da Costa. Quo-ted in Lemos, *Cartas da Guerra do Paraguai*, 113.

54. See Viscount of Porto Alegre to João Lustosa da Cunha Paranaguá, Oct. 19, 1866. IHGB, Lata 312 pasta 12.

55. For an analysis of center–periphery relations during the Argentinean state-building process, see Chiaramonte, *Ciudades, provincias, estados*, 231–46.

56. Allub, "Estado y sociedad civil," 109–57.

57. Brazilians retained the command of the fleet.

58. Those numbers represent an estimate, as it is currently impossible to ob-tain accurate data concerning the number of combatants in the three forces.

59. Rock, *Argentina, 1516–1982*, 129.

60. For a personal description of living conditions of immigrant soldiers in the Argentinean army, see Lopacher and Tobler, *Un suizo en la Guerra del Paraguay;* Burton, *Letters from the Battle-Fields of Paraguay*, 325, 362.

61. Alberdi, *Bases y puntos de partida para la organización política de la república Argentina*.

62. Alberdi's works on the Paraguayan War are "Las disensiones de las repu-blicas del Plata y las maquinaciones del Brasil" (The Rio de La Plata Republics and Brazilian Machinations; March 1865); "Los intereses Argentinos en la guerra del Paraguay con el Brasil" (Argentinean Interests in the War between Paraguay and Brazil; July 1865); "Crisis permanente en las republicas del Plata" (Permanent Crisis of the Rio de La Plata Republics; February 1866); "Texto y comentario del Tratado Secreto de la Triple Alianza contra el Paraguay" (Text of and Comments on the Secret Treaty of the Triple Alliance against Paraguay; May 1866). In 1869, these articles were edited and collected in *La Guerra del Paraguay* (The Paraguayan War). References here are to the 1988 Argentinean edition, published in Buenos Aires by Editorial Hispanoamerica.

63. Braganzas was the lineage of the Brazilian royal family, a dynasty with Portuguese, French, and Austrian antecedents.

64. This geographically deterministic approach was strong even among American newspapers. The *New York Herald,* the major interpreter of the war in the United States, also sympathized with the Paraguayan cause.

65. For a general account of the relationship between racism and geographical determinism, see Drescher, "The Ending of the Slave Trade and the Evolution of European Scientific Racism," 275–311.

66. During the war, the Paraguayan government published small brochures in Europe. One of them, *La politique du Brésil ou la fermeture des fleuves* (The Politics of Brazil and the Closure of Rivers) published in Paris in 1867, defended the hypothesis that Brazil made war with the aim of closing all South American rivers. This anti-blockade position was clearly in accordance with the Paraguayan struggle against the river blockade, a major aspect of the war.

67. *Cabichui,* Paso Pucu/Paraguay, Jan. 23, 1868, 2.

68. Benjamin Constant to Cláudio Luís da Costa, April 11, 1867, in Teixeira Mendes, *Benjamin Constant,* 140. See also Izecksohn, *O cerne da discórdia,* 140; Lemos, *Cartas da Guerra do Paraguai,* 155.

69. Notwithstanding the persistent outbreak of provincial revolts, the tide turned in the direction of pro-center forces, resulting in complete Unitarian hegemony in most provinces. Yet, total hegemony was established in the 1880s. See Moreno, "Incorporación de la Argentina al mercado mundial (1880–1930)," 215–33.

70. This subject was extensively treated in the private correspondence of the Marquis of Caxias with the Minister of War. See ANRJ, Codices 932 and 934, Correspondences of the High Command with Diverse Authorities.

71. Argentina remained a nominal partner in the Triple Alliance after 1867. According to some accounts, this situation prevailed because of secret threats from Brazil that any move toward a separate peace would be treated as a casus belli. See Cardozo, "Paraguay Independiente," 173–264.

72. João da Costa Paranaguá to Homem de Mello, Feb. 7, 1867. AHRS, Códices B1070—Avisos do Ministério da Guerra.

73. Carvalho, *Teatro de sombras,* 107–38; Martins, *A velha arte de governar,* 255–328.

74. Other questions, not directly linked to the war, addressed problems resulting from the war. Such was the case with emancipation, discussed in two crucial meetings during the month of April 1867, as well as the country's financial situation and the need to create new taxes, likewise discussed in April 1867.

75. *Atas,* 6:81.

76. Councilors Viscount of Abaeté, Pimenta Bueno, Sousa Franco, Viscount of Sapucí, and Nabuco de Araújo favored it, while Councilors Viscount of Jequitinhonha, Viscount of Itaboraí, Marquis of Olinda, Paranhos, and Torres Homes voted against it.

77. All those sectors referred to state-related activities.

78. The public farms were located in Santa Cruz, a distant district of Rio de Janeiro. For a complete report on the situation of these farms during the 1860s, see ANRJ, RMF, 1866, especially Map 116. On the slaves of the nation, see Mamigonian, "Conflicts over the Meanings of Freedom," 235–64.

79. In this particular sense, Brazilian contrabands resembled Confederate slaves received into Union fortifications during the Civil War, although similarities end here.

80. AHEX requerimentos n. 650/1863. It is impossible to know whether Antônio was freed or not, but the officer's remarks attest that his information was true, emphasizing his good behavior while serving in the army. One year later, military officers were still adjudicating his request.

81. According to a Confederate observer, slaves from the Santa Cruz farm enjoyed better living conditions. They received daily payments and education. Their children had a band that could play the anthems of the United States, England, and France. See John Codman, *Ten Months in Brazil* (Boston: R. Grant and Son, 1867), quoted in Conrad, *The Destruction of Brazilian Slavery, 1850–1888*, 73.

82. *Atas*, 6:84. There is great disagreement on the treatment of African-born slaves. According to Agostinho Marques Perdigão Malheiro, they were treated worse than Creole slaves. See Perdigão Malheiro, *A escravidão no Brasil: ensaio histórico-jurídico-social*, 2 vols. (São Paulo: Edições Cultura, [1866–67] 1944), 2:70–72. Quoted in Conrad, *The Destruction of Brazilian Slavery, 1850–1888*, 68.

83. *Atas*, 6:72–73.

84. Reports concerning the ironworks and farms of Ypanema in São Paulo show a population of 49 men and 26 women of all ages.

85. ANRJ, RMF, 1866, Annexes, table 108. The emperor also owned a number of slaves (slaves from the Imperial House) employed in domestic tasks. These servants were the first to be freed. It is impossible to discover the number of women freed as a consequence of the Imperial decision.

86. Estimates made by Councilor Viscount of Abaeté, *Atas*, 6:72.

87. The Catholic Church, as the Crown's official religion, was also committed to the conversion of non-Catholic groups. Historically, this had worked as a functional defense of slavery. In this ambivalent situation, its main intellectual goal was the reconciliation of Christian morals with the interests of the Imperial state.

88. *Atas*, 6:89.

89. See Nabuco, *The Abolitionism*, 132. Joaquim Nabuco was the son of one of the Imperial councilors, Senator Nabuco de Araújo.

90. According to Conrad, in 1862 it was estimated that if all proprietors suddenly needed to prove legal ownership of their servants, three-fourths of all Brazilian slaves would be considered free. *The Destruction of Brazilian Slavery, 1850–1888*, 55.

91. For an appreciation of the meaning of slavery in Brazil as a cross-class institution, see Schwartz, *Sugar Plantations in the Formation of Brazilian Society*, 439–67. Analysis of inventories and testaments shows that even the poor and freed sectors occasionally possessed slaves. The expression "Seeing like a State" refers to the

title of James C. Scott's book: *Seeing Like a State: How Certain Schemes to Improve the Human Condition Have Failed.*

92. The Viscount of Abaeté, a councilor deeply committed to the use and generalization of statistics, defended that position.

93. *Atas,* 6:81–85.

94. In his book *O Negro no Brasil,* the journalist Julio José Chiavenatto erroneously interpreted this perspective as the final result of the recruitment process. The enlistment of the Brazilian slaves was viewed as a sort of "Final Solution" for the racial plurality prevailing in the empire.

95. *Atas,* 6:73–75.

96. For extensive discussions concerning slavery and recruitment in the South American republics, see Lasso, "Race War and Nation in Caribbean Gran Colombia, Cartagena, 1810–1832," 336–61, and Sales de Bohigas, *Sobre esclavos, reclutas y mercaderes de quintos,* 59–135. On the Afro-Argentinean population, see Andrews, *The Afro-Argentines of Buenos Aires, 1800–1900.* The mobilization for the war against Paraguay is discussed on 113–37.

97. Burton, *Letters from the Battle-Fields of Paraguay,* 122. For a recent approach to the relation between slavery and military service in Spanish America, see Mallo and Telesca, "Negros de la Patria."

98. For a detailed account of Afro-Paraguayan communities, see Cooney, "Abolition in the Republic of Paraguay," 149–66; Saeger, "Survival and Abolition," 59–85.

99. This position was very ambiguous. For practical purposes, it would never be possible to split one perspective from the other. In addition, there was no news of racially oriented rebellions in the mass of soldiers serving at the front.

100. Anonymous to Marquis de Paranaguá, Minister of War, 20 November 1866. ANRJ, SPE, Codice 572, doc. 6, fl. 19.

101. According to a document released in April 1867, six of the Carmelite's slaves were working on farms rented to private individuals. See AHMI, DPP—96—I—25.4867.

102. The final distribution of Carmelite slaves freed by the province was: Para (17), Court (14), São Paulo (14). Of these 6 were rented to private owners. See AHMI, DPP-96—25.04.867.

103. Frier Fausto de Monte Carmelo to Marquis de Paranaguá, AHMI, DPP—96—I—25.04.1867—Mon.c.

104. According to the Report of the Ministry of War from 1872, the total number of slaves coming from the convents and monasteries amounted to just 95 individuals, or 2.4 percent of the total number of troops listed in that Report. See "Mappa da Força que cada uma das províncias do Império concorreu para a guerra do Paraguay. . . . ," ANRJ, RMW, 1872.

105. Joaquim José de Souza Breves to Esperidião Eloy de Barros Pimentel, Feb. 2, 1867. ANRJ, IG1 146, cx. 582, fl. 663.

106. José Tavares Bastos to João Lustosa da Cunha Paranaguá, March 2, 1867. ANRJ/SPE/IG-1 159 cx. 587, maço 1867, fl. 820.

107. ANRJ/SPE/IG1-40 (CE), no. 20, Diogo Velho Cavalcante de Albuquerque to Barão de Muritiba, Fortaleza, Jan. 23, 1869.

108. Recent research has emphasized the lack of uniformity in prices of slaves freed in order to enlist. Souza, *Escravidão ou morte*, 72, has in the Court (Rio de Janeiro City) an average 1:985$000 (US$913.00). Graden, "From Slavery to Freedom in Bahia, Brazil, 1791–1900," 172, has the median price in Bahia as 1:300$000 (US$600.00), and concludes that slave owners were paid top prices. Kraay, "Slavery, Citizenship, and Mobilization in Brazil's Mobilization for the Paraguayan War," 240, has the following average prices: Maranhão 1: 272$542 (US$585.00); Pará: 1:133$333 (US$604.00); Pernambuco: 1:382$979 (US$610.00). Prices in Rio de Janeiro and Bahia oscillated depending on the period. According to Moreira, *Faces da liberdade, máscaras do cativeiro*, 65, for the city of Porto Alegre (Rio Grande do Sul's capital), prices varied between 800$000 (US$368.00) and 1:300$000 (US$598.00). Finally, Salles, *Guerra do Paraguai: escravidão e cidadaia na formação do exército*, 68, suggests that the cost of slaves in 1870 differed from 2:000$000 to 3:000$000 (or from US$920 to US$1,380).

109. Pla, *Hermano Negro*, 159–72.

110. Parallels between the Cuban and Brazilian abolition processes are many, including the slow path of each nation. On the process of abolition in Cuba, see Scott, *Slave Emancipation in Cuba*, and Bergad, *The Comparative Histories of Slavery in Brazil, Cuba, and the United States*, 273–90.

111. Quoted in Lyra, *História do Império de Dom Pedro II*, 235–36.

112. *Anais do Parlamento Brasileiro*, 96. The "Speeches of the Throne" were traditional events of Brazilian Imperial politics. Through his "Speeches," the emperor announced major legislation as well as state goals for the forthcoming year.

113. Nabuco, *The Abolitionism*, 49.

114. Analyzing the positions of different groups of planters during the "Agrarian Council" debates, held in Rio de Janeiro in 1878, Peter L. Eisenberg concluded that Brazilian farmers, as with any other class in history, faced internal divisions. However, these divisions did not conform to geographical divisions. According to Eisenberg, there were no strong differences among Brazilian regional power groups concerning the status of labor. "A Mentalidade dos Fazendeiros no Congresso Agrícola de 1878," 167–94.

115. Carvalho, "Escravidão e razão nacional," 299–302.

116. Thomas Dew is commonly credited with writing the first systematic pro-slavery tract in 1832. For a broad view, see Elliott, *Cotton Is King*, and *Pro-slavery Arguments*. George Fitzhugh was the best known defender of slavery in the antebellum South, and his writings went far beyond his native Virginia. Some of his comparisons between slave and wage work are still very useful for research concerning working conditions and productivity in slave as well as early industrial societies. His most important works are *Cannibals All! or Slaves Without Masters;* and *Sociology for the South, or The Failure of Free Society*. Analyses of Fitzhugh's works include Wish, *George Fitzhugh, Propagandist of the Old South;* Genovese, *The World the Slaveholders Made*, especially part 2 "The Logical Outcome of the

Slaveholders' Philosophy," 118–246; and Faust, *The Ideology of Slavery*, 168–205, 272–300.

117. J Alencar, "Novas Cartas de Erasmo," 7. For a summary appreciation of Alencar's ideas concerning slavery, see the following texts: "Carta ao Visconde de Itaboraí sobre a crise financeira de 1866" in *Obras completas*, 4:113–23; *A propriedade*; and especially the introduction by Santos under the title, "A teoria da democracia proporcional de José de Alencar," 9–50.

## Conclusion

1. I define "national unity" as the preservation of territorial integrity, that is, the consolidation and maintenance of administrative control of larger portions of an extensive territory by a political center. It includes the creation of a differentiated and autonomous set of institutions that claim sovereignty and a monopoly over the tasks of coercion and extraction. This control was historically achieved through the diffusion and acceptance of the central authority by different groups of inhabitants in specific regions. It involved enhancing national symbols, rituals, and costumes. Thus was forged a larger conception of nationality based on territorial integration that grew concurrently with the swelling pride of being part of a larger structure. Two good accounts on this subject are Hobsbawm and Ranger, *The Invention of Tradition*, and Hobsbawm, *Nations and Nationalism since 1780*.

2. In Brazil a new recruitment law passed in 1874 by Minister Oliveira Junqueira abolished corporal punishment and made military service compulsory. A lottery would select those men for service, thus minimizing the problems of conscription. The law had no practical effect. In practice, Brazilian recruitment was modified only in 1916, during the First World War. Schulz, *O exército na política* 76–93; Dudley, "Reform and Radicalism in the Brazilian Army, 1870–1889," 126–80. For the law of 1916, see McCann, "The Nation in Arms," 211–43.

3. *O cearence*, Fortaleza CE, Feb. 7, 1865, quoted in Souza, "Impactos da Guerra do Paraguai na Província do Ceará (1865–1870)," 31.

4. The Confederate vice president Alexander Stephens quoted in Degler, "The American Civil War and the German Wars of Unification," 63.

5. Abraham Lincoln, "Annual Message to Congress, Dec. 1, 1862," in Fehrenbacher, *Abraham Lincoln*, 202–3.

6. *O cearence*, Fortaleza CE, March 8, 1869, 3, quoted in Souza, "Impactos da Guerra do Paraguai na Província do Ceará (1865–1870)," 15.

7. Of course, this particular interpretation of European liberalism, associated with property rights and social and racial exclusion, did not go so far as to defend individual rights. Planters behaved as a collective body that saw the state as a defender of national interests, that is, their interests in keeping their slaves.

8. These elements were described in chapter 1.

9. Of course, there was Paraguay. The reconstruction of Paraguay was analyzed in Warren, *Paraguay and the Triple Alliance*. Unfortunately, it is not possible to follow developments in the Paraguayan Reconstruction in this work.

10. On Brazilian railroads, see Summerhill "Railroads in Imperial Brazil, 1854–1889," 383–405.

11. Codman, *Ten Months in Brazil*, 210.

12. Graham, *Patronage and Politics in Brazil*, 195–238.

13. Royster, *The Destructive War*, 39.

14. Tilly, "States and Nationalism in Europe, 1492–1992," 131–46.

15. Scott, *Seeing Like a State*," 53–84.

16. Centeno, *Blood and Debt*, 20–26.

# Bibliography

## Archives

Arquivo Histórico do Exército, Rio de Janeiro
Arquivo Histórico do Museu Imperial, Petrópolis
Arquivo Histórico do Rio Grande do Sul, Porto Alegre
Arquivo Nacional, Rio de Janeiro
Arquivo Público do Estado do Rio de Janeiro, Rio de Janeiro
Arquivo Público do Estado do Rio Grande do Sul, Porto Alegre
Gilder Lehrman Institute of American History, New York City
Instituto Histórico e Geográfico Brasileiro, Rio de Janeiro
Museu Casa de Benjamin Constant, Rio de Janeiro
Museu Histórico Nacional, Rio de Janeiro

## Newspapers

*A sentinela do sul,* 1865–67, Porto Algre, Brazil
*A semana ilustrada,* 1866–71, Rio de Janeiro, Brazil
*Cabichui,* 1867–68 Passo Pucú, Paraguay;
*Charleston Mercury,* 1860–61, South Carolina
*Congressional Globe,* Washington, D.C.
*Douglass' Monthly,* 1861–62, Rochester, N.Y.
*El centinela,* 1867–68, Asunción, Paraguay
*Frank Leslie's Illustrated Newspaper,* 1861–65, New York City
*Madison Wisconsin Daily State Journal,* 1861
*New York Times,* 1861–65
*O cabrião,* 1866–68, São Paulo, Brazil
*Vida fluminense,* 1866, Rio de Janeiro, Brazil

## Published Sources

Abente, Diego. "The War of The Triple Alliance: Three Explanatory Models." *Latin American Research Review* 22, no. 2 (1987): 47–67.

Adams, Virginia M., ed. *On the Altar of Freedom: A Black Soldier's War Letters from the Front; Corporal James Henry Gooding.* Amherst: University of Massachusetts Press, 1991.

Agulhon, Maurice. "La 'statuomanie' et la Histoire." *Ethnologie Française* 8 (1978): 145–72.

Alberdi, Juan Bautista. *Bases y puntos de partida para la organización política de la república Argentina.* Buenos Aires: Editorial Plus Ultra, 1990.

———. *La Guerra del Paraguay.* Buenos Aires: Editorial Hispanoamerica, 1988.

Alencar, José de. *Ao imperador: novas cartas de Erasmo.* Rio de Janeiro: Tipografia de Pinheiro e Co., 1867.

———. *A propriedade.* Rio de Janeiro, Garnier, 1883.

———. "Ao Visconde de Itaboraí: Carta de Erasmo sobre a crise financeira de 1866," in José de Alencar. *Obra completa,* vol. 4. Rio de Janeiro: Editora Aguilar Ltda, 1960, 1113–23.

Alencastro. "Memórias da Balaiada: Introdução ao Relato de Gonçalves de Magalhães." *Novos estudos CEBRAP* 23 (March 1989): 7–13.

Allub, Leopoldo. "Estado y sociedad civil: patrón de emergencia y desarrollo del Estado Argentino (1810–1930)," in *Estado nacional y sociedad en el Pensamiento Nacional: antologia conceptual para el analysis comparado,* edited by Waldo Ansaldi and Jose Luis Moreno, 109–57. Buenos Aires: Cantaro, 1996.

Almada, Vilma Paraíso Ferreira. *Escravismo e transição. O Espírito Santo (1850–1888).* Rio de Janeiro: Graal, 1984.

*Anais do Parlamento Brasileiro* (Records of the Brazilian Parlament), Câmara dos Senhores Deputados, 10. ano da 3a. Legislatura, Sessão de 1867, Tomo 1. Rio de Janeiro: Typografia Imperial e Constitucional de J. Villeneuve, 1867.

Anderson, Fred. *A People's Army: Massachusetts Soldiers and Society in the Seven Years' War.* Chapel Hill: University of North Carolina Press for the Institute of Early American History and Culture, Williamsburg, Va., 1984.

Andrew, John A. *Address of His Excellency John A. Andrew to the two branches of the Legislature of Massachusetts. January 9, 1863.* Boston: Wright & Potter, State Printers, Jan. 8, 1864.

Andrews, George Reid. *The Afro-Argentines of Buenos Aires, 1800–1900.* Madison: University of Wisconsin Press, 1980.

Andrews, J. Cutler. *The North Reports the Civil War.* Pittsburgh: University of Pittsburgh Press, 1955.

Ansaldi, Waldo, and Jose Luis Moreno. *Estado nacional y sociedad en el pensamiento nacional: antologia conceptual para el analysis comparado.* Buenos Aires: Cantaro, 1996.

Ashworth, John. *Slavery, Capitalism, and Politics in the Antebellum Republic.* 2 vols. New York: Cambridge University Press, 1995–2008.

Atas do Conselho de Estado Pleno, direção geral, organização e introdução de José Honório Rodrigues. 14 vols. Brasília: Centro Gráfico do Senado Federal, 1973–78.

Azevedo. Celia Maria M. Onda negra, medo branco: O negro no imaginário das elites. Século XIX. Rio de Janeiro: Paz e Terra, 1995.

Baez, Adolfo J. Yatayty-Corá: una conferencia histórica. Buenos Aires: Imprenta y Papelería Juan Perroti, 1929.

Baldwin, Lawrence M., and Michel Grimaud. "How New Naming Systems Emerge: The Prototypical Case of Columbus and Washington." Names: Journal of the American Name Society 40, no. 3 (Sept. 1992): 153–66.

Barman, Roderick J. Brazil: The Forging of a Nation, 1798–1852. Stanford: Stanford University Press, 1988.

———. Citizen Emperor: Pedro II and the Making of Brazil, 1825–1891. Stanford: Stanford University Press, 1999.

Barnes, Thurlow Weed. Memoir of Thurlow Weed by His Grandson Thurlow Weed Barnes. Boston: Houghton, Mifflin and Company, 1884.

Barton, Michael. Goodmen: The Character of Civil War Soldiers. State College: Pennsylvania State University Press, 1981.

Basset, George W. A Warning for the Crises Or Popular Errors Involved in the Present War. An Address Delivered at the Court House at Ottawa, Illinois on February 2nd, 1863. Ottawa, Ill.: I. H. Legget, 1863.

Bearman, Peter S. "Desertion as Localism: Army Unit Solidarity and Group Norms in the U.S. Civil War." Social Forces 70, no. 2 (Dec. 1991): 321–41.

Beattie, Peter M. "Conscription versus Penal Servitude: Army Reform's Influence on the Brazilian State's Management of Social Control, 1870–1930." Journal of Social History 32, no. 4 (Summer 1999): 847–73.

———. The Tribute of Blood: Army, Honor, Race, and Nation in Brazil, 1864–1945. Durham, N.C.: Duke University Press, 2001.

Bellows, Henry W. Historical Sketch of the Union League Club of New York. Its Origin, Organization and Work, 1863–1879. New York: Press of G. P. Putnam's sons, 1879.

Belz, Herman. Emancipation and Equal Rights: Politics and Constitutionalism in the Civil War Era. New York: W. W. Norton, 1978.

———. "Law, Politics, and Race in the Struggle for Equal Pay during the Civil War." Civil War History 22 (1976): 197–222.

Bender, Thomas. A Nation among Nations: America´s Place in World History. New York: Hill and Wang, 2006.

Bensel, Richard F. Yankee Leviathan: The Origins of Central State Authority in America, 1859–1877. New York: Cambridge University Press, 1990.

Bergad, Laird W. The Comparative Histories of Slavery in Brazil, Cuba, and the United States. New York: Cambridge University Press, 2007.

Berlin, Ira. Slaves Without Masters: The Free Negro in the Antebellum South. New York: Pantheon Books, 1974.

Berlin, Ira, ed. The Black Military Experience. Freedom, A Documentary History of Emancipation, 1861–1867, 2nd ser. New York: Cambridge University Press, 1982.

Berlin, Ira, ed. *The Destruction of Slavery: Freedom, A Documentary History of Emancipation, 1861–1867*, 1st ser., vol. 1. New York: Cambridge University Press, 1985.

Berlin, Ira, et al. *Slaves No More: Three Essays on Emancipation and the Civil War*. New York: Cambridge University Press, 1992.

Berlinger, Richard E., Herman Hattaway, Archer Jones, and William N. Still Jr. *Why the South Lost the Civil War*. Athens: University of Georgia Press, 1986.

Bernstein, Iver. *The New York City Draft Riots: Their Significance for American Society and Politics in the Age of the Civil War*. New York: Oxford University Press, 1990.

Berrance de Castro, Jeanne. "O Negro na Guarda Nacional." *Anais do Museu Paulista* 23 (1969): 149–72.

Berry, Mary Frances. *Military Necessity and Civil Rights Policy: Black Citizenship and the Constitution, 1861–1868*. Port Washington, N.Y.: Kennikat Press, 1977.

Bezerra Neto, José Maia. "Nos bastidores da guerra: fugas escravas e fugitivos na época da Guerra do Paraguai (Grão-Pará: 1864–1870)." *História & Perspectivas* 20/21 (Uberlândia, Minas Gerais; Jan.–Dec. 1999): 85–115.

Black, Andrew K. "In the Service of the United States: Comparative Mortality among African-American and White Troops in the Union Army." *Journal of Negro History* 79, no.4 (Fall 1994): 317–33.

Blassingame, John W. "The Recruitment of Colored Troops in Kentucky, Maryland, and Missouri." *Historian* 29 (1967): 533–45.

———, ed. *Slave Testimony: Two Centuries of Letters, Speeches, Interviews, and Autobiographies*. Baton Rouge: Louisiana State University Press, 1977.

Blinn Reber, Vera. "Commerce and Industry in Nineteenth-Century Paraguay." *The Americas* 42, no. 1 (1985): 29–53.

———. "The Demographics of Paraguay: A Reinterpretation of the Great War, 1864–70." *Hispanic American Historical Review* 68, no. 2 (1988): 283–319.

Bogue, Allan G. *The Congressman's Civil War*. New York: Cambridge University Press, 1989.

———. *The Earnest Men: Republicans of the Civil War Senate*. Ithaca: Cornell University Press, 1981.

Bolster, Jeffrey W., and Hilary Anderson. *Soldiers, Sailors, Slaves, and Ships. The Civil War Photographs of Henry P. Moore*. Concord: New Hampshire Historical Society, 1999.

Boxer, C. R. *The Golden Age of Brazil, 1865–1750: Growing Pains of a Colonial Society*. Berkeley: University of California Press, in cooperation with the Sociedade de Estudos Históricos Dom Pedro Segundo, Rio de Janeiro, 1962.

———. *The Portuguese Seaborne Empire, 1415–1825*. New York: Alfred A. Knopf, 1969.

Browning, Orville Hickman. *The Diary of Orville Hickman Browning*, vol. 1: *1850–1864*, edited by Theodore Calvin Pease and J. G. Randall. Springfield: Trustees of the Illinois State Historical Library, 1925.

Bryant, James Kenneth, II. "A Model Regiment: The 36th United States Colored Infantry in the Civil War." MA thesis, University of Vermont and State Agricultural College, 1996.

Buckley, Roger Norman. *Slaves in Red Coats: The British West India Regiments, 1795–1815.* New Haven, Conn.: Yale University Press, 1979.

Burt, Silas Wright. *My Memoirs of the Military History of the State of New York during the War for the Union, 1861–1865.* Albany: J. B. Lyon Company, State Printers, 1902.

Burton, Richard Francis. *Letters from the Battle-Fields of Paraguay.* London: Tinsley Brothers, 1870.

Cabral de Mello, Evaldo. *Olinda restaurada: guerra e açúcar no nordeste, 1630–1654.* São Paulo: Editora 34, 2007.

———. *Rubro Veio: o imaginário da restauração Pernambucana.* Rio de Janeiro: Topbooks, 1997.

Capdevila, Luc. *Una guerra totale: Paraguay, 1864–1870.* Buenos Aires: Sb, 2010.

Capistrano de Abreu, João. *Chapters of Brazil's Colonial History, 1500–1800.* Translated by Arthur Brakel. New York: Oxford University Press, 1997.

Cardozo, Efrain. "Paraguay Independiente." In *Historia de America y de los Pueblos Americanos,* vol. 21, edited by Antonio Ballesteros y Beretta, 173–264. Barcelona: Salvat Editores, 1949.

Carneiro da Cunha, Manuela. "Silences of the Law: Customary Law and Positive Law on the Manumission of Slaves in Nineteenth-century Brazil." *History and Anthropology* 1, no. 2 (1985): 427–43.

Carvalho, José Murilo de. "Escravidão e razão nacional." *Revista DADOS* 31, no. 3 (1988): 287–309.

———. *Teatro de sombras: a política imperial.* Rio de Janeiro: Vértice/IUPERJ, 1988.

Castro, Celso. "Entre Caxias e Osório: a criação do culto ao patrono do exército brasileiro." *Estudos Históricos* 14, no. 25 (2000): 103–18.

Centeno, Miguel A. *Blood and Debt: War and the Nation-State in Latin America.* University Park: Pennsylvania State University Press, 2002.

———. "The Centre Did Not Hold: War in Latin America and the Monopolization of Violence," in *Studies in the Formation of the Nation State in Latin America,* edited by James Dunkerley, 54–76. London: Institute of Latin American Studies, 2002.

———. "Symbols of State Nationalism in Latin America." *European Review of Latin American and Caribbean Studies* No. 66 (June 1999): 74–106.

Cerqueira, Dionísio. *Reminiscências da campanha do Paraguai.* Rio de Janeiro: Bibliex, 1980.

Channing, Steve. *Crisis of Fear: Secession in South Carolina.* New York: Simon and Schuster, 1970.

Cheek, William, and Aimee Lee Cheek. "White Over Black in Union Blue." *Reviews in American History* 18, no. 3 (1990): 104–27.

Chiaramonte, José Carlos. *Ciudades, provincias, estades: orígenes de la nación Argentina (1800–1846).* Buenos Aires: Emecé, 2007.

Chiavenatto, Julio José. *O Negro no Brasil: da senzala à Guerra do Paraguai.* São Paulo: Brasiliense, 1982.

Cimprich, John, and Robert C. Mainfort Jr. "The Fort Pillow Massacre: A Statistical Note." *Journal of American History* 76, no. 3 (Dec. 1989): 830–39.

Codman, John. *Ten Months in Brazil*. Boston: R. Grant and son, 1867.

Conrad, Robert Edgar. *The Destruction of Brazilian Slavery, 1850–1888*. Berkeley: University of California Press, 1972.

Cooney, Jerry W. "Abolition in the Republic of Paraguay: 1840–1870." *Jahrbuch fur Geschichte von Staat Wirtschaft und Gesellschaft* No. 11 (1974):149–66.

———. "Economy and Manpower: Paraguay at War, 1864–69," in *I Die with My Country: Perspectives on the Paraguayan War, 1864–1870*, edited by Hendrik Kraay and Thomas L. Whigham, 23–43. Lincoln: University of Nebraska Press, 2004.

Cooper, Susan. "Records of Civil War African American Troops Inspire Major Archival Project." *The Record* 3, no. 2 (Nov. 1996): 9–11.

Cornish, Dudley Taylor. *The Sable Arm: Negro Troops in the Union Army, 1861–1865*. Lawrence: University Press of Kansas, 1987.

Costa, Dora L., and Matthew E. Kahn. *Heroes and Cowards: The Social Face of War*. Princeton: Princeton University Press, 2008.

Costa, Fernando Dores. "Os problemas do recrutamento militar no final do século XVIII e as questões da construção do estado e da nação." *Análise Social* 20, no. 130 (1995): 121–55.

Costa, Wilma Peres. *A espada de Dâmocles: o exército, a Guerra do Paraguai e a crise do império*. São Paulo: Hucitec/Unicamp, 1996.

Cotta, Francis A. "No rastro dos Dragões: universo militar luso-brasileiro e as políticas de ordem nas Minas setecentistas," PhD diss., Universidade Federal de Minas Gerais.

Crofts, Daniel W. *Reluctant Confederates: Upper South Unionists in the Secession Crisis*. Chapel Hill: University of North Carolina Press, 1989.

Curry, Leonard P. *Blueprint for Modern America: Non-Military Legislation of the First Civil War Congress*. Nashville: Vanderbilt University Press, 1968.

———. "Congressional Democrats, 1861–1863." *Civil War History* 12 (Sept. 1966): 213–19.

Curry, Richard O. "The Union as It Was: A Critique of Recent Interpretations of the 'Copperheads.'" *Civil War History* 13 (March 1967): 25–39.

Davis, David Biron. *The Problem of Slavery in the Age of Revolution, 1770–1823*. Ithaca: Cornell University Press, 1975.

Dean, Warren, *Rio Claro: um sistema brasileiro de grande lavoura*. Rio de Janeiro: Paz e Terra, 1977.

Degler, Carl N. "The American Civil War and the German Wars of Unification: The Problem of Comparison," in *On the Road to Total War: The American Civil War and the German Wars of Unification, 1861–1871*, edited by Stig Förster and Jorg Nagler, 53–74. New York: Cambridge University Press, 1997.

———. *Neither Black nor White: Slavery and Race Relations in Brazil and the United States*. New York: Macmillan, 1971.

De la Fuente, Ariel. *Children of Facundo: Caudillo and Gaucho Insurgency during the Argentine State-Formation Process (La Rioja, 1853–1870)*. Durham: Duke University Press, 2000.

Dew, Charles B. *Apostles of Disunion: Southern Secession Commissioners and the Causes of the Civil War.* Charlottesville: University of Virginia Press, 2002.

Donald, David Herbert, ed. *Gone for a Soldier: The Civil War Memoirs of Private Alfred Bellard; from the Alec Thomas Archives.* Boston: Little, Brown, 1975.

——, ed. *Inside Lincoln's Cabinet: The Civil War Diaries of Salomon P. Chase.* New York: Longmans, Green, 1954.

Doratioto, Francisco. *General Osorio: a espada liberal do império.* São Paulo: Cia. das Letras, 2008.

——. *Maldita Guerra: nova história da Guerra do Paraguai.* São Paulo: Cia. Das Letras, 2002.

Douglass, Frederick. *The Life and Writings of Frederick Douglass,* edited by Philip S. Foner. 4 vols.; New York: International Publishers, 1982.

Doyle, Don H. *Nations Divided: America, Italy, and the Southern Question.* Athens: University of Georgia Press, 2002.

Drescher, Seymour. "Brazilian Abolition in Comparative Perspective," in *The Abolition of Slavery and the Aftermath of Emancipation in Brazil,* edited by Rebecca J. Scott, 23–54. Durham: Duke University Press, 1988.

——. "The Ending of the Slave Trade and the Evolution of European Scientific Racism," in *From Slavery to Freedom: Comparative Studies in the Rise and Fall of Atlantic Slavery,* edited by Seymour Drescher, 275–311. New York: New York University Press, 1999.

Duarte, Paulo de Queirós. *Os voluntários da pátria na Guerra do Paraguai.* Rio de Janeiro: Bibliex, 1981.

Dubois, Laurent. *Avengers of the New World: The Stroy of the Haitian Revolution.* Cambridge, Mass.: Belknap Press of Harvard University Press, 2004.

——. *A Colony of Citizens: Revolution and Slave Emancipation in the French Caribbean, 1787–1804.* Chapel Hill: University of North Carolina Press for the Omohundro Institute of Early American History and Culture, Williamsburg, Va., 2004.

Dudley, William S. "Reform and Radicalism in the Brazilian Army, 1870–1889." PhD diss., Columbia University, 1972.

Duncan, J. MacLeod. *Slavery, Race, and the American Revolution.* New York: Cambridge University Press, 1974.

Duncan, Julian Smith. *Public and Private Operations of Railways in Brazil.* New York: Columbia University Press, 1932.

Duncan, Russel, ed. *Blue-Eyed Child of Fortune: The Civil War Letters of Colonel Robert Gould Shaw.* Athens: University of Georgia Press, 1992.

Durden, Robert F. *The Gray and the Black.* Baton Rouge: Louisiana State University Press, 1972.

Einsenberg, Peter L. "Ficando livre: as alforrias em Campinas no século XIX." *Estudos Econômicos* 17, no. 2 (May–Aug. 1976): 175–226.

——. "A mentalidade dos fazendeiros no congresso agrícola de 1878," in *Modos de produção e realidade brasileira,* edited by José Roberto do Amaral Lapa, 167–94. Petrópolis: Vozes, 1980.

Elliott, E. N., ed. *Cotton Is King, and Pro-slavery Arguments: Comprising the Writings of Hammond, Harper, Christy, Stringfellow, Hodge, Bledsoe, and Cartwright, on This Important Subject.* New York: Johnson Reprint Corp., 1968.

Emilio, Luis F. *A Brave Black Regiment: The History of the Fifty-fourth Regiment of Massachusetts Volunteer Infantry, 1863–1865.* New York: Da Capo Press, 1995.

Evans, Ira C. *Revised Register of the Soldiers and Sailors of New Hampshire in the War of the Rebellion, 1861–1866.* Concord, N.H.: Ira C. Evans, 1895.

*Fala Dirigida À Assembléia Legislativa Provincial das Alagoas no Dia 05 de Maio de 1865 pelo Ex. Sr. Desembargador João Baptista Gonçalves Campos Presidente da Província.* Maceió: Typografia Progressista, 1865. (Report from the President of Alagoas.)

Farinatti, Luis Augusto. "Cabedais militares: os recursos sociais dos potentados da fronteira meridional (1801–1845)," in *Gente de guerra e fronteira: estudos de história militar do Rio Grande do Sul*, edited by Paulo Possamai, 81–100. Pelotas: Editora da Universidade de Pelotas, 2010.

Faust, Drew Gilpin. *The Creation of Confederate Nationalism: Ideology and Identity in the Civil War South.* Baton Rouge: Louisiana State University Press, 1988.

Faust, Drew Gilpin, ed. *The Ideology of Slavery: Proslavery Thought in the Antebellum South, 1830–1860.* Baton Rouge: Louisiana State University Press, 1981.

Fehrenbacher, Don E., ed. *Abraham Lincoln: A Documentary Portrait through His Speeches and Writings.* Stanford: Stanford University Press, 1964.

Ferraro, William Michael. "Lives of Quiet Desperation: Community and Polity in New England over Four Centuries; The Cases of Portsmouth and Foster, Rhode Island." PhD diss., Brown University, 1991.

Fitzhugh, George. *Cannibals All! or Slaves Without Masters.* Cambridge, Mass.: Belknap Press of Harvard University Press, 1960.

———. *Sociology for the South, or The Failure of Free Society.* New York: B. Franklin, 1965.

Florentino, Manolo, and José Roberto Góes. *A paz nas Senzalas: famílias escravas e tráfico atlântico, Rio de Janeiro, c.1770–c.1850.* Rio de Janeiro: Civilização Brasileira, 1997.

Flory, Thomas. *Judge and Jury in Imperial Brazil, 1808–1871: Social Control and Political Stability in the New State.* Austin: University of Texas Press, 1981.

Foner, Eric. "The Causes of the American Civil War: Recent Interpretations and New Directions." *Civil War History* 20 (Sept. 1974): 215–28.

———. *Free Soil, Free Labor, Free Men: The Ideology of the Republican Party before the Civil War.* New York: Oxford University Press, 1979.

———. *Politics and Ideology in the Age of the Civil War.* New York: Oxford University Press, 1980.

———. *Reconstruction: America's Unfinished Revolution, 1863–1877.* New York: Harper & Row, 1988.

Foner, Philip, and Ronald Lewis, eds. *The Black Worker: From Colonial Times to 1869; A Documentary History.* Philadelphia: Temple University Press, 1969.

Forest, Alan. *Soldiers of the French Revolution*. Durham, N.C.: Duke University Press, 1990.

Förster, Stig, and Jorg Nagler, eds. *On the Road to Total War: The American Civil War and the German Wars of Unification, 1861–1871*. Washington, D.C.: German Historical Institute; New York: Cambridge University Press, 1997.

Fragoso, João. "A nobreza vive em bandos: a economia política das melhores famílias da terra do Rio de Janeiro, século XVI, algumas notas de pesquisa." *Tempo* 8, no. 15 (July–Dec. 2003): 11–35.

Franklin, John Hope. *The Emancipation Proclamation*. Garden City, N.Y.: Doubleday, 1963.

Fredrickson, George M. *The Black Image in the White Mind*. Hanover, N.H.: Wesleyan University Press, 1987.

———. *The Inner Civil War: Northern Intellectuals and the Crisis of the Union*. New York: Harper & Row, 1965.

———. "A Man But Not a Brother: Abraham Lincoln and Racial Equality." *Journal of Southern History* 41, no 1 (1975): 30–58.

Freehling, William W. *The South vs. the South: How Anti-Confederate Southerners Shaped the Course of the Civil War*. New York: Oxford University Press, 2001.

Freehling, William W., and Craig M. Simpson. *Secession Debated: Georgia's Showdown in 1860*. New York: Oxford University Press, 1992.

Freidel, Frank, ed. *Union Pamphlets of the Civil War, 1861–1865*. Cambridge, Mass.: Belknap Press of Harvard University Press, 1967.

Frey, Sylvia R. *Water from the Rock: Black Resistance in a Revolutionary Age*. Princeton: Princeton University Press, 1991.

Friedrich, Otto. "We Will Not Do Duty Any Longer for Seven Dollars per Month." *American Heritage* 39, no. 1 (Feb. 1988): 64–73.

Frost, Dan R. "Blacks and Emancipation: The Decisive Factors That Resulted in Union Victory in the Civil War," MA thesis, Fullerton State University, 1987.

Gallagher, Gary W. *The Confederate War: How Popular Will, Nationalism, and Military Strategy Could Not Stave Off Defeat*. Cambridge, Mass.: Harvard University Press, 1997.

Geary, James W. "Blacks in the American Military: A Review Essay." *Ethnic Forum* 11, no. 1 (1991): 59–68.

———. "The Enrollment Act in the Thirty-seventh Congress." *Historian* 46, no. 4 (Aug. 1984): 562–82.

———. *We Need Men: The Union Draft in the Civil War*. Dekalb: Northern Illinois University Press, 1991.

Geggus, David Patrick. "Slavery, War, and Revolution in the Greater Caribbean, 1789–1815," in *A Turbulent Time: The French Revolution and the Greater Caribbean*, edited by David Barry Gaspar and David Patric Geggus, 1–50 Bloomington: Indiana University Press, 1997.

Genovese, Eugene D. *Roll, Jordan, Roll: The World the Slaves Made*. New York: Pantheon, 1974.

———. *The World the Slaveholders Made: Two Essays in Interpretation*. Middletown, Conn.: Wesleyan University Press, 1969.

Gerteis, Louis. *From Contraband to Freedmen: Federal Policy toward Southern Blacks, 1861–1865*. Westport, Conn.: Greenwood Press, 1969.

Glatthaar, Joseph T. *Forged in Battle: The Civil War Alliance of Black Soldiers and White Officers*. New York: Meridian, 1990.

———. *Partners in Command: The Relationships between Leaders in the Civil War*. New York: Free Press, 1994.

Góes e Vasconcellos, Zacarias de. *Da natureza e limites do poder moderador*. Rio de Janeiro: Laemmert, 1862.

Goldman, Noemi, and Salvatore Ricardo, eds. *Caudilhismos rioplatenses: nuevas miradas a un viejo problema*. Buenos Aires: Eudeba, 2005.

Graden, Dale T. "From Slavery to Freedom in Bahia, Brazil, 1791–1900." PhD diss., University of Connecticut, 1991.

Graebner, Norman A., ed. *The Enduring Lincoln: Sesquicentennial Lectures at the University of Illinois*. Urbana: University of Illinois Press, 1959.

Graham, Richard. *Patronage and Politics in Brazil*. Stanford: Stanford University Press, 1990.

Grimsley, Mark. "Conciliation and Its Failure, 1861–1862." *Civil War History* 39, no. 4 (Dec. 1993): 317–35.

Gross, Robert. *The Minutemen and Their World*. New York: Hill and Wang, 1976.

Haas, Ernest. "The Balance of Power: Prescription, Concept, and Propaganda," in *International Politics and Foreign Policies: A Reader in Research and Theory*, edited by James N. Rosenau, 318–29. New York: Free Press, 1961.

Hahn, Steven. *The Roots of Southern Populism: Yeoman Farmers and the Transformation of the Georgia Upcountry, 1850–1890*. New York: Oxford University Press, 1983.

Hale, Laura Virginia. *Four Valiant Years in the Lower Shenandoah Valley, 1861–1865*. Strasburg, Va.: Shenandoah Publishing House, 1975.

Hallock, Judith Lee. "The Role of Community in Civil War Desertion." *Civil War History* 29, no. 29 (1983): 123–34.

Hancock, Harold Bell. *Delaware during the Civil War: A Political History*. Wilmington: Historical Society of Delaware, 1961.

Harris, J. William. *Plain Folk and Gentry in a Slave Society: White Liberty and Black Slavery in Augusta's Hinterlands*. Middletown, Conn.: Wesleyan University Press, 1985.

Hattaway, Herman, and Archer Jones. *How the North Won: A Military History of the Civil War*. Urbana: University of Illinois Press, 1991.

Hay, John. *Lincoln and the Civil War in the Diaries and Letters of John Hay: Selected and with an Introduction by Tyler Dennet*. New York: Dodd, Mead & Company, 1939.

Herrera, Ricardo Adolfo. "Guarantors of Liberty and Republic: The American Citizen Soldier and the Military Ethos of Republicanism, 1775–1861," PhD diss., Marquette University, 1998.

Hess, Earl J. *Liberty, Virtue, and Progress: Northerners and Their War for the Union.* New York: New York University Press, 1988.

Hesseltine, William Best. *Lincoln and the War Governors.* Gloucester, Mass.: Peter Smith, 1972.

Hicken, Victor. "The Record of Illinois' Negro Soldiers in the Civil War." *Journal of the Illinois State Historical Society* 56, no. 3 (Autumn 1963): 529–51.

Higginson, Thomas Wentworth. *Army Life in a Black Regiment.* Boston: Beacon Press, 1970.

Hobsbawm, E. J. *Nations and Nationalism since 1780: Program, Myth, Reality.* New York: Cambridge University Press, 1990.

———. *Primitive Rebels: Studies in Archaic Forms of Social Movement in the 19th and 20th Centuries.* New York: Praeger, 1963.

Hobsbawm, E. J., and Terence Ranger. *The Invention of Tradition.* New York: Cambridge University Press, 1992.

Holloway, Thomas H. *Policing Rio de Janeiro: Repression and Resistance in a 19th-Century City.* Stanford: Stanford University Press, 1993.

Howard, Victor "The Civil War in Kentucky: The Slave Claims His Freedom." *Journal of Negro History* 67 (1982): 245–56.

Hubbel, John T. "Abraham Lincoln and the Recruitment of Black Soldiers." *Papers of the Abraham Lincoln Association* 2 (1980): 6–21.

Huch, Ronald K. "Fort Pillow Massacre: The Aftermath of Paducah." *Journal of the Illinois State Historical Society* 66, no.1 (1973): 62–70.

*Instituto Brasileiro de Geografia e Estatísticas, Estatísticas históricas do Brasil;* 2nd ed. Rio de Janeiro: IBGE, 1990.

Izecksohn, Vitor. *O cerne da discórdia: a Guerra do Paraguai e o núcleo profissional do exército.* Rio de Janeiro: E-Papers, 2002.

———. "Recrutamento militar no Rio de Janeiro durante a Guerra do Paraguai," in *Nova história militar brasileira,* edited by Celo Castro, Vitor Izecksohn, and Hendrik Kraay, 179–208. Rio de Janeiro: FGV/Bom Texto, 2004.

Izecksohn, Vitor, and Peter M. Beattie. "The Brazilian Home Front during the War of the Triple Alliance, 1864–1870," in *Daily Lives of Civilians in Wartime Latin America: From the Wars of Independence to the Central American Civil Wars,* edited by Pedro Santoni, 123–46. Westport, Conn: Grenwood Press, 2008.

Jackson, Andrew. *Correspondence of Andrew Jackson,* edited by John Spencer Basset. 6 vols.; Washington, D.C.: Carnegie Institution of Washington, 1926.

Jimerson, Randall. *The Private Civil War: Popular Thought during the Sectional Conflict.* Baton Rouge: Louisiana State University Press, 1988.

Johnson, Michael *Toward a Patriarchal Republic: The Secession of Georgia.* Baton Rouge: Louisiana State University Press, 1977.

Jordan, Ervin L., Jr. *Black Confederates and Afro-Yankees in Civil War Virginia.* Charlottesville: University Press of Virginia, 1995.

Jordan, Winthrop. *Tumult and Silence at Second Creek: An Inquiry into a Civil War Slave onspiracy.* Baton Rouge: Louisiana State University Press, 1993.

————. *White Over Black: American Attitudes toward the Negro, 1550–1812*. Baltimore: Penguin Books, 1969.

Joshi, Manoj K., and Joseph P. Reidy. "To Come Forward and Aid in Putting Down This Unholy Rebellion: The Officers of Louisiana's Free Black Native Guard during the Civil War Era." *Southern Studies* 21, no. 2 (1983): 326–42.

Kagan, Donald. *On the Origin of War and the Preservation of Peace*. New York: Anchor Books, 1996.

Karash, Mary C. *Slave Life in Rio de Janeiro, 1808–1850*. Princeton: Princeton University Press, 1987.

Katz, William Loren, ed. *U.S. Department of Commerce, Bureau of the Census, Negro Population in the United States, 1790–1915*. New York: Arno Press, 1968.

Keegan, John. *The Face of Battle*. Hammondsworth: Penguin, 1978.

Kinsley, Rufus. *Diary of a Christian Soldier: Rufus Kinsley and the Civil War*, edited by David C. Rankin. New York: Cambridge University Press, 2004.

Kraay, Hendrik. "Em outra coisa não falavam os pardos, cabras e crioulos: o 'recrutamento' de escravos na guerra de independência da Bahia." *Revista Brasileira de História* 22, no. 43 (2002): 109–26.

————. "Os companheiros de Dom Obá: os Zuavos Baianos e outras companhias negras na Guerra do Paraguai." *Afro-Ásia* 46 (2012): 121–61.

————. "Reconsidering Recruitment in Imperial Brazil." *The Americas* 55, no. 1 (July 1998): 1–33.

————. "The Shelter of the Uniform: The Brazilian Army and Runaway Slaves, 1800–1888." *Journal of Social History* 29, no. 3 (March 1996): 637–57.

————. "Slavery, Citizenship, and Mobilization in Brazil's Mobilization for the Paraguayan War." *Slavery and Abolition* 18, no. 3 (Dec. 1997): 228–56.

————. "Soldiers, Officers, and Society: The Army in Bahia, Brazil, 1808–1889," PhD diss., University of Texas at Austin, 1995.

Kraay, Hendrik, and Thomas L. Whigham, eds. *I Die with My Country: Perspectives on the Paraguayan War, 1864–1870*. Lincoln: University of Nebraska Press, 2004.

Kynoch, Gary. "Terrible Dilemmas: Black Enlistment in the Union Army during the American Civil War." *Frank Cass Journal* 18, no. 2 (Aug. 1997): 104–27.

Lara, Silvia Hunold. *Campos da violência: escravos e senhores na capitania do Rio de Janeiro, 1750–1808*. Rio de Janeiro: Paz e Terra, 1988.

Lasso, Marixa. "Race War and Nation in Caribbean Gran Colombia, Cartagena, 1810–1832." *American Historical Review* 111, no. 2 (2006): 336–61.

Ledman, Paul L. "A Town Responds: Cape Elizabeth, Maine, in the Civil War," MA thesis, University of New Hampshire, 1999.

Lee, Basil Leo, F.S.C. *Discontent in New York City, 1861–1865*. Washington, D.C.: Catholic University of America Press, 1943.

Lemos, Renato, ed. *Cartas da Guerra do Paraguai: Benjamin Constant na campanha do Paraguai*. Rio de Janeiro: IPHAN, 1999.

Leuchars, Chris. *To the Bitter End: Paraguay and the War of the Triple Alliance*. Westport, Conn.: Greenwood Press, 2002.

Levine, Bruce. *Confederate Emancipation: Southern Plans to Free and Arm Slaves during the Civil War.* New York: Oxford University Press, 2006.

Levine, Peter. "Draft Evasion in the North during the Civil War, 1863–1865." *Journal of American History* 67 (May 1981): 816–34.

Lieber, Francis. *No Party Now but All for Our Country.* Philadelphia: Chrissy and Markley, 1863.

Lima, Carlos A. M. "Escravos de Peleja: a instrumentalização da violência escrava na América Portuguesa (1580–1850)." *Revista de Sociologia e Política* No. 18 (2002): 131–52.

Lincoln, Abraham. *The Collected Works of Abraham Lincoln,* edited by Roy P. Basler. 9 vols. to date; New Brunswick, N.J.: Rutgers University Press for the Abraham Lincoln Association, Springfield, Ill., 1953–.

Linderman, Gerald F. *Embattled Courage: The Experience of Combat in the American Civil War.* New York: Free Press, 1987.

Litwack, Leon F. *North of Slavery: The Negro in the Free States, 1790–1860.* Chicago: University of Chicago Press, 1961.

Long, E. B., and Barbara Long. *The Civil War Day by Day: An Almanac 1861–1865.* Garden City, N.Y.: Doubleday, 1971.

Lonn, Ella. *Desertion in the Civil War.* Gloucester, Mass.: Peter Smith, 1966.

Lopacher, Ulrich, and Alfred Tobler. *Un suizo en la Guerra del Paraguay.* Asunción: Editorial del Centenario, 1969.

López-Alves, Fernando. *State Formation and Democracy in Latin America, 1810–1900.* Durham, N.C.: Duke University Press, 2000.

Lyra, Heitor. *História do império de Dom Pedro II.* 3 vols.; São Paulo: Melhoramentos, 1940.

Macdonald, John. *Great Battles of the Civil War.* New York: Collier Books, 1992.

Magalhães, Domingos José Gonçalves de. "Memória histórica e documentada da revolução da Província do Maranhão," *Novos Estudos CEBRAP* 23 (1989): 14–66.

Magalhães, Raimundo, Jr. *D. Pedro II e a Condessa de Barral.* Rio de Janeiro: Civilização Brasileira, 1956.

Mallo, Silvia C., and Ignacio Telesca. *"Negros de la Patria": los Afrodescendientes en las luchas por la Independencia en el Antiguo Virreinato del Río de La Plata.* Buenos Aires: SB, 2010.

Mamigonian, Beatriz G. "Conflicts over the Meanings of Freedom: The Liberated Africans' Struggle for Emancipation in Brazil (1840s–1860s)," in *Paths to Freedom: Manumission in the Atlantic World,* edited by Rosemary Brana-Shute and Rand J. Sparks, 235–64. Columbia: University of South Carolina Press, 2009.

Martins, Maria Fernanda. *A velha arte de governar: um estudo da política e elites a partir do Conselho de Estado (1842–1889).* Rio de Janeiro: Presidência da República, Arquivo Nacional, 2007.

Marvel, William. "New Hampshire and the Draft, 1863." *Historical New Hampshire* 36 (1981): 58–72.

Maslowski, Peter. "National Policy toward the Use of Black Troops in the Revolution." *South Carolina Historical Magazine* 73 (1972): 1–17.

Mattos, Hebe. "Henrique Dias: expansão e limites da justiça distribuitiva no Império Português," in *Retratos do Império Trajetórias individuais no mundo português nos séculos XVI a XIX*, edited by Ronaldo Vainfas, Georgina Silva dos Santos, and Guilherme Pereira das Neves, 29–45. Niterói: Editora da Universidade Federal Fluminense, 2006).

Mattos, Ilmar Rohloff de. *O tempo saquarema*. São Paulo: Hucitec, 1988.

May, Thomas. "Continuity and Change in the Labor Program of the Union Army and the Freedman's Bureau." *Civil War History* 17, no. 3 (1971): 245–54.

Mayo, James M. "War Memorials as Political Memory." *Geographic Review* 78, no. 1 (1988): 62–75.

Mays, Joe H. "Black Americans and Their Contribution toward Union Victory in the American Civil War, 1861–1865," PhD diss., Middle Tennessee State University, 1983.

McCann, Frank D. "The Nation in Arms: Obligatory Military Service during the Old Republic," in *Essays Concerning the Socioeconomic History of Brazil and Portuguese India*, edited by Dauril Alden and Warren Dean, 211–43. Gainesville: University Press of Florida, 1977.

McClellan, George B. *The Civil War Papers of George B. McClellan: Selected Correspondence, 1860–1865*, edited by Stephen W. Sears. New York: Ticknor & Fields, 1989.

McDonnel, Michael A. *The Politics of War: Race, Class, and Conflict in Revolutionary Virginia*. Chapel Hill: University of North Carolina Press, 2007.

McKitrick, Eric L. "Party Politics and the Union and Confederate War Efforts," in *The American Party Systems: Stages of Political Development*, edited by William Nisbet Chambers and Walter Dean Burham, 117–51. New York: Oxford University Press, 1975.

McLynn, Franklin J. "The Causes of the Triple Alliance: An Interpretation." *Inter-American Economic Affairs* 23, no. 2 (Autumn 1979): 21–44.

McPherson, James M. *Battle Cry of Freedom: The Civil War Era*. New York: Ballantine Books, 1988.

———. *For Cause and Comrades: Why Men Fought in the Civil War*. New York: Oxford University Press, 1997.

———. *The Negro's Civil War: How American Blacks Felt and Acted during the War for the Union*. New York: Ballantine Books, 1991.

———. *The Struggle for Equality: Abolitionists and the Negro in the Civil War and Reconstruction*. Princeton: Princeton University Press, 1964.

Mendes, Fábio F. "O tributo de sangue: recrutamento militar e construção do estado no Brasil imperial," PhD diss., Instituto Universitário de Pesquisas do Rio de Janeiro, 1997.

———. *Recrutamento militar e construção do estado no Brasil imperial*. Belo Horizonte: Argumentum, 2010.

Mendes, Raimundo Teixeira. *Benjamin Constant—esboço de uma apreciação sintética da vida e da obra do fundador da república brasileira*, vol. 2: *(Peças justificativas)*. Rio de Janeiro: Igreja Positivista do Brazil, 1894.

Menezes, Alfredo da Mota. *A Guerra é nossa: a Inglaterra não provocou a Guerra do Paraguai*. São Paulo: Editora Contexto, 2012.

*Message of the President of the United States to the Two Houses of Congress at the Commencement of the Second Section of the Thirty-Seventh Congress. December, 3 1861. . . .*, vol. 2. Washington, D.C.: Government Printing Office, 1861.

Metzer, Jacob. "The Records of the U.S. Colored Troops as a Historical Source: An Exploratory Examination." *Historical Methods* 14, no. 3 (Summer 1981): 123–32.

Meznar, Joan E. "The Ranks of the Poor: Military Service and Social Differentiation in Northeast Brazil, 1839–1875." *Hispanic American Historical Review* 72, no. 3 (1992): 335–51.

*Miscellaneous Documents of the Senate of the United States for the First Session Thirty-Eighth Congress, The*. Washington, D.C.: Government Printing Office, 1864.

Mitchell, Reid. *Civil War Soldiers: Their Expectations and Their Experiences*. New York: Touchstone, 1988.

Moore, Albert Burton. *Conscription and Conflict in the Confederacy*. New York: Macmillan, 1924.

Moreira, Paulo R. S. *Faces da liberdade, máscaras do cativeiro: experiências de liberdade e escravidão percebidas através das cartas de alforria—Porto Alegre (1858–1888)*. Porto Alegre: Arquivo Público do Estado/EDIPUCRS, 1996.

Moreno, Jose Luis. "Incorporación de la Argentina al Mercado Mundial (1880–1930)," in *Estado nacional y sociedad en el pensamiento nacional: antologia conceptual para el analysis comparado*, edited by Waldo Ansaldi and Jose Luis Moreno, 215–33. Buenos Aires: Cantaro, 1996.

Murdock, Eugene C. *One Million Men: The Civil War Draft in the North*. Madison: State Historical Society of Wisconsin, 1971.

———. *Patriotism Limited, 1862–1865: The Civil War and the Bounty System*. Kent, Ohio: Kent State University Press, 1967.

Murphy, Fred. "Latin American State Formation in Regional Context." *Working Paper*. New School of Social Research No. 71 (May, 1998): 1–28.

Murrin, John M. "War, Revolution, and Nation Making: The American Revolution versus the Civil War." *Research Paper, Philadelphia Center for Early American Studies*, 1984.

Nabuco, Joaquim. *The Abolitionism: The Brazilian Antislavery Struggle*. Chicago: University of Chicago Press, 1977.

———. *Um estadista do império: Nabuco de Araújo, sua vida, suas opiniões, sua época*. São Paulo: Cia. Editora Nacional, 1936.

Nash, Gary B. *Freedom by Degrees: Emancipation in Philadelphia and Its Aftermath*. New York: Oxford University Press, 1991.

Needell, Jeffrey D. "Party Formation and State-Making: The Conservative Party and the Reconstruction of the Brazilian State, 1831–1840." *Hispanic American Historical Review* 81, no. 2 (2001): 259–308.

———. *The Party of Order: The Conservatives, the State, and Slavery in the Brazilian Monarchy, 1831–1871*. Stanford: Stanford University Press, 2006.

Neimeyer, Charles Patrick. *America Goes to War: A Social History of the Continental Army*. New York: New York University Press, 1996.

Nelson, Jacquelyn Sue. *Indiana Quakers Confront the Civil War*. Indianapolis: Indiana State Historical Society, 1991.

Nevins, Allan. *The War for the Union: The Organized War to Victory, 1864–1865*. New York: Charles Scribner's Sons, 1960.

Nieman, Donald G. *Promises to Keep: African-Americans and the Constitutional Order, 1776 to the Present*. New York: Oxford University Press, 1991.

Niven, John. *Connecticut for the Union: The Role of the State in the Civil War*. New Haven, Conn.: Yale University Press, 1965.

O'Leary, Juan E. *El Paraguay en la unificación Argentina*. Asunción: Instituto Paraguayo de Cultura, 1976.

Oliveira, Manuel Lucas de. *Diário do Coronel Manuel Lucas de Oliveira*, edited by Paulo S. Moreira and Jorge R. Petersen. Porto Alegre: Edições EST, 1997.

Osher, David. "Soldier Citizens for a Disciplined Nation: Union Conscription and the Construction of the Modern American Army," PhD diss., Columbia University, 1992.

O'Sullivan, John, and Alan M. Mecler, eds. *The Draft and Its Enemies: A Documentary History*. Urbana: University of Illinois Press, 1974.

Palacios, Guillermo. *A Guerra dos Marimbondos: uma revolta camponesa no Brasil escravista. (Pernambuco 1851–1852)*. Rio de Janeiro: CPDA/UFRJ, Mimeo, 1989.

Palladino, Grace. *Another Civil War: Labor, Capital, and the State in the Anthracite Regions of Pennsylvania, 1840–68*. Urbana: University of Illinois Press, 1990.

Paludan, Phillip Shaw. *A People's Contest: The Union and the Civil War, 1861–1865*. Lawrence: University Press of Kansas, 1996.

Paradis, Michael James. "Strike the Blow: A Study of the Sixth Regiment of United States Colored Infantry," PhD diss., Temple University, 1995.

Parker, Geoffrey. *The Military Revolution: Military Innovation and the Rise of the West, 1500–1800*. Cambridge: Cambridge University Press, 2002.

Pena, Maria Valério Junho. "O surgimento do imposto de renda: um estudo sobre a relação entre estado e mercado no Brasil." *Revista Dados* 35, no. 3 (1992): 337–70.

Perkins, Howard Cecil, ed. *Northern Editorials on Secession*. New York: D. Appleton-Century Company, 1942.

Pla, Josefina. *Hermano negro: la esclavitud en el Paraguay*. Madrid: Paraninfo, 1972.

Possamai, Paulo, ed. *Gente de guerra e fronteira: estudos de história militar do Rio Grande do Sul*. Pelotas: Editora da Universidade de Pelotas, 2010.

Potter, David M. *The Impending Crisis, 1848–1861*. New York: Harper & Row, 1973.

———. *Lincoln and His Party in the Secession Crisis*. New Haven: Yale University Press, 1942.

———. *The South and the Sectional Conflict*. Baton Rouge: Louisiana State University Press, 1968.

Preisser, Thomas E. "The Virginia Decision to Use Negro Soldiers in the Civil War, 1864–1865." *Virginia Magazine of History and Biography* 82, no. 1 (1975): 98–113.

*Proposta e Relatório do Ministério da Fazenda Apresentados à Assembléa Geral Legislativa na Quarta Sessão da Décima Segunda Legislatura pelo Ministro e Secretário de Estado dos Negócios da Fazenda, João da Silva Carrão*. Rio de Janeiro: Typografia Nacional, 1866.

Quarles, Benjamin. *The Negro in the American Revolution*. Chapel Hill: University of North Carolina Press, 1961.

———. *The Negro in the Civil War*. New York: Da Capo, 1953.

Rankin, David C. "The Impact of the Civil War on the Free Colored Community of New Orleans." *Perspectives in American History* 11 (1977–78): 379–416.

Redkey, Edwin S. *A Grand Army of Black Men: Letters from African American Soldiers in the Union Army, 1861–1865*. New York: Cambridge University Press, 1991.

Reis, João José, and Eduardo Silva. *Negociação e conflito: a resistência negra no Brasil escravista*. São Paulo: Companhia das Letras, 1989.

*Relatório Apresentado à Assembléa Geral Legislativa na Primeira Sessão da Décima Terceira Legislatura pelo Respectivo Ministro e Secretário de Estado Martin Francisco Ribeiro de Andrada*. Rio de Janeiro: Typografia do Correio Mercantil, 1867.

*Relatório apresentado Á Assembléa Geral Legislatva na Quarta Sessão da Décima-Quarta Legislatura pelo Ministro e Secretario de Estado Interino dos Negócios da Guerra Visconde do Rio Branco*. Rio de Janeiro: Typographia Universal de Laemmert, 1872.

*Relatório Apresentado à Assembléa Geral Legislativa na Quarta Sessão da Décima Segunda Legislatura pelo Ministro e Secretário de Estado dos Negócios da Guerra Angelo Moniz da Silva Ferraz*. Rio de Janeiro: Typographia Nacional, 1866.

*Relatório Apresentado á Assembléa Geral Legislativa na Terceira Sessão da Décima Segunda Legislatura pelo Ministro e Secretário de Estado dos Negocios da Guerra Visconde de Camamú*. Rio de Janeiro: Typographia Universal de Laemmert, 1865.

*Relatório apresentado á Assembléa Legislativa Provincial do Rio de Janeiro na primeira sessão da decima-oitava legislatura no dia 15 de outubro de 1868 pelo presidente da mesma provincia, o conselheiro Benvenuto Augusto de Magalhães Taques*. Rio de Janeiro: Typographia do Correio Mercantil, 1868.

*Relatório Apresentado a Assembleia Geral Legislativa na Primeira Sessão da Décima Terceira Legislatura pelo Respectivo Ministro e Secretário de Estado Martim Francisco Ribeiro de Andrada*. Rio de Janeiro: Typografia do Correio Mercantil, 1867.

*Relatório Apresentado à Assembleia Geral na Primeira Sessão da Décima Terceira Legislatura, pelo Ministro e Secretário d'Estado dos Negócios da Guerra, João Lustosa da Cunha Paranaguá*. Rio de Janeiro: Typografia Nacional, 1867.

*Relatório Apresentado A Assembléia Legislativa Provincial da Bahia pelo Excelentíssimo Senhor Presidente o Comendador Manuel Pinto de Souza Dantas no Dia 10. de Março de 1866*. Bahia: Typografia de Tourinho e C.e.

*Relatório com que o Dr. Esperidião Eloy de Barros Pimentel, Presidente da Província das Alagoas Entregou a Administração da Mesma Província no dia 10 de Abril de 1866, ao 10. Vice-Presidente Dr. Galdino Augusto da Natividade e Silva*. Maceió: Typografia do Bacharel Félix da Costa Moraes, 1866.

# Bibliography

*Relatório com que o Sr. Conselheiro de Estado Bernardo de Souza Franco passou a Administração da Província do Rio de Janeiro à José Tavares Bastos.* Nicterói: May 10, 1865.

*Relatório da Repartição dos Negócios Estrangeiros apresentado Á Assembléa Geral Legislativa na Terceira Sessão da Decima-Segunda Legislatura pelo respectivo Ministro e Secretário João Pedro Dias Vieira.* Rio de Janeiro: Typografia Universal de Laemmert, 1865.

*Relatório do Ministério da Justiça apresentado a Assembléia Geral Legislativa na Quarta-Sessão da Décima-Segunda Legislatura pelo Respectivo Ministro e Secretário de Estado José Thomas Nabuco de Araújo.* Rio de Janeiro: Typografia Universal Laemmert, 1866.

*Relatório do Ministério da Justiça Apresentado à Assembléia Geral Legislativa na Segunda Sessão da Décima Terceira Legislatura pelo Respectivo Ministro e Secretário de Estado Martim Francisco Ribeiro de Andrada.* Rio de Janeiro: Typografia Perserança, 1868.

*Relatório que à Assembléia Legislativa Provincial de Minas Gerais Apresentou no Ato da Abertura da Sessão Ordinária de 1865 o Desembargador Pedro de Alcântara Cerqueira Leite, Presidente da mesma Província.* Ouro Preto: Typografia de Minas Gerais, 1865.

*Relatório que Apresentou ao Ex. Sr. Vice-Presidente da Província de Minas Gerais Dr. Elias Pinto de Carvalho por Ocasião de Passar a Administração em 3 de Julho de 1867.* Rio de Janeiro: Typographia Perseverança, 1867.

Resquin, Francisco Isidoro. *Datos historicos de la Guerra del Paraguay contra la Triple Alianza.* Asunción: Compañia Sud-Americana de Billetes de Banco, 1895.

Ribeiro, José Iran. "'Tudo isto é indiada coronilha ( . . . ) não é como essa cuscada lá da corte': O serviço militar na cavalaria e a afirmação da identidade riograndense durante a Guerra dos Farrapos," in *Gente de guerra e fronteira: estudos de história militar do Rio Grande do Sul,* edited by Paulo Possamai, 117–37. Pelotas: Editora da Universidade de Pelotas, 2010.

Roberts, Timothy M. *Distant Revolutions: 1848 and the Challenge to American Exceptionalism.* Charlottesville: University of Virginia Press, 2009.

Rock, David. *Argentina, 1516–1982: From Spanish Colonization to the Falklands War.* Berkeley: University of California Press, 1985.

Rollins, Richard, ed. *Black Southerners in Gray: Essays On Afro-Americans in Confederate Armies.* Murfreesboro, Tenn.: Southern Heritage Press, 1994.

Rose, Willie Lee. *Rehearsal for Reconstruction: The Port Royal Experiment.* Indianapolis: Bobbs-Merrill, 1964.

Rothman, Adam. "West India Regiments at the Battle of New Orleans and Beyond." Paper presented to the American Historical Association Annual Meeting, Washington, D.C., Jan. 7–10, 1999.

Royster, Charles. *The Destructive War: William Tecumseh Sherman, Stonewall Jackson, and the Americans.* New York: Alfred A. Knopf, 1991.

Rudé, George F. E. *The Crowd in History: A Study of Popular Disturbances in France and England, 1730–1848.* New York: Wiley, 1964.

Rutherford, Phillip. "Revolt in the Corps D'Afrique." *Civil War Times Illustrated* 24, no. 2 (May 1985): 20–23.

Saeger, James Schofield. *Francisco Solano López and the Ruination of Paraguay: Honor and Egocentrism.* New York: Rowman & Littlefield, 2007.

———. "Survival and Abolition: The Eighteenth Century Paraguayan Encomienda." *The Americas* 38, no. 1 (July 1981): 59–85.

Saint-Hilaire, August de. *Viagem pelas Províncias do Rio de Janeiro e Minas Gerais.* Rio de Janeiro: Cia. Editora Nacional, 1938.

Sales de Bohigas, Núria. *Sobre esclavos, reclutas y mercaderes de Quintos.* Barcelona: Editorial Ariel, 1974.

———. "Some Opinions on Exemption from Military Service in Nineteenth-Century Europe." *Comparative Studies in Society and History* 10, no. 3 (April 1968): 261–89.

Salles, Ricardo. *E o vale era escravo: Vassouras, século XIX—senhores e escravos no coração do Império.* Rio de Janeiro: Civilização Brasileira, 2008.

———. *Guerra do Paraguai: escravidão e cidadania na formação do exército.* Rio de Janeiro: Paz e Terra, 1990.

———. *Guerra do Paraguai: memórias e imagens.* Rio de Janeiro: Biblioteca Nacional, 2003.

Santos, Wanderley Guilherme dos. "A Guerra do Paraguai: lição para os conflitos contemporâneos." *Dados* 30, no. 3 (1987): 311–24.

———. "A teoria da democracia proporcional de José de Alencar," in Wanderley Guilherme dos Santos, ed., *Dois escritos democráticos de José de Alencar,* 9–50. Rio de Janeiro: UFRJ, 1991.

Schneider, Louis. *A Guerra da Tríplice Aliança contra o Paraguai.* Porto Alegre: Editora Pradense, 2009.

Schulz, John. *O exército na política.* São Paulo: Edusp, 1994.

Schwartz, Stuart B. *Sugar Plantations in the Formation of Brazilian Society: Bahia 1550–1835.* Cambridge: Cambridge University Press, 1985.

Schwartz, Thomas F. "Salmon P. Chase Critiques First Reading of the Emancipation Proclamation of President Lincoln." *Civil War History* 33, no. 1 (1987): 84–87.

Scott, James. *Seeing Like a State: How Certain Schemes to Improve the Human Condition Have Failed.* New Haven, Conn.: Yale University Press, 1998.

Scott, Rebecca J. *Slave Emancipation in Cuba: The Transition to Free Labor, 1860–1899.* Princeton: Princeton University Press, 1986.

Seraile, William. "The Struggle to Raise Black Regiments in New York State, 1861–1864." *New-York Historical Society Quarterly* 58 no. 3 (1974): 215–33.

Seymour, Horatio. *Public Record: Including Speeches, Messages, Proclamations, Official Correspondence and Other Public Utterances of Horatio Seymour,* edited by Thomas Cook and Thomas Knox. New York: I. W. England, 1868.

Shanon, Fred A. *The Organization and Administration of the Union Army, 1861–1865.* 2. vols. Gloucester, Mass.: Peter Smith, 1965.

Silber, Nina, ed. *Yankee Correspondence: Civil War Letters between New England Soldiers and the Homefront.* Charlottesville: University Press of Virginia, 1996.

Silbey, Joel H. *A Respectable Minority: The Democratic Party in the Civil War Era, 1860–1868*. New York: W. W. Norton, 1977.

Silva, Eduardo. *Prince of the People: The Life and Times of a Brazilian Free Man of Color*. London: Verso, 1993.

Silveira, Mauro Cesar. *A batalha de papel: a Guerra do Paraguai através da caricatura*. Porto Alegre: L&PM, 1996.

Skowronek, Stephen. *Building a New American State: The Expansion of National Administrative Capacities, 1877–1920*. New York: Cambridge University Press, 1982.

Slenes, Robert W. "The Demography and Economics of Brazilian Slavery, 1850–1880," PhD diss., Stanford University, 1976.

Smith, John David, "The Recruitment of Negro Soldiers in Kentucky, 1863–1865." *Register of the Kentucky Historical Society* 72, no. 4 (1974): 364–90.

Smith, Michael O. "Raising a Black Regiment in Michigan: Adversity and Triumph." *Michigan Historical Society Review* 16, no. 2 (1990): 22–41.

Souza, Jorge Prata de. *Escravidão ou morte: os escravos brasileiros e a Guerra do Paraguai*. Rio de Janeiro: Mauad/Adesa, 1996.

Souza, Maria Regina Santos de. "Impactos da Guerra do Paraguai na Província do Ceará (1865–1870)," PhD diss., Universidade Federal do Ceará, 2007.

Stampp, Kenneth M., ed. *The Causes of the Civil War*. New York: Simon & Schuster, 1991.

Stampp, Kenneth. *And the War Came: The North and the Secession Crisis, 1860–1861*. Baton Rouge: Louisiana State University Press, 1967.

———. *The Peculiar Institution: Slavery in the Ante-Bellum South*. New York: Vintage Books, 1956.

Stanchak, John E. *Leslie's Illustrated Civil War*. Jackson: University of Mississippi Press, 1992.

Stark, William C. "Forgotten Heroes: Black Recipients of the United States Congressional Medal of Honor in the American Civil War, 1863–1865." *Lincoln Herald* 88, no. 1 (1986): 70–80.

*Statutes at Large, Treaties, and Proclamations of the United States of America*. 17 vols. Boston: Little, Brown and Company, 1850–73.

Stein, Arthur A., and Bruce M. Russet. "Evaluating War: Outcomes and Consequences," in *Handbook of Political Conflict: Theory and Research*, edited by Ted Robert Gun, 399–422. New York: Free Press, 1980.

Stein, Stanley J. *Vassouras: A Brazilian Coffee County, 1850–1900*. Princeton: Princeton University Press, 1985.

Stephen, Martin. *Jailed for Peace: The History of American Draft Law Violators, 1658–1985*. Westport, Conn.: Greenwood Press, 1986.

Sterling, Robert E. "Civil War Draft Resistance in the Middle West," PhD diss., Northern Illinois University, 1974.

Strickland, Arvarh E. "The Illinois Background of Lincoln's Attitude toward Slavery and the Negro." *Journal of the Illinois State Historical Society* 56, no. 3 (1963): 474–94.

Summerhill, William R. "Railroads in Imperial Brazil, 1854–1889," in *Latin America and the World Economy since 1800*, edited by John H. Coastworth and Alan M. Taylor, 383–405. Cambridge, Mass.: Harvard University Press and the David Rockefeller Center for Latin American Studies, 1998.

Tannenbaum, Frank. *Slave and Citizen*. Boston: Beacon Press, 1992.

Taunay, Alfredo D'Escragnole. *A retirada da laguna*. São Paulo: Editorial Tecnoprint, 1946.

———. *Cartas da campanha de Mato Grosso*. Rio de Janeiro: Biblioteca Militar, 1944.

———. *Memórias*. São Paulo: Instituto Progresso Editorial, 1948.

Taylor, Susie King. *Reminiscences of My Life: A Black Woman's Civil War Memories*, edited by Patricia W. Romero and Willie Lee Rose. New York: Markus Wiener Publisher, 1988.

Thompson, E. P. *Customs in Common*. New York: New Press; distrib. by W. W. Norton, 1991.

Thompson, George. *A Guerra do Paraguai: com um esboço histórico do país e do povo paraguaio, e notas sôbre a engenharia militar durante a guerra*. Rio de Janeiro: Conquista, 1968.

Thucydides. *History of the Peloponnesian War*. London: Penguin, 1972.

Tilly, Charles. *Coercion, Capital, and European States, AD 990–1992*. Cambridge, Mass.: Blackwell, 1992.

———. "States and Nationalism in Europe, 1492–1992." *Theory and Society* 23, no. 1 (1994): 131–46.

Toral, André A. de. *Imagens em Desordem: a iconografia da Guerra do Paraguai (1864–1870)*. São Paulo: Humanitas/FFLCH/USP, 2001.

Trudeau, Noah Andre. *Like Men of War: Black Troops in the Civil War, 1862–1865*. Boston: Little, Brown, 1998.

Tunnel, Ted. "Free Negroes and the Freedmen: Black Politics in New Orleans during the Civil War." *Southern Studies* 19, no. 1 (1980): 5–28.

Urwin, Gregory J. W. "'We Cannot Treat Negroes . . . as Prisoners of War': Racial Atrocities and Reprisals in Civil War Arkansas." *Civil War History* 42, no. 3 (Sept. 1996): 193–210.

Vandiver, Frank E. *The Long Loom of Lincoln*. Fort Wayne, Ind.: Louis A. Warren Lincoln Library and Museum, 1987.

Vasconcellos, Zacarias de Góes e. *Da natureza e limites do poder moderador*. Rio de Janeiro: Laemmert, 1862.

Voegeli, V. Jacque. *Free But Not Equal: The Midwest and the Negro during the Civil War*. New York: Harper and Row, 1977.

Voelz, Peter M. *Slave and Soldier: The Military Impact of Blacks in the Colonial Americas*. New York: Garland Publishing, 1993.

Vorenberg, Michael . "Abraham Lincoln and the Politics of Black Colonization." *Journal of the Abraham Lincoln Association* 14, no. 2 (1993): 23–45.

———. *Final Freedom: The Civil War, the Abolition of Slavery, and the Thirteenth Amendment*. New York: Cambridge University Press, 2001.

*War of the Rebellion: A Compilation of the Official Records of the Union and Confederate Armies.* 128 vols. Washington, D.C.: Government Printing Office, 1889–1901.

Warren, Harrys Gaylord. *Paraguay and the Triple Alliance: The Postwar Decade, 1869–1878.* Austin: University of Texas Press, 1978.

Welles, Gideon. *Diary of Gideon Welles: Secretary of the Navy under Lincoln and Johnson,* edited by Howard K. Beale. 3 vols.; New York: Norton, 1960.

Westwood, Howard C. "Captive Black Union Soldiers in Charleston—What to Do?" *Civil War History* 21, no. 1 (1982): 29–44.

———. "The Cause and Consequence of a Union Black Soldier's Mutiny and Execution." *Civil War History* 31, no. 3 (1985): 222–36.

———. "Lincoln's Position on Black Enlistments." *Lincoln Herald* 86, no. 2 (1984): 101–12.

Whigham, Thomas L. *The Paraguayan War,* vol. 1: *Causes and Early Conduct.* Lincoln: University of Nebraska Press, 2002.

Whigham, Thomas L., and Barbara Pottash. "The Paraguayan Rosetta Stone: New Insights into the Demographics of the Paraguayan War, 1864–1870." *Latin American Research Review* 34, no. 1 (1999): 174–86.

White, David O. *Connecticut's Black Soldiers, 1775–1783.* Chester: Connecticut Historical Commission, 1973.

White, Shane. *Somewhat More Independent: The End of Slavery in New York City.* Athens: University of Georgia Press, 1991.

Wiebe, Robert H. *The Search for Order, 1877–1920.* New York: Hill and Wang, 1995.

Wiley, Bell Irvin. *The Life of Billy Yank: The Common Soldier of the Union.* Baton Rouge: Louisiana State University Press, 1992.

Williams, John Hoyt. *The Rise and Fall of the Paraguayan Republic, 1800–1870.* Austin: University of Texas Press, 1979.

———. "A Swamp of Blood: The Battle of Tuyuti." *Military History* 17, no. 1 (April 2000): 58–64.

Wilson, Joseph T. *The Black Phalanx: African American Soldiers in the War of Independence, the War of 1812, and the Civil War.* New York: Da Capo Press, 1994.

Wilson, Mark. *The Business of Civil War: Military Mobilization and the State, 1861–1865.* Baltimore: Johns Hopkins University Press, 2006.

Wish, Harvey. *George Fitzhugh, Propagandist of the Old South.* Baton Rouge: Louisiana State University Press, 1943.

Woodward, William E. *Meet General Grant.* New York: Liveright, 1946.

Zikmund, Joseph, II. "National Anthems as Political Symbols." *Australian Journal of Politics and History* 15, no. 3 (Dec. 1969): 73–80.

# Index

*Page numbers in italics refer to illustrations.*

Abaeté, Viscount of, 152, 209n76, 211n92

abolitionism, abolitionists, 31, 32, 37, 94, 101, 113, 161, 170, 196n26; Andrew as, 33, 111–12; in Brazil, 150, 154, 155; Emancipation Proclamation and, 49; gradual, 106; Higginson as, 111; Lovejoy as, 198n44; movement for, 98, 121; Nabuco and, 152; opposed, 197n40; Port Royal Experiment and, 102–3; societies of, 126; white officers as, 123, 204n142

African Americans: camp deaths of, 123; casualties of, 202n115, 204n139; changing status of, 94, 95; as citizens, 112, 118, 164, 168; Congressional Medal of Honor and, 201n106, 202n116; controversy over enlistment of, 37–39; crossing Union lines, 198n55; draft of, 58; Dred Scott Decision and, 98; emancipation of, 195n8; federal control of, 171, 198n43, 198n47; fragmentation of, 121; impressment of, 117–18; military pay of, 204n150; population of, 203n132; public opinion of, 126; racism against, 184n44; recruitment of, 2, 23, 186n75, 186–87n81, 200n91, 202–3n123,

203n127; regiments of, 200n83, 200n85, 200–201nn91–92, 202n117, 203n134; rights of, 112; as soldiers, 104–6, 116, 121–23, 196n27, 197n35, 201n92, 202n108, 202n111, 202n119, 204n139, 204n145; as substitutes, 118–21, 202–3n123, 203n129, 203n131

agriculture: in Brazil, 5, 152, 165, 169; in Paraguay, 14; recruitment and, 44; slave labor in, 113, 152, 153, 161; war and, 165; women in, 13. *See also names of crops*

Agrippa, Menenio, 71, 172

Alagoas province, 63, 73–74, *74*, 77, 83–85

Alberdi, Juan Bautista, 143–144, 208n62

Alencar, José Martiniano de, 161, 172

Almeida, Felinto Henrique de, 61

American Civil War (1861–65), 5, 23–24, 58–59, 89, 165; casualty figures of, 1, 27; compared to Brazilian war, 4–5, 26–27, 70, 71, 90–91, 134, 139, 141, 176; civilians and, 2, 176; dynamics of, 39–45; political engineering of, 55; as reference for Brazil, 154, 160; shift in nature of, 28, 94–95, 107, 108; as total war, 171; as war for freedom, 49–50; as war for union, 37, 38–39, 51, 99

Browning, Orville Hickman, 92–93
Bueno, Pimenta, 82, 140, 152–53, 154,
    209n76
Buenos Aires, Argentina, 17, 142, 143, 155
Bull Run, second battle of, 49
Burnside, Gen. Ambrose, 49
Burt, Silas Wright, 45
Burton, Richard, 155
Butler, Gen. Benjamin, 102, 104–5, 118

Cabinet, Brazilian, 3, 61, 64, 70, 94, 169,
    200n80
Câmara, Lt. Col. Eufrazio Arruda, 60
Câmara, Francisco Antônio de Arruda, 60
Cameron, Simon, U.S. secretary of war,
    28–29, 36, 186n68
Capdevila, Luc, 13, 20
Carmelite Order, 156, 211nn101–2
Carney, Sgt. William H., 201n106
Catholic Church, Catholics, 13; evasion of
    draft and, 189n124; as immigrants, 35;
    Irish, 34, 54; slave ownership of, 150,
    156, 210n87. *See also names of specific
    Orders*
caudillos, 15, 17
cavalry, 17, 88, 107, 117, 140, 201n92,
    202n119, 208n48
Caxias, Marquis de. *See* Silva, Luís Alves
    de Lima e, Marquis de Caxias
Ceará province, 65, 84, 157
Centeno, Miguel Angel, 21, 90, 175
centralization, 2, 7, 10, 17, 68, 116–17,
    142, 163, 195n6; demand for, 29;
    draft and recruitment and, 26, 57,
    95–96; of economic interests, 173,
    176; Enrollment Act and, 53, 167; of
    government, 5, 13, 27, 45, 51, 61, 93;
    military, 110, 163, 166–67; opposition
    to, 52, 167, 174; political, 3, 28, 29, 142;
    Republicans and, 173–74
Cerro Cora, battle of, 20, 21
Cerro León, Paraguay, 15
Cisplatine Province (Uruguay), 15, 165
citizenship, citizens, 47, 117, 126, 132; of
    African Americans, 101, 112, 116, 118,
    168, 169, 172; in Brazil, 16, 44; draft
    and, 95; Dred Scott Decision and, 98;
    government and, 27, 28, 29, 54, 59,

91, 112; immigrants and, 58; military
    service and, 26, 61, 94, 96; militia
    open to, 96, 97, 98; national, 164, 168;
    recruitment and, 45, 140; as soldiers,
    36, 59, 133, 152
civic culture, 5, 32; American, 171;
    Brazilian, 89–91; civic responsibility
    and, 35, 66, 167; civic virtue and, 10,
    52, 98
civilians, 12, 24, 27, 30, 51, 61, 89, 103,
    126, 166; conscription of, 2; military
    and, 7, 42
civil liberties, 49, 133
class, 56, 58, 62, 89, 188n99, 189n5,
    198n50; of blacks, 121; in Brazil, 65;
    draft resistance and, 54; governing,
    38; lower, 55, 180n4; planter, 103,
    161, 191n25; recruitment and, 180n4,
    185n59
Cobb, Gen. Howard, 99–100
Cobb, Thomas R. R., 31
Cobble, Samuel, 122
Coimbra, Mato Grosso, 18
Colorados, 16, 17, 18
commutation, 53, 54, 58, 119, 167, 174,
    203n126
compensation, 92; expropriation without,
    151; for freed slaves, 93, 131, 133–34,
    152, 156; for slave labor, 100
Confederacy, 4, 104, 116, 185n62, 199n58;
    advantages of, 40–41, 42; blacks
    and, 99–100; Border States and, 40;
    compared to Paraguayan situation,
    179n1; conscription and recruitment
    in, 41, 179n1, 182n5, 185n59; defeated
    and occupied, 94, 168, 175; destruction
    of, 45, 51; Fort Sumter and, 32–33;
    independence and nationalism of,
    32, 185n61, 191n33; population of,
    189n125; total war against, 42, 44
Connecticut, 41–42, 47, 50, 112–13, 117,
    201n92, 203n132
conscription, 24, 27, 108, 166; African
    Americans and, 118; armed resistance
    against, 60–61; in Confederacy, 41,
    182n5; Conscription Act, 184n38;
    lottery for, 109; national system of, 28,
    47; opposed by Peace Democrats,

quotas for enlistments, 36, 44, 46, 48,
109, 121, 167, 174; blacks and, 95, 115;
of Border States, 185n57; in Brazil,
61, 75; failure to meet, 48, 53; slave
recruitment and, 109; state, 95, 114,
115, 118, 119; of towns and cities, 54, 57

race, races, 125, 171; citizenship and,
98; construction of racial identity
and, 3; equality of, 126; exclusion by,
195n3, 213n7; issues of, 121; mixture
of, 162; mobilization of, 89; Southern
relations of, 118; transformations of,
169, 197n40. See also racism, racial
prejudice
racism, racial prejudice, 2, 37, 56, 124,
125, 138, 163; American stereotypes
of, 38; in Brazil, 93–94, 96, 130, 132,
144, 152–53, 211n94; combating of,
171; in Confederacy, 100, 168; draft
riot as pogrom of, 57; enrollment of
black soldiers and, 58, 110; hierarchies
of, 39, 164; imagination of whites
and, 101; justice of, 101; in local
communities, 56; military service
and, 96, 99; minorities of, 58; in
Northern states, 98, 100, 170, 200n91;
pervasive, 196n26; policies of, 40;
racial determinism and, 144; racial
segregation in early Brazil and, 21, 96,
139; restrictions based on, 91, 97, 98;
South American assumptions of, 24,
141, 144, 146; of white officers, 123,
126–27
railroads: in Brazil, 71, 172–73;
exemptions for employees of, 47, 79;
in Northern United States, 32; in
Paraguay, 14, 15; standardization of,
173, 176
Rebouças, André, 126
recruitment, 2; bounty system
and, 187n86, 188n108, 196n27;
centralization of, 26, 163, 166; class
and, 180n4, 185n59; communal
organizations and, 36; compulsory,
23; federal caution of, 185n57; local
party structures and, 35; mass, 3;
method of, 9–10; resentment of, 163;

of slaves, 154, 179n1; substitutes in,
188n97, 188n108, 192n50, 192n52,
203n129. See also conscription;
draft; enlistment; recruitment in
Brazil; recruitment in Northern
United States; recruitment of African
Americans
recruitment in Brazil, 65, 72; as cause
of revolts, 193n76; as challenge to
traditions, 27; as coercive, 190n9,
192n53, 196n15; compared to Union
recruitment, 66, 83, 91, 93–96,
106, 113–14, 171–72; as compulsory,
213n2; crisis of, 90; early success of,
64; efforts to increase efficiency of,
64–65; enrollment of free blacks and
freed slaves, 95–96, 131, 168–69, 170;
growing resistance to, 71, 76; hostile
environment for, 77–78; liberation of
slaves for, 62, 175; medical exams and,
205n5; of mercenaries, 153, 196n20;
during Paraguayan campaign, 62–68;
politics and, 80–82, 84; rates of
voluntary, 207n39; rebellions against,
82–84; slavery and, 93, 128, 129, 130,
147–48, 152–53, 155, 156–59, 159;
substitution in, 157, 192n50; system
of, 191n25, 196n15; targets of, 44;
third wave of, 76, 77; unfairness in, 53;
unpopularity of, 61, 131
recruitment in Northern United States,
42, 43, 65; compared to Brazilian
recruitment, 66, 83, 91, 93–96, 106,
113–14, 171–72; exemptions in, 192n57,
194n92, 196n14; extended range of,
45; failure of volunteerism and, 28;
of former slaves, 154, 162, 168, 174,
200n85, 200n89; opposition to, 55,
56; by states, 47. See also recruitment
of African Americans
recruitment of African Americans,
37–38, 92–127; completion of process
of, 110; controversy over, 93–94;
demographics of, 115–16; immediate
consequences of, 125–27; in Kentucky,
114; as lesser evil, 111; nationalization
of, 118; in Northern states, 111–12;
official, 109–10; sources of, 115;